Principles and Politics in Contemporary Britain

Second Edition

Mark Garnett

imprint-academic.com

First edition published by Addison Wesley Longman Ltd, 1996

This edition published 2006 in the UK by
Imprint Academic, PO Box 200, Exeter EX5 5YX, UK

This edition published 2006 in the USA by
Imprint Academic, Philosophy Documentation Center
PO Box 7147, Charlottesville, VA 22906-7147, USA

ISBN 184540 026 7
ISBN-13 9781845400262

A CIP catalogue record for this book is available from the
British Library and US Library of Congress

Contents

List of Abbreviations   vi

Acknowledgements   viii

Introduction: Principles and Politics   **1**
The nature of ideology   3
Ideology and political action   7
Ideology and institutions   9
Ideology in UK politics   10
Summary   18

1   **A Decade of Discontent?**
   The Labour Party, 1970–79   **21**
Background   21
Socialists and social democrats   24
What went wrong?   30
In opposition, 1970–74   32
Back in office, 1974–79   34
The IMF loan   37
What went wrong – this time?   40
Conclusion   43

2   **From Selsdon Man to Grantham Woman:**
   The Conservative Party, 1970–79   **48**
Background   48
Post-war conservatism   52
In opposition, 1964–70   56
In office, 1970–74   58
Defeats and recrimination, 1974–75   62
The crusade begins, 1975–79   68
Conclusion   71

3   The Liberals and their Allies, 1970–2006   **79**
       Background   79
       Looking for allies, 1970–81   84
       Realignment, 1981   90
       Partnership of principle,
             or marriage of convenience? 1981–92   92
       'Owenism' and the SDP   99
       Equidistance? 1992–99   102
       Another false dawn? 1999–2006   104
       Conclusion   107

4   Thatcherism and its Legacy, 1979–90   **111**
       Opening shots, 1979–83   111
       Second innings, 1983–87   118
       Hubris, 1987–90   123
       The nature of Thatcherism   133
       Conclusion   138

5   Socialism or Social Democracy?
       The Labour Party, 1979–92   **144**
       Settling scores, 1979–83   144
       Confrontation, 1983–87   153
       Consolidation, 1987–92   157
       Conclusion: the betrayal of socialism?   164

6   Nationalism in UK Politics   **169**
       Scottish nationalism   171
       Welsh nationalism   175
       Nationalism in Northern Ireland   179
       English nationalism   184
       The immigration question   185
       The European controversy   191
       Conclusion: varieties of nationalism   194

7   The Conservatives since Thatcher, 1990–2006   **200**
       Background: Thatcher to Major   200
       In Thatcher's shadow   208
       Divisions over Europe   212
       Nationalism and nostalgia, 1997–2006   217
       Conclusion   229

8	**'New' Labour**	**232**
	'New' Labour in opposition	236
	'New' Labour in government	240
	Iraq	246
	Blair and Thatcherism	249
	Conclusion: a new consensus?	253
9	**Pressure Groups and the Rise of Apathy**	**260**
	Feminism	264
	The Campaign for Nuclear Disarmament	269
	Environmental movements	273
	Animal rights	279
	Conclusion: the politics of alienation?	283
	Conclusion: Principles and Politics since 1970	**287**
	The Conservative Party	287
	Labour	290
	Liberal Democrats	293
	A crisis of party politics	294
	Index	295

List of Abbreviations

ACAS	Advisory Conciliation and Arbitration Service
AES	Alternative Economic Strategy
ALF	Animal Liberation Front
ASI	Adam Smith Institute
BNP	British National Party
BSE	Bovine Spongiform Encephalopathy
CAP	Common Agricultural Policy
CBI	Confederation of British Industry
CDS	Campaign for Democratic Socialism
CLPD	Campaign for Labour Party Democracy
CND	Campaign for Nuclear Disarmament
CPRS	Central Policy Review Staff
CPS	Centre for Policy Studies
CRD	Conservative Research Department
CSA	Campaign for a Scottish Assembly
DEA	Department of Economic Affairs
DOE	Department of the Environment
DTI	Department of Trade and Industry
DUP	Democratic Unionist Party
EC	European Community
EC	European Communities
EEC	European Economic Community
EMS	European Monetary System
ERM	Exchange Rate Mechanism
EU	European Union
FOE	Friends of the Earth
GLC	Greater London Council
IEA	Institute of Economic Affairs
IMF	International Monetary Fund
IRA	Irish Republican Army

LCC	Labour Co-ordinating Committee
LSC	Labour Solidarity Campaign
MP	Member of Parliament
MSP	Member of the Scottish Parliament
NF	National Front
NATO	North Atlantic Treaty Organisation
NEB	National Enterprise Board
NEC	National Executive Committee
NEDC	National Economic Development Council
NF	National Front
NHS	National Health Service
NICRA	Northern Ireland Civil Rights Association
NUM	National Union of Mineworkers
NUPRG	New Ulster Political Research Group
OMOV	One Member One Vote
PFI	Private Finance Initiative
PLP	Parliamentary Labour Party
RFMC	Rank and File Mobilising Committee
RSPCA	Royal Society for the Prevention of Cruelty to Animals
SCLV	Socialist Campaign for Labour Victory
SDLP	Social Democratic and Labour Party
SDP	Social Democratic Party
SEA	Single European Act
SHAC	Stop Huntingdon Animal Cruelty
SLP	Scottish Labour Party
SNP	Scottish Nationalist Party
SPD	Social Democratic Party (Germany)
SWP	Socialist Workers' Party
TUC	Trades Union Congress
UK	United Kingdom
UKIP	United Kingdom Independence Party
USA	United States of America
UUP	Ulster Unionist Party
VAT	Value Added Tax
VFS	Victory for Socialism
WLM	Women's Liberation Movement

Acknowledgements

For this second edition, my chief debts are to Keith Sutherland and Anthony Freeman at Imprint Academic, who have been remarkably resourceful and supportive as ever. I salute their indefatigability. Prior to publication, the whole of the first edition was read with care and patience by Philippa Sherrington. Individual chapters were scrutinized by Ian Gimour, David Marquand, William Wallace and Gerry Taylor. Tony Benn, Michael Foot and Robert Garner were willing to give up their time to answer my questions.

In first edition I acknowledged more general debts, and after more than a decade these should still be recorded. Without the guidance and encouragement of Bernard Crick and Iain Hampsher-Monk, the book would never have been written. Since then, I have followed the practice of most fellow-Britons by accumulating additional debts which cannot easily be repaid. Confining the cluttered field to academic influences and friends, I owe a great deal to John Benyon, Andrew Denham, Andrew Gamble, John Gibbins, Philip Lynch, Michael Oliver, Richard Weight, and Mark Wickham-Jones. James Douglas, Ben Pimlott and my PhD supervisor, Henry Tudor, have passed away but they are certainly not forgotten.

Despite all of these debts, any errors of fact and interpretation in this book are entirely my own responsibility.

INTRODUCTION

Principles and Politics

This book has two main purposes. First, it explores the impact of ideology on UK politics, attempting to bring some clarity to a subject which almost invariably generates confusion. The analysis presented here challenges many common assumptions about the ideological allegiances of prominent politicians and the main UK parties. Second, the chapters build a concise survey of key developments in British political history since 1970. While ideas influence political events, it is equally true that events help to shape political thinking. The relationship between the two is complex, but it is impossible to understand either one of them in isolation from the other. Although individual chapters are devoted to specific parties and principles, the structure of the book is chronological as well as thematic. It is designed primarily for students following courses on UK Politics; Contemporary British History; and Ideologies. However, it tackles a topic that is highly relevant to non-students with a general interest in the politics of the UK, and the book has been written with their requirements in mind.

Although a great deal has been written about ideology, and several good books on contemporary British political history are available, few scholars have attempted to write about the recent past from the ideological perspective. In part, this reflects prevailing academic practice; ideology is usually taught in a rather abstract way, and, despite its obvious importance for citizens of any healthy democracy, contemporary political history is not taught widely enough. Probably, though, the most effective deterrent is the nature of the subject. Ideology is a forum for endless contestation.

During some of the party battles since 1970, ideological labels have been used as insults or as badges of honour. If the various meanings which have been attached to the terms were to be taken at face value, lucid discussion would soon become impossible. For example, most Labour leaders since 1970 have been attacked by their own party members for allegedly 'betraying' socialism. By contrast, critics in other parties have regularly claimed that Labour acts in accordance with an extreme socialist agenda; Margaret Thatcher, for example, once publicly branded Neil Kinnock as a 'crypto-communist'. For her own part, Thatcher was often accused of departing from a distinctive conservative approach to government, while her supporters claimed that she had rescued conservatism from her heretical predecessors. Obviously such disputes chiefly affect practising politicians, but media commentators and even academics have not been immune. Even now, when the main parties are generally presumed to be in broad agreement on basic principles, ideological terms tend to confuse more than they clarify.

The problem of terminology is serious enough for anyone writing about political ideas; but to make matters worse, the concept of ideology itself is warmly contested. Various conflicting definitions have been suggested. On the Marxist view, ideology is distorted thinking, generated by the unequal distribution of economic power. Thus, for example, in a capitalist society the ruling ideas are those that serve the interests of the dominant class. An alternative approach to ideology identifies it with extreme, dogmatic thought of all kinds. This view of ideology is particularly characteristic of people who have associated themselves with the conservative tradition. They argue that their own approach to politics is 'pragmatic', allowing them to deal flexibly with problems as they arise. In their eyes, ideologues are people who seek to impose change in accordance with a pre-determined plan, and try to make reality conform to their theories.

The problem with these interpretations of ideology is that they are themselves part of ideological debate. Marxists and conservatives rarely agree, but their combined efforts have left ideology with negative connotations in the UK context. As a result, it has become a useful political tactic to accuse one's opponents of ideological inclinations. Ironically, though, the concept of ideology was originally introduced as an attempt to foster a more rational and objective approach to politics. The French philosopher, Antoine Destutt de Tracy (1754–1836) was the first person to use the term, to denote a 'science of ideas' which would eradicate biased thinking of all kinds.

If de Tracy's hopes had been fulfilled, politics as we know it would probably no longer exist; disagreement, after all, is the soul of debate, and this would wither away if it was really possible to identify a single, 'objective' truth in political questions. However, something useful can be taken from de Tracy's approach. Even if it is a mistake to expect the removal of bias from political disputation, we can at least try to study the varying views of political agents in an objective spirit. In this respect, the concept of ideology is as at least *potentially* a useful explanatory tool rather than a political insult.

The nature of ideology

Although there is still plenty of disagreement about the nature of ideology, some basic propositions are accepted by most academic commentators. On this view, 'ideologies are bodies of concepts, values and symbols which incorporate conceptions of human nature and thus indicate what is possible or impossible for humans to achieve'[1]. It is not difficult to demonstrate that conceptions of human nature are central to political beliefs. This is certainly true of political philosophers, who typically build their theories on characterisations of human nature. Obviously, most practising politicians are far less systematic than great thinkers like Plato or Thomas Hobbes. However, when they do try to explain their principles, almost invariably their appeals

---

[1]   Andrew Vincent, *Modern Political Ideologies*, 2nd edition, Blackwell, 1995, 16.

reflect specific assumptions about human conduct and motivation.

In turn, there is an obvious connection between views of human nature and preferred social arrangements. Thus, for example, someone who thinks that human beings are naturally co-operative will tend to oppose institutions which embody competitiveness. By the same token, those who argue that human beings are competitive by instinct can be expected to dislike 'collectivist' institutions, particularly when these are backed by the compulsive force of the state. We would be mistaken if we expected politicians to be wholly consistent in these matters. But in the absence of explicit declarations about human nature, views of society can be taken as reliable indications of ideological allegiance. Such evidence can emerge in a variety of situations. Personal statements of belief often feature in leadership contests[2], or at the annual party conferences. Often politicians will appeal to underlying principles when they recommend controversial change in a specific policy area, or respond to unexpected developments. Politicians who defect from one party to another usually try to justify their actions in terms of principle, and the ensuing exchange of views with their former colleagues can shed important light on their respective positions.

However, students of ideology should also pay close attention to the general tendency of party policy, and check it against explicit declarations of principle. It is too much to expect that all of the policies pursued by a party in government or opposition will reflect a consistent view of human nature. Even the most radical politician usually finds that the scope for constructive action is limited, and will have to accept policies which have been introduced by their predecessors. Thus, although it is obvious from her habitual pronouncements that Mrs Thatcher disliked the welfare state (which, in her view, produced a 'dependency culture') a

---

[2]   Indeed, both Michael Howard and David Cameron have made declarations of faith *after* being chosen as successive Conservative Party leaders.

frontal assault on its principles would have courted electoral disaster. The only realistic option was the gradual infiltration of a pseudo-market mentality, which 'New' Labour has continued in its approach to public service reform since 1997. It can also be argued that 'New' Labour has been forced to accept the 40 per cent top rate of income tax which was established by the Conservatives in 1988, against a background of outraged protest from the parliamentary opposition. However, Tony Blair's warm acceptance of wealth accumulation demonstrates that he, at least, would not have increased the top rate of income tax even if he felt that such a move would be popular. In other words, careful sifting of the evidence allows us to distinguish between cases in which existing policies have the effect of thwarting even the most radical reformers, and other occasions when they are used as excuses for inaction.

This approach is much more profitable than taking on trust the labels which politicians claim for themselves, or which they try to pin on others in the pursuit of partisan advantage. More generally, when judging political utterances students of ideology have to distinguish between rhetorical flourishes and sincere statements of belief. This depends on a fairly sophisticated understanding of the relevant context. There are times when politicians are prepared to say almost anything in the hope of winning a standing ovation, or of avoiding a demonstration of discontent. The usual venue for such outbursts of insincerity is the party conference. However, in certain circumstances politicians exploit the occasion to appeal to the nation at large over the heads of their internal critics. Notable examples during our period are Mrs Thatcher's 'The Lady's not for Turning' speech in 1981, and Neil Kinnock's attack on the Militant Tendency four years later. Tony Blair also developed the habit of using his conference speech to disappoint party members who continued to hope for signs that the 'New' Labour project was running out of steam.

The student of ideology, then, is looking for the 'core' values that underpin policies and pronouncements, and must learn to distinguish evidence of genuine commitment from a mass of conflicting signals. Although it is persuasive in itself, this method of assessing ideological allegiance also promotes a reasonable degree of objectivity, which is more than can be said for the alternatives on offer. On this view, for example, the conservative equation of ideology with dogmatic thinking can be refuted. If ideology is about conceptions of human nature, conservatives deserves the label no less than their socialist and liberal opponents. Politicians may indeed judge every political dilemma on its merits; but it is a mistake to assume that even 'pragmatic' decisions are entirely free from presumptions about human nature. A pragmatist, after all, tries to take the most effective decision in specific circumstances; but a policy is likely to backfire if it is based on a misconception of human conduct. One can still say that some politicians are *more* ideological than others; but in most cases this really means that the politician in question is more *conscious* of ideological motivation, and more anxious to take decisions which conform to a system of belief. As a general rule, those who repeatedly justify their decisions by reference to a specific interpretation of human nature are those who want to promote a radical change in the way that people currently conduct themselves. But this does not necessarily mean that their views are any more 'dogmatic' than those which are advanced in favour of the *status quo*, or to advocate moderate reform.[3]

The focus on human nature is also a significant improvement on the Marxist interpretation of ideology. On examination, this turns out to be just as partisan as the conservative approach. It implies that Marxism is the *only*

---

[3]   Ironically, the first great exponent of conservative views, Edmund Burke (1729–97) provides an excellent illustration of this point. Burke produced the most explicit account of his ideas (his *Reflections* on the French Revolution [1790]) when he believed that the existing British constitution was under threat. The crisis in British politics in the wake of the French Revolution provoked him to make an eloquent expression of his views on human nature and society. Those ideas were widely held at the time, and Burke had argued on similar lines in earlier works; but his passionate rhetoric in the *Reflections* allowed critics to claim that he had suddenly become a 'reactionary' ideologue.

objective approach to politics, whereas to non-Marxists it appears to be even more biased than rival ideologies, because it demands a thorough transformation of the way in which people behave in capitalist societies. There is certainly a significant element of truth in the Marxist idea that the most powerful people in any society tend to encourage support for the existing dispensation. It is also mistaken to claim that the failure of Marxist regimes in the twentieth century somehow *proves* that Marx's view of human nature was wrong. Equally, though, there is no reason to accept the characteristic Marxist claim that their opponents are victims of 'false consciousness', endorsing the ideas of the ruling class even when these run counter to their own interests. In short, Marxism is very much like the other ideologies: its ideas are persuasive to those who embrace them, and either wrong-headed or downright dangerous to every else.

Ideology and political action

The approach adopted in the present study implies that ideology should be regarded as an inescapable aspect of political life, rather than a curse which could (and should) be eradicated. Almost everyone is to some extent influenced by ideology; that is, most people have ideas about human nature, whether these ideas are shaped by experiences in their everyday lives or inspired by magisterial works of political philosophy.

Another proposition concerning ideology which wins general acceptance is that it is 'action-oriented'. In other words, beliefs about human nature help to inspire political participation, at all levels. In the most obvious cases, many revolutions have been undertaken in the name of political principles, even if some of their original supporters have been disappointed by the ultimate outcomes. At a more mundane level, politicians who compete for votes are often accused of opportunism, advocating popular policies even if these represent significant deviations from their professed beliefs. However, even on the most cynical view of political life, most politicians have at least *embarked* upon their careers because of genuine ideological commitment. Apart from inspiring people to join political parties, ideology also affects other forms of participation, such as voting and pressure-group activity. Even when voters attribute their choices to seemingly accidental factors like the allegiance of their parents, it might well be the case that this feeling of familial loyalty is reinforced by agreement with the basic principles of their favoured party.

However, the problem of political apathy, which has become more serious over the years since 1970, suggests a refinement to the idea that ideology is invariably connected with positive *action*. More accurately, it can be argued that ideology provides a *framework for political evaluation*, from which action may or may not arise. Some people may hold beliefs which are incompatible with the form of society in which they find themselves, and decide that no existing political organisation reflects their thinking. In these circumstances, they might try to establish their own parties or pressure groups; equally, though, they might decide that political activity of any kind is utterly pointless. Thus it can be argued that as the principles espoused by the main UK parties become more difficult to distinguish, ideology increasingly becomes a recipe for *inaction* for the voters.

Political apathy cannot simply be attributed to the narrowing of electoral choice over recent years. However, it is impossible to deny that the main political parties have adopted broadly similar policies. The reasons for this phenomenon — which include the perceived demands of a volatile electorate, and the context of a globalised, competitive economic system — will be addressed in the following chapters. It is important to realise, though, that this does not make ideology less important as a factor in UK politics. If anything, when the main parties seem to agree on fundamental principles, and differ only on the details of policy, it is more important than ever to understand the characteristics of the dominant ideology.

Ideology and institutions

When discussing the views espoused by political parties and pressure groups, there is an obvious danger of misleading generalisations. For example, there is a temptation to make statements like 'Labour became more socialist between 1979 and 1983', or that 'the Conservative Party adopted classical liberalism after Margaret Thatcher became leader in 1975'. Such judgements are obviously flawed. In the first instance, many Labour Party members, including prominent MPs, continued to oppose socialism between 1979 and 1983; and although resistance to Mrs Thatcher's ideas within the Conservative Party did decline over the years, stubborn ideological opponents like Edward Heath were still in parliament when she was toppled in 1990. However, it is difficult to avoid excessive generalisations in a relatively brief study, and including the necessary provisos and qualifications would tend to become tedious. The best course is to avoid sweeping statements wherever possible, and to hope that the reader will pardon them when they sneak in.

By contrast, some students of ideology will dispute the approach of the present study because it places too much emphasis on the beliefs of specific individuals. The respective importance of individuals and institutions is a topic for perennial debate among political scientists, and some scholars believe that there is no room for compromise. There is a strong case for the argument that social and political institutions have a crucial effect on the thinking of individuals. Senior politicians, in particular, learn to operate within a framework of reference which includes well-defined institutions like parties and parliament. However, individuals react to institutions in different ways. The majority decide that they should never do anything which offends against an institutional ethos; but others make a conscious attempt to transform their parties. Obvious examples in recent years include Mrs Thatcher and (to an even greater extent) Tony Blair. On some occasions, politicians decide that their parties cannot be reformed, and take the drastic step of defection. In other words, the contrasting characteristics of certain individuals do make a difference. The attempt to explain these differences in terms of other formative institutions (eg social class) are often pertinent. But socio-economic factors cannot explain (for example) why some Labour MPs decided to join the Social Democratic Party (SDP) while others remained loyal in the hope that their party could be reformed.

However, there is one institution whose influence on political ideas can hardly be exaggerated. For regular participants in UK elections, the procedures are so familiar that it is easy to overlook an inbuilt ideological bias. Countries like the UK might not conform to an ideal model of liberal democracy; for example, the first-past-the-post electoral system does not give equal weight to the decisions of every voter. However, democratic political campaigning focuses on *individual choice*. From this perspective, it is significant that the main UK political parties have tended over recent years to present policy programmes which are designed to appeal to 'rational', self-interested individuals — thus reflecting the view of human nature associated with classical liberalism (see below). It can be argued that this is a natural development, although it has happened gradually as participants in the democratic process have digested the true implications of the system. This is not to say that members of rival ideological 'families' have no chance of prospering in mature liberal democracies, regardless of the circumstances. But under any electoral system they are most unlikely to secure an overall majority; and in countries which have not adopted proportional representation their prospects even of winning a share of power at national level look increasingly slim.

Ideologies in UK politics

This book is mainly concerned with the ideologies which have played the most important role in British politics since 1970. Some views are not discussed at all, but that is no reflection on their intrinsic interest. For example, anarchism is a fascinating ideology; but its effect on UK politics has always been marginal. Feminism and environmentalism are included, and a separate chapter is devoted to nationalism. However, a subsidiary purpose of this book is to argue that the latter three positions are not really ideologies at all — that is to say, in their most common forms they do not fulfil the characteristics of an ideology as outlined in this book. Many of the radical ideas which have recently been advanced in the name of Islam certainly fit within the present framework of analysis. However, as yet their influence on British politics has largely been *negative*: that is, their most important impact has been to inspire tough new laws against terrorist activity.

Ideological debates are often discussed in terms of 'left' and 'right'. This terminology can be defended as a kind of short-hand to characterise relative positions. In specific contexts, a reference to 'the left of the Labour Party' or 'right-wing Liberal Democrats' can make perfect sense; and this approach has obvious attractions for hard-pressed media commentators. However, the terms cannot really help to analyse the underlying beliefs of various party factions. As such, they have generally been avoided in this book.

The main ideologies covered here are conservatism; socialism; social democracy; classical liberalism; and new liberalism. Although these ideologies will be examined in greater detail in the relevant chapters, some preliminary sketches are necessary.

- *conservatism.* This is the most controversial and confusing of the main ideologies. In part, this is because the word denotes a political party as well as an ideology. In recent years, prominent members of the Conservative Party have speculated about adopting a new name. Whether or not this would affect their electoral fortunes, it would certainly be applauded by students of ideology. Some commentators get around the terminological problem by equating 'conservatism' with the beliefs espoused by the Conservative Party at any given time. However, this is an unprofitable approach, since it forces students of ideology to say that 'conservatism' is subject to constant change, under different party leaders or even from one year to the next. To anticipate one of the book's major themes, since 1975 commentators who take this view have had to argue that 'conservatism' shares many characteristics with classical liberalism. This is an obvious nonsense. It takes at face value the conservative (ideological) claim to flexibility, and attributes the same characteristics to members of the Conservative Party. But the ideas adopted by members of the Conservative Party at a specific time might be extremely *inflexible*. This was certainly true of Margaret Thatcher, who found it necessary to compromise on occasion but always believed in the intrinsic truth of her ideas.[4]

In this book, the core principle of conservative ideology is taken to be a belief that human nature is imperfect. In particular, conservatives are sceptical about any claims concerning human *rationality*. On this view, people are and always will be creatures of passion rather than reason. Some conservatives take this position further, and focus on the human capacity for wickedness. Others simply assert that people are essentially unpredictable; those who are basically good are still capable of wicked actions, while others who tend to be malevolent can be prone to occasional fits of morality.

The main political implication of this viewpoint is a deep distrust of programmes which promise radical reform. Even with the best of intentions, conservatives believe, reformers are likely to encounter unforeseen difficulties because they are dealing with human beings, not machines. The best that politicians can hope to do is to 'muddle through', tackling specific problems as they arise. For the most part, conservatives believe that the practices of the past are the best guide. Institutions have evolved over time, and thus represent the accumulated wisdom of many generations. It is foolish — even blasphemous — for individual politicians to imagine that their own thinking is any better.

The conservative viewpoint supports the idea of social

---

[4]   A further source of confusion is the tendency of politicians in the United States (usually members of the Republican Party) to claim the 'conservative' label. This problem is not of direct concern in the present book, which focuses on ideology in the UK. From this perspective, party-political debate in the US appears to be a conflict between *liberals* of various kinds. On examination, US 'conservatives' turn out to be hard-line classical liberals, who (for example) have a strictly limited interest in the traditional conservative goal of social stability.

hierarchy. Equality is an impossible dream; in fact, it is unjust because it would mean that relative goodness, and relative evil, would meet the same earthly reward. For conservatives, society is a network of relationships in which some find it natural to take decisions, while others are only capable of obedience. If the weakest members of society should ever overthrow their natural leaders, the result would be bad government, or a state of anarchy. The best that can be hoped is that leaders are nurtured from an early age to recognise the interests of the weak as well as the strong. It is no accident that conservative ideology seemed most persuasive in the pre-democratic age. Indeed, its conscious resistance to rapid change makes it most suitable for pre- industrial societies, governed by aristocrats who owe their position to the accident of birth.

- *socialism.* The core principles of socialism are that social conditions have a decisive effect on human nature, but that people are naturally co-operative. That is, if people find themselves in circumstances where the prevailing practices and ideas promote competition, they will tend to be competitive. But this situation is both unjust (because the 'winners' monopolise social resources), and inefficient, because most people are prevented from devoting their full talents to the service of society as a whole. While socialists have criticised other socio-economic arrangements, their main target is the capitalist system. This rests upon the exploitation of workers who often have to labour in degrading conditions. It also leads to a perverse allocation of productive power, so that workers who lack basic necessities are forced to produce goods which the rich could easily live without.

On this basis of these principles, socialists seek to abolish any institutions which promote competition. Some socialists have followed Karl Marx (1818–83) in believing that capitalists cannot be persuaded by peaceful means to relinquish their dominant position. For them, the transformation of society can only be achieved by a violent revolution. In the early years of the twentieth century some of Marx's followers argued that radical change could be effected through the ballot-box. However, the ultimate goal of these *democratic socialists* remained the same. For them, there can be no social justice while the means of production remain in private hands. So the state should confiscate such property, and ensure that production is geared towards the genuine needs of the population as a whole.

- *social democracy*. As we shall see, socialist views have been a major source of controversy within the Labour Party, especially between 1979 and 1987. However, for most of the period the party has been led by politicians who are best understood as representatives of the social democratic tradition. Social democracy, which first became influential in Britain during the 1950s, marked a real ideological shift from socialism. The leading British advocate of social democracy, Anthony Crosland (1918–77), argued that developments within industry were making socialist assumptions obsolete. Ownership of the means of production was less relevant now that the most powerful firms had become too large and complex to be dominated by a handful of rich capitalists who knew nothing about the productive process. Instead, industrial power was passing into the hands of highly-educated technicians and gifted managers. Often the best-qualified specialists were those who had risen from relatively humble positions within the firm. As such, they had every reason to know that the best workers are those who enjoy satisfactory pay and conditions. Under their influence, exploitation in the workplace was diminishing, and it was likely that this process would continue.

  Socialists argue for something like 'equality of outcome', where all members of society would have a common standard of living, adjusted to take account of special needs. For social democrats, by contrast, the priority was to move towards genuine 'equality of opportunity'. They argued that the state should continue to run major utilities, like gas, water and electricity, mainly because they were essential providers of the basic necessities for civilised life. There should also be a tax-funded health service which guaranteed that everyone would be treated without charge in the event of illness. But the main purpose of the state was to ensure high quality education for all children, regardless of family income. Social democrats have accepted a degree of social inequality; but it is essential for them that differences of income should be based on real merit, not on the chances of birth.

  The social democratic position has been a source of confusion within the Labour Party, not least because for many years its supporters continued to call themselves 'socialists' for tactical reasons. Social democrats often argued that they shared socialist aspirations, and that the only difference was that socialists had failed to take account of socio-economic change which meant that their goals were already being achieved by a better-educated electorate. However, there was a crucial difference. Social democrats did not want to abolish competition; they merely insisted that competition should be *fair*, and should not result in excessive economic inequality. Although they wanted certain industries to remain under state control, they accepted a 'mixed economy', in which most firms would still be privately owned. By contrast, in socialist eyes the question of ownership remained as important as ever, despite changes within the workplace. Private firms were still interested in making profits, rather than fulfilling social needs; and the quest for profit required exploitation, of workers and consumers alike.

- *classical liberalism*. The central proposition of classical liberalism is that all individuals are driven by self-interest. In other words, people are competitive, rather than co-operative, by nature. They are also rational, at least to the extent that they can be trusted to know best what is good for them. They want to be free to make their own decisions, up to the point where their actions do real harm to others. If they transgress these limits, the state should punish them. But for classical liberals, the punishment of serious wrong-doing and defence against foreign enemies is the only justified state activity. If the state strays outside this sphere, claiming that it has undertaken an action on behalf of 'society', it should be resisted. The agents of the state, after all, are self-interested individuals, hoping to extend their personal power. 'Society' is a fiction, which is almost invariably dangerous because it makes people think that there is a collective interest which should over-ride individual preferences.

   This brand of liberalism is particularly associated with the British thinkers John Locke (1632–1704) and Adam Smith (1723–90). Locke argued that government was based on a voluntary agreement between individual citizens; if the government failed to protect life, liberty and property, it should be dissolved. Though Locke was regarded as a radical during his lifetime, his ideas underlie the contemporary practices of liberal democracies like the US and the UK. Adam Smith's greatest work, *An*

Enquiry into the Nature and Causes of the Wealth of Nations (1776), argued against extensive state interference in the economy.[5]

This tradition of thought — justly called *classical* liberalism, because of its age and also because it has inspired so many great thinkers — seemed to have been eclipsed by the end of the Second World War. During that conflict, the state had taken on numerous responsibilities, including controls over industry and consumption. This development was not driven by a theoretical commitment to the supposed interests of 'society'; arguably, if the British state had not imposed strict limits on a variety of individual freedoms, it could not have succeeded in protecting its citizens from foreign conquest between 1939 and 1945. As the scope of state action tended to increase after the end of the war, the survival of classical liberalism as a relevant ideology came into question. However it retained some talented and vocal advocates, and revived under different circumstances in the 1970s. Nowadays its supporters are often described as '*neo*-liberals', but their thinking remains faithful to the classical tradition in all essentials.

- *new liberalism*. The idea that the state should restrict itself to keeping the peace at home and abroad came under considerable pressure in the second half of the nineteenth century. The characteristic arguments of classical liberalism had been developed before the industrial revolution. But from early in the nineteenth century, a series of social commentators deplored the tendency of rural workers to flock into the towns and cities. Even if they found regular employment on higher wages, their quality of life was usually diminished; and the great new industrial cities faced enormous pressures associated with poor hygiene and limited amenities. Towards the end of the nineteenth century, relative economic decline led to periods of rising unemployment, when even 'respectable' workers found themselves unable to support their families.

  New liberalism was a response to these dilemmas. After 1850 the state began to take on additional responsibilities, contravening the classical liberal belief that it

---

[5]   There is a danger that Smith's message can be taken out of context; his main target was the fashionable idea that a nation could prosper at the expense of other countries, and it is possible to use his work as a rationale for the collective provision of essential public services.

should confine itself to questions of war and peace and law and order. At least in part, law-makers were acting out of self-interest; they were at some risk themselves from the spread of contagious diseases, not to mention the possibility that impoverished workers would begin to embrace revolutionary ideas. But there was also a genuine element of philanthropy, directed in particular towards children who were forced to work at an early age in order to supplement the family income. As a result, parliament took action to limit working hours for children, but there were other measures of reform intended to make life more tolerable for all industrial workers.

Since classical liberalism provided no realistic solution to these problems, thinkers who sympathised with the liberal tradition began to modify their views. John Stuart Mill (1806–73) even expressed sympathy with socialist objectives in his later writings. But the most constructive response came from the Oxford academic Thomas Hill Green (1836–82). Green was certainly no advocate of an over-mighty state; but his work did provide a distinctively liberal rationale for the extension of government activity which was already under way in Britain. Like the classical liberals, Green based his thinking on the concept of the rational individual with a thirst for freedom. But Green's followers argued that the state has a duty to ensure that *all* individuals should enjoy the chance to maximise their rational faculties, whereas unrestrained capitalism apparently limited those opportunities to a fortunate few. Thus the state should provide at least minimal guarantees against ill-health and involuntary unemployment. More importantly, it should also subsidise education, without which most of its citizens would remain in ignorance.

This brief survey suggests several points of relevance to the following chapters. First, conservatism and socialism have not played a major part in political developments since 1970. They are included as 'major' ideologies because their importance is assumed in the common-place rhetoric of politicians, and in media commentaries. This is not to say that the views of conservatives and socialists are irrelevant to the concerns of contemporary life; on the contrary, it remains perfectly possible to question the human capacity for rational thought, and the socialist insistence that the profit motive generates injustice and waste has lost none of its force. It can be argued, though, that these ideologies no longer inform the policy suggestions of the major UK parties because it is perceived that, for one reason or another, they would have a detrimental effect on electoral prospects.

A further conclusion is that social democracy and new liberalism are quite closely related. Both provide a principled basis for accepting the profit motive within limits, and both justify an active role for the state, especially in the provision of education in order to ensure equal opportunity. However, a crucial difference remains. The starting point for social democratic thought is the good of society as a whole; new liberals, by contrast, are primarily concerned with *individual* fulfilment. In practice, though, it is worth noting that new liberalism seems better adapted to electoral requirements in the contemporary context, since voters make their choices as individuals.

Finally, although there are significant differences between all of these ideological positions, in the context of contemporary British politics one feature, in particular, stands out. To varying degrees, socialism, social democracy, new liberalism and conservatism are antagonistic towards the capitalist ethos. Socialism seeks its abolition; social democrats and new liberals want to humanise it; and even if conservatives can accept the social inequalities it produces, they deplore the incessant changes which it has provoked over the last two centuries. By contrast, some classical liberals treat the capitalist system with an enthusiasm which borders on religious veneration, seeing it as a guarantor of all human freedoms worthy of the name. This means that in the crucial area of economics, if classical liberalism came to dominate the political agenda in any country there would be a tendency for the advocates of rival ideologies to feel alienated from the democratic process.

Summary

The present study is an attempt to identify the underlying ideas which have informed British politics since 1970. It focuses on ideologies, which are taken to be systems of thought which ultimately arise from different views of human nature. This approach suggests that most people have ideological views of some kind, even if they are unaware themselves of their reasons for thinking as they do. In general, politicians can be expected to have entered public life with distinctive visions of the social arrangements which are most likely to accommodate human nature as they understand it. Even when we find their views unacceptable, students of politics have a duty to understand them.

Often focusing on tacit assumptions rather than explicit declarations by political actors, the conclusions offered here are unlikely to win universal acceptance. But if we wish to understand the role of ideas in political life we need to establish some ground-rules for analysis. Contemporary usage of ideological terms is usually unhelpful, and under-lines the need for a concerted attempt to map the various categories of belief onto the irregular terrain of political life. Even if readers find this version difficult to reconcile with their own impressions, at least it should encourage them to undertake the same exercise. In turn, this will enhance their appreciation and understanding of contemporary politics. Although political decisions are informed by a variety of factors, the role of ideas should never be discounted.

Further reading

On ideology, Andrew Heywood's *Political Ideologies: An Introduction* (3rd edition, Palgrave Macmillan, 2003) and Andrew Vincent's *Modern Political Ideologies* (2nd edition, Blackwell, 1995) are strongly recommended. Readers should also consult Robert Eccleshall, Alan Finlayson, Vincent Geoghegan, Michael Kenny, Moya Lloyd and Rick Wilford (eds) *Political Ideologies: An Introduction* (3rd edition, Routledge, 2001); Michael Freeden (ed) *Reassessing Political Ideologies: Transition and Durability* (Routledge, 2001); and Barbara Goodwin, *Using Political Ideas* (4th edition, John Wiley, 1997).

Ian Adams, *Ideology and Politics in Britain Today* (Manchester University Press, 1998), and Robert Leach, *Political Ideology in Britain* (Palgrave Macmillan, 2002) provide useful introductions to the influence of specific ideologies on British political debate. A more ambitious study, W.H. Greenleaf's *The British Political Tradition:*

Volume 11, *The Ideological Heritage* (Methuen, 1983) is based on impressive scholarship, but focuses more on political ideas than on practice.

Among the available surveys of contemporary history, Alan Sked and Chris Cook's *Post-War Britain: A Political History* (4th edition, Penguin, 1993) is strongly recommended. Contrasting interpretations of Britain's post-war fortunes are presented in George L Bernstein, *The Myth of Decline: The Rise of Britain Since 1945* (Pimlico, 2004), and Andrew Gamble, *Britain in Decline* (4th edition, Macmillan, 1994).

CHAPTER 1

A Decade of Discontent: The Labour Party, 1970–79

Background

In 1964, Harold Wilson's Labour Party came into office with ambitious plans and a slender parliamentary majority of four seats over all other parties. In contrast to the Conservatives, who had allegedly 'wasted' their years of power since 1951, Wilson confronted the electorate as the apostle of dynamic change. Under Labour, he promised, technology would be harnessed for the good of the people; renewed economic strength would be used to create 'a fairer order of society' (Wilson, 1974, 17).

Although the further general election called in 1966 rewarded Labour with a majority of ninety-five, by 1970 most commentators agreed that the hopes of 1964 had not been realised. With hindsight, the most surprising thing about the 1970 election is that Labour were clear favourites to win. The party's defeat led to an unhappy post-mortem — the first of many conducted over the next two decades.

Labour's difficulties did not begin in 1964, however. In many respects they were built into the party at the foundation of the Labour Representation Committee in 1900. At that time, it was recognised that instead of relying on the Liberal Party for parliamentary support, organised labour needed its own elected representatives. Yet this initial incentive for unity could not disguise the contrasting ideas held within the fledgling party. Although the vast majority of party members were committed to peaceful, as opposed to revolutionary, change, some had a clear vision of a socialist society and a determination to bring it about. Such activists mingled uneasily with others who either disliked theorising of any kind, or were broadly content with things as they were. The party was not socially uniform, containing both working-class trade unionists and middle-class intellectuals, notably those associated with the Fabian Society. These class differences did not coincide precisely with differences of principle, but they were not calculated to assist the long-term prospects for unity within the party. From the outset, then, the Labour Party was a coalition (or a 'broad church', as its members preferred to say). Over the years, as Labour's popularity grew and the Liberal Party declined, the diversity of principles held by its members tended to increase rather than diminish. In a party system where Labour seemed to be the only electable alternative to the Conservatives, ambitious politicians who might have been congenial recruits for a strong Liberal Party decided that joining Labour was their only realistic option. For example, Harold Wilson was a member of the Liberal Party for part of his undergraduate career.

After the First World War, the party adopted a programme and constitution which seemed to represent a conclusive move towards a coherent socialist position. The programme (Labour and the *New Social Order*) denounced the 'monstrous inequalities' produced by capitalism, and promised that a Labour government would do nothing to prop up such an unjust system. In its place, the party would promote 'deliberately planned co-operation in production and distribution', with the intention of producing 'a healthy equality of material circumstances' for all human beings (Coates, D, 1975, 14). The constitution included Clause IV, section 4, which committed Labour to remove the means of production, distribution and exchange from private hands. In pursuit of these goals, *Labour and the New Social Order* spoke of the immediate nationalisation of transport, mining and electricity, and promised that nationalisation of land would not be far away.

Despite these radical aspirations, the first Labour government, formed by Ramsay MacDonald in 1924, made very little progress towards a socialist society. Admittedly, this was a short-lived minority administration, and it could be argued that, as a relatively new party, Labour would need experience of power before it could realise its intentions. The second MacDonald government, however, was a different matter. In 1931, faced with an economic slump and the prospect of cuts in unemployment benefit, the Cabinet resigned. This failure to produce an imaginative response to what could be interpreted as the inevitable final crisis of capitalism would have been bad enough; what made matters worse was Ramsay MacDonald's decision, encouraged by King George V, to remain in office with Conservative support. In the eyes of Labour loyalists, MacDonald's action transformed him from hero to traitor. As the immediate shock wore off, his past record was reinterpreted; the suggestion that he had never really been a socialist seemed to be proved by his long-standing appreciation of aristocratic society. While MacDonald remained true to his party, his social life had been tolerated; after 1931, it was remembered as a sure sign that he had always wanted to go over to the enemy. The suspicion that party leaders might be tempted to repeat such a betrayal has remained alive ever since.

The 1945-51 government of Clement Attlee has generally been regarded as the most successful Labour administration. Even this legacy, however, has promoted ideological dispute. Labour's nationalisation of basic industries such as coal, steel and electricity could be regarded either as a useful step towards the fulfilment of the 1918 programme, or as the completion of a more limited exercise which marked the proper boundaries of state ownership. In 1959 Hugh Gaitskell, the then Labour leader, unsuccessfully urged the party to take the latter view. He wanted the abandonment of Clause IV, on the grounds that Labour's constitutional attachment to complete nationalisation of the means of production gave a misleading and counter-productive impression. After Gaitskell's failure, the party remained opposed on paper to the private ownership of industry. Among his opponents in 1959 was Harold Wilson, who always wished to avoid divisions within the party. This stance left Wilson well placed to succeed Gaitskell, and he won the leadership after the latter's death in 1962.

Socialists and social democrats

Socialists

Although Labour's divisions (like those of other parties) are often simply denoted by the terms 'left', 'right' and 'centre', even commentators who use the words usually admit that they are little better than convenient shorthand which does not tell us enough about the *nature* of the beliefs in question. The importance of differing loyalties and personality clashes within the modern Labour Party adds to the normal problems of providing a tidy ideological map; Henry Drucker has also argued that the 'ethos' of the party should be examined along with its 'doctrine' (Drucker, 1979). Bearing in mind these complications, however, in a brief survey primarily concerned with questions of belief it is still possible to illustrate the party's divisions through the categories of 'socialist' and 'social democrat'.

Herbert Morrison, the main architect of the Attlee government's nationalisation programme, once famously defined socialism as whatever the Labour Party did. Similarly, it has been a regular tactic of Conservative leaders to simply call Labour 'the socialist party', in the hope that this word alone would be enough to discredit it. Clearly these approaches to the question are inadequate, and even though complete precision is impossible, some broad fundamental principles can be identified.

Gaitskell's defeat over Clause IV demonstrated the strong emotional pull of socialist ideas on the Labour Party of 1959–60. Socialists oppose private ownership of the means of production because the profit motive entails the exploitation of workers whose labour is only partly rewarded. Also, the capitalist system encourages people to regard one another as competitors; for socialists, this competition impoverishes human nature, which can thrive only in a system of harmonious co-operation. The distribution of rewards under capitalism is also markedly unjust; indeed, cunning and deceit are rewarded more often than genuinely commendable traits such as generosity. Socialists are committed to a thorough transformation of capitalist society, involving a decisive shift of power from employers to workers. The vast majority of socialists within the Labour Party have always believed that this goal can be achieved through parliamentary action. Revolutionary writers such as Karl Marx have often been admired, but more for their ethical commitment to a fairer society than for their advocacy of revolutionary action. Hence, British socialists normally describe themselves as 'democratic socialists', and their beliefs stem from a conviction that a socialist society would be morally superior to the capitalist alternative.

Between 1964 and 1970 the truly socialist element within the Labour Party, which included Members of Parliament (MPs) such as Ian Mikardo, Frank Allaun and Judith Hart, was unable to exert a significant influence on policy. Perhaps the main reason for this was its lack of a recognised charismatic leader. Aneurin (Nye) Bevan, founder of the National Health Service (NHS) and a superb rallying orator, had died in 1960. Although Bevan's friends shared the general distrust of Harold Wilson, most were content to see him elected as Gaitskell's successor. Wilson had at one time been closely associated with the 'Bevanites', and resigned from the Cabinet with Bevan in 1951 over the introduction of National Health charges. In the absence of a more reliable alternative candidate throughout the 1960s, the socialist grouping within the Labour Party (mainly those associated with the newspaper *Tribune*) were by no means the most dangerous of many plotters against Wilson's authority.

Recriminations began even before Labour lost the 1970 election. In the *Political Quarterly* the moderate Reg Prentice, who had served in the Wilson government, claimed that the party had not been socialist enough. Prentice spoke for many socialists when he denounced the government's 'surrender to anti-trade union prejudices' in its 1969 White Paper *In Place of Strife* as the worst blot on its record (Prentice, 1970). The White Paper was a carrot-and-stick approach to the unions; certain rights were protected in return for a clamp-down on unofficial strikes, enforced through twenty-eight-day cooling off periods and pre-strike ballots. Barbara Castle, the Employment Secretary, won support for her proposals from Wilson, Chancellor Roy Jenkins and the Minister of Technology, Tony Benn, but there was a widespread feeling within the labour movement that unions were being used as a scapegoat for the government's own failings. The Home Secretary James Callaghan led a Cabinet attack on the measures, and legislation was abandoned in exchange for a voluntary (albeit 'solemn and binding') agreement between government and unions. Although socialists could applaud this as a victory for workers, the government's initial proposals generated lasting suspicion.

The 1964-70 government gave socialists little to celebrate in other areas. In 1964 a Department of Economic Affairs (DEA) was set up to challenge the supremacy of the Treasury, which had always been regarded as a powerful obstacle to socialist policies. Yet apart from a desire to maintain the impression of a dynamic government, the main inspiration behind the creation of this department was Harold Wilson's desire to provoke hostility between his main internal rivals, George Brown (who headed the new department) and the then Chancellor, James Callaghan. The DEA produced a National Plan which owed more to the goal of industrial efficiency than the dismantling of capitalism, and even this was abandoned in 1966. In foreign affairs, socialists were dismayed by Wilson's apparent eagerness to please the US President Lyndon Johnson, although he did keep British troops out of the Vietnam War. Wilson also seemed helpless in the face of defiance from the racist Rhodesian government led by Ian Smith. Against this record, the renationalisation of the steel industry in 1967 was too meagre a bone to satisfy socialists.

Social democrats

Since the fall of the Attlee government in 1951, the main intellectual impetus within the Labour Party undoubtedly came from its 'revisionist' wing. Most of the revisionists continued to identify themselves as socialists until the 1970s, but it would be more accurate to describe them as social democrats. The most prominent contribution to the social democratic case was Anthony Crosland's book *The Future of Socialism*, first published in 1956. Crosland argued that recent developments in industry meant that Britain was no longer a truly capitalist nation. Although the question of ownership was still relevant, *control* of industry had passed from shareholders to managers. This development promised to solve the problem of class exploitation without the need for a social upheaval. For Crosland, nationalisation could be justified only as a means to the end of a morally fair social order. This approach was now outdated, and socialists needed to readjust to changed realities (Crosland, 1964). Complete equality of rewards was not possible, but in a fairer society incomes would gradually flatten out. Governments could act to redistribute wealth and guarantee real equality of opportunity within a 'mixed' economy.

Crosland's ideas, then, represented at least a major revision or updating of socialism. For his numerous supporters, the continued attachment of the Labour Party to the principle of nationalisation was an irrational nuisance. The persuasiveness of Crosland's views depended crucially on the consistent achievement of high economic growth-rates. Without this, wealth distribution would meet with resistance from the better-off. Growth would be heavily dependent upon the performance of the private sector; if this was threatened by the prospect of further nationalisation, shareholders would be reluctant to provide adequate investment. Apart from threatening the achievement of high growth-rates, because of its perceived inefficiency, nationalisation had never been very popular with the electorate. During this period of Cold War politics, the association of state ownership with the Soviet Union was hardly likely to bring extra support for any British party. Since Hugh Gaitskell agreed with Crosland, it is not surprising that he was so keen to abandon Clause IV in the late 1950s. His move coincided with the decision of the German Social Democratic Party (SPD) to renounce any lingering allegiance to Marxist ideas at its 1959 Bad Godesberg Congress (Padgett and Paterson, 1991, 29).

Although in practice the immediate goals of the social democrats did not seriously conflict with those of their socialist colleagues within the Labour Party, Crosland's view that capitalism had been reformed was regarded by socialists as naive at best. Crosland admitted that class divisions were still important, but he did not share the socialist view that owners of capital and their representatives throughout the British establishment would fight stubbornly to retain their advantages. As Aneurin Bevan justifiably claimed, the controversy within the Labour Party was 'between those who want the mainsprings of economic power transferred to the community and those who believe that private enterprise should still remain supreme but that its worst characteristics should be modified by liberal ideas of justice and equality' (Greenleaf, 1983, 470). In short, socialists thought that Crosland's proposals would merely throw a veil of decency over a system which was itself irredeemably unfair. For socialists, only the nationalisation of at least the 'commanding heights' of the British economy could ensure a just society. Under Hugh Gaitskell, the bitterness generated by this internal debate led to the formation within the party of the Campaign for Democratic Socialism (CDS), which was opposed by the smaller Victory for Socialism (VFS). Crosland privately urged Gaitskell to expel the 'hard-boiled extreme left' from the party; the depth of hatred felt for the socialists among Gaitskell's friends can be measured by the fact that it was originally proposed to call the CDS 'Victory for Sanity' (Dorril and Ramsay, 1992, 22–9).

As Bevan hinted, social democracy owes as much to the liberal tradition as it does to socialism. Towards the end of the nineteenth century, liberal thinkers (notably Thomas Hill Green) had concluded that in an increasingly complex and anonymous industrial society, individuals needed state support to ensure that they were given a fair chance of a meaningful life. Green and his 'New liberal' followers thus retained the liberal focus on the individual, but recognised that the old attachment to the free market must be modified by some collective action in view of its tendency to fail. This point had been emphasised by Britain's economic decline at the end of the nineteenth century, and was graphically illustrated by the poor health of working-class volunteers for the Boer War. Green's ideas were an important inspiration for the social reforms of the Liberal Asquith government (1906–16). Ultimately they lay behind the economic and social proposals of John Maynard Keynes and William Beveridge, which did so much to shape politics after the Second World War.

The social democrats' admiration for Keynes and Beveridge brought them close to this new liberal tradition (see also Chapter 3). Important differences remained; social democrats had a positive view of the state, while New liberals were still apprehensive that it might begin to endanger important freedoms. But the fact that Roy Jenkins, a leading social democrat, had written an appreciative biography of the Liberal Asquith could only increase the socialist suspicion that the social democrats were concerned to humanise capitalism rather than to work seriously for fundamental changes. To add to their misgivings, Jenkins shared Ramsay MacDonald's penchant for aristocratic society.

In Harold Wilson's Cabinets between 1964 and 1970, social democrats were powerfully represented. Jenkins rapidly advanced to the Home Office, before succeeding Callaghan as Chancellor in 1967. Crosland himself held posts in the DEA, the Department of Education and the Board of Trade; he ended up as Secretary of State for Local Government and Regional Planning. Other talented social democrats within the Labour Party included Shirley Williams, Roy Hattersley, David Marquand, William Rodgers, David Owen and John Mackintosh.

Rightly or wrongly the 1964–70 government was identified as predominantly social democratic in its leanings. In spite of this common perception, few social democrats were entirely content with Labour's record in government. At the Home Office, Roy Jenkins consistently supported 'permissive' private members' legislation on issues such as abortion and homosexuality; moves to outlaw racial and sexual discrimination were equally welcome to social democrats. Yet their most urgent priorities, concerning education and wealth distribution, were not realised. The relative position of the poor improved very marginally, if at all, during these years, and in 1968 proposals to raise the school leaving age fell victim to Jenkins' spending cuts. Anthony Crosland requested local education authorities to plan for the phasing out of selective schooling in 1965, but ironically more progress towards this aim was made under Edward Heath's Conservative government (with Margaret Thatcher at the Department of Education). Finally, growth in the UK economy remained sluggish at an average rate of 2.2 per cent, well below the forecast included in the ill-fated National Plan, and languishing behind the prosperity experienced in countries of the European Economic Community (EEC). The key assumption of *The Future of Socialism* — that high levels of growth would be achieved, and reduce the pain of wealth distribution — was already looking over-optimistic.

What went wrong?

By 1970, socialists and social democrats were at least united in their disappointment. The burden of explanation, however, fell more heavily on the social democrats. For them, the government's failure could be traced to Harold Wilson's refusal to devalue the pound sterling on taking office in 1964, or at least when the question was canvassed again in 1966 (Marquand, 1992, 155–65). In defence of sterling's exchange value, Wilson had consistently chosen to deflate the economy, and to sacrifice social democratic priorities such as raising the school leaving age. The high interest rates established to uphold the pound choked off industrial investment, and an over-valued currency made British exports uncompetitive. Wilson clearly did not want to continue Labour's reputation as the party of devaluation (earned at the time of the Attlee government, of which he had been a member). For the social democrats, it was more damaging to be seen as a party which reneged on its promises.

Wilson himself subsequently claimed that 'economic constraints' had thwarted 'the social revolution to which we were committed'. Under the circumstances, 'we achieved far more than most would have expected' (Wilson, 1974, 17–18). This was a tacit admission that the advocates of devaluation had been right. But Wilson's memoirs blamed his government's record on the mess left behind by the Conservatives in 1964, particularly the severe balance of payments deficit. This defence did not impress many Labour supporters. Throughout his premiership, Wilson had posed as a conciliator between Labour's two main ideological groupings. As a result, electoral defeat left him vulnerable to assault from both sides. Whatever energy was left to ministers after their frequent bouts of crisis management expended itself in bitter faction-fighting, which Wilson's own suspicions only exacerbated. With neither the socialists nor the social democrats in full control of the party's direction, the most serious friction occurred within, rather than between, the factions. Since Wilson carefully avoided identification with any consistent ideological position, he could count only on an element of personal loyalty within the Cabinet which wore very thin over the years. Often the question seemed not to be whether Wilson would fall, but who from each faction would be best placed to challenge for the leadership when he was toppled. Personal ambitions thus helped to reinforce the impression that the government lacked any firm principles of any kind.

In opposition, 1970–74

Between the defeat of June 1970 and the return to office in February 1974 the Labour Party adopted a recognisably socialist programme. This happened for several reasons. First, whatever their own feelings, the social democratic wing of the party was more compromised by the failure of the previous government. Wilson had not been one of them, but he was perceived as standing closer to their views than he did to socialism. If this handicap were not enough for them, they soon found themselves distracted by the controversy which developed when it became clear that the United Kingdom's renewed application for membership of the EEC was not going to be vetoed by France, as it had been in 1963 and 1967. For social democrats, the prosperous community offered a promising solution for the growth problem of the 1960s. By contrast, many socialists regarded it as a capitalist club, which would divert attention from the wider human community and deprive Britain's government of the sovereign power it would need if a transformation of society were to be successfully implemented. On this issue the social democratic position was defeated within the party, and Roy Jenkins resigned from the deputy leadership in 1972 when the party committed itself to holding a referendum on EEC membership.

While the social democrats were occupied with this issue, other forces were working on behalf of the socialists. The election of what was perceived to be a right-wing Conservative government led to a polarisation of politics. A growing sense of militancy developed inside the trade unions as they fought against the Heath Government's Industrial Relations Act (Ferris, 1972). In the late 1960s there had been a notable shift towards radicalism in the trade union hierarchy; Hugh Scanlon, once a member of the Communist Party, replaced a moderate at the head of the Engineers' Union, while Jack Jones, who had fought for the Republicans in the Spanish Civil War, was elected leader of the Transport Workers. With the trade union 'block vote' exerting significant leverage over the Labour Party Conference, this shift in opinion was transmitted to all sections of the party. The student unrest experienced throughout Western Europe and the United States in the late 1960s also acted to renew interest in socialist alternatives to unimaginative government policies; notably in Britain, it inspired a group of young 'New Left' academics to write *May Day Manifesto 1968* (Williams, 1968). After his 1970 defeat Harold Wilson was not in a position to temper this mood. Thus, although important books by Roy Jenkins and Anthony Crosland showed that social democracy had not lost its intellectual edge in the early 1970s, the socialist momentum was irresistible (Jenkins, 1972; Crosland, 1974). Finally, a newly-radicalised Tony Benn held the chairmanship of the party in 1971-72, and, freed from the need to maintain loyal silence during the difficult years of Labour government, the *Tribune* group increased its membership and began to make itself heard (Warde, 1982, 171–6).

These factors culminated in what has been called Labour's 'most radical programme since the war' — *Labour's Programme 1973*, approved by its annual conference held in Blackpool (Whitehead, 1985, 120). The centrepiece of the programme was the proposed extension of state ownership. Although Harold Wilson blocked a specific plan to nationalise twenty-five of Britain's largest companies, a National Enterprise Board (NEB) was to be set up, with powers to invest throughout the economy. Planning agreements were to be drawn up with private sector firms, and worker participation in management was advocated. These policies were designed to combat the modern development which socialists identified as the greatest menace to their ideals — the growth of the multinational firm, able to avoid the impact of socialist policies simply by transferring their operations to another country. Economic and social equality was to be a priority of the next Labour government, and along with wealth, power over all forms of production would be shifted significantly towards working people and their families.

Back in office, 1974–79

The Heath Government's confrontation with the National Union of Mineworkers (NUM) brought about the early general election of February 1974 (see Chapter 2). On the key issue of relations with the unions, Labour was very well placed. Since the brief but bitter quarrel over *In Place of Strife*, the election of Mr Heath had presented Labour and the unions with a unifying enemy. The rekindled friendship was cemented through meetings of the Trades Union Congress (TUC) and the Labour Party leadership which agreed to a list of proposals known as the 'Social Contract'. The unions were granted concessions over pensions, housing and child benefits; subsidies and other price controls would help to keep down living costs. In addition, the unions received a promise that the Industrial Relations Act would be repealed, and an Advisory Conciliation and Arbitration Service (ACAS) set up to defuse labour disputes. Unlike the 1964–70 administration, the next Labour government would not impose statutory limitations on wages, but the union contribution to the deal was clearly intended to be a responsible attitude in pay negotiations. As far as they went, these policies coincided with short-term socialist aspirations. Overall, even though the socialists within the Labour Party did not get everything that they had wanted in the manifesto for February 1974, their reasons for satisfaction can be inferred from the fact that Roy Jenkins did not think that his party deserved to win this particular election (Jenkins, 1994, 364).

The Labour Party was undoubtedly helped in February 1974 by its perceived harmony with the trade unions. Yet its chances of forming a successful government were thrown into doubt by the election result which turned the Conservatives out of office. Between February and October 1974, when Labour asked the country for a stronger mandate, it governed without a majority. Even after October, its parliamentary position was worse than it had been in 1964 – the overall majority was only three seats. Labour also inherited a precarious economic situation, worse than the one it had faced ten years earlier. A worldwide rise in commodity prices in 1973, followed by the near-quadrupling of the cost of oil between October 1973 and January 1974, helped to produce a massive balance of payments deficit, and a year-on-year inflation rate of 13 per cent at the time of the February election. Unemployment had risen sharply in the early years of the Heath government, and although urgent measures subsequently brought the figure down, the underlying problems of the UK economy remained.

In fact, Labour's combination of electoral and economic constraints probably would have been enough to thwart the idealistic 1973 programme, even if the leadership had been wholeheartedly behind it. Only something more radical, which bravely ignored the Treasury view of economic realities, might have worked to the satisfaction of socialists. After the publication of Stuart Holland's *The Socialist Challenge* (1975), such a platform began to emerge in the shape of the Alternative Economic Strategy (AES), which advocated selective import controls as a means of protecting a real socialist experiment in Britain. The AES ran the risk of isolating the UK from an increasingly globalised economic system. By that time, however, there was little reason to imagine that the leadership would contemplate such a course. Any changes from the approach of Labour's first few months in power would be in a very different direction.

Despite the ominous background, Wilson's third government actually made a promising start for both socialists and social democrats. These groups agreed that the worst off in society should not bear the heaviest cost for the restoration of Britain's damaged prospects. Denis Healey's first budget included pension increases, and other benefits were raised. The scope of Value Added Tax (VAT) was extended, but food subsidies were increased. Allowances were lifted, to ensure that 1.5 million people escaped income tax entirely, but the basic rate was raised by 3 per cent (to 33 per cent; subsequently it was lifted again, to 35 per cent) and a reform of the tax structure left the rate on the highest earned incomes at 83 per cent. The Chancellor's promise in opposition to target the rich was fulfilled by the introduction of a 98 per cent band for the greatest 'unearned' incomes. These figures would be quoted against Labour for the next two decades. But such measures could be seen as down-payments on the Social Contract. They were supplemented by a July mini-budget which reduced the rate of VAT from 10 to 8 per cent, introduced reliefs on local taxation, increased food subsidies and encouraged employment in depressed regions. In the mean time the hated Industrial Relations Act had been repealed, and the miners' strike ended with a 29 per cent settlement.

Criticism from the Tribune group was understandably muted at this time, but for socialists these policies were only the icing – significant nationalisation would be the cake. On this crucial subject they were to be disappointed yet again. Concessions wrested from the Labour leadership in the weakness of opposition could be easily evaded when they were back in office. Although the Industry ministry was entrusted to the sympathetic Tony Benn and Eric Heffer, the vaunted Industry Act did not become law until December 1975, and even then represented a watered-down version of the original proposals. The NEB had a theoretical budget of £1 billion, which was far below socialist expectations. Instead of buying a significant share of profitable enterprises, the Board seemed to be designed as a prop for failing concerns – a view reinforced when a non-socialist businessman, Sir Don Ryder, was appointed as its chairman. Whatever faith socialists might still have had in the policy by 1975 was crushed when Harold Wilson grasped the occasion of the 'Yes' vote in the European Referendum to sack the anti-marketeer Tony Benn. Eric Heffer had already left office over the same issue. Eric Varley, Benn's replacement, had no comparable zest for nationalisation. Of the planning agreements which were an essential accompaniment to the socialist programme, only one was actually signed with a private company. This was the American-owned Chrysler car manufacturer, which received bountiful cash hand-outs in return for co-operation, before selling their British operation to Peugeot without consulting the government.

Soon after Benn's abrupt removal to the Department of Energy, the government took action to control wage rises which were now easily outstripping inflation. According to the Labour leadership, this could result only in workers 'pricing themselves out of jobs', and British industry becoming still less competitive. Certainly overseas confidence in Britain was low, and the pound was under pressure again. In April of the same year, Denis Healey had begun to unravel the Social Contract, cutting food and housing subsidies and raising taxes with less discrimination against the rich than he had previously contrived. This was an inauspicious time to begin asking the TUC to keep its side of the bargain on pay struck before the 1974 election, but the government negotiated a flat rate limit of £6 to run for a year from August 1975 (higher earners were to have their pay frozen). This at least looked egalitarian, as the low paid did comparatively well out of it; Hugh Scanlon and Jack Jones, the union leaders most closely associated with the Social Contract, urged their members to accept. In subsequent years, however, percentage increases were restored, ending with a 5 per cent limit for Stage IV of the incomes policy in 1978. Although the trade union leaders had loyally supported the pay policy up until that time, the patience of their members had been pushed too far. The result was a succession of strikes which ensured that these months would be remembered as 'The Winter of Discontent'. Having been elected because of its alliance with the unions, Labour could not survive this breakdown in industrial relations, which mainly affected low-paid workers in the public sector. The government, now led by James Callaghan, was defeated in a House of Commons vote of confidence, then turned out of office at the ensuing general election of 3 May 1979.

The IMF loan

Although the Labour Party remained in office until 1979, it effectively lost any independent powers in December 1976, when it agreed to strict International Monetary Fund (IMF) economic instructions in return for a loan to support the ailing pound on the foreign exchange markets. This represented the culmination of a process of economic retrenchment which had begun in April 1975. Harold Wilson escaped from the government's difficulties by resigning on 16 March 1976, just after his sixtieth birthday; the arrival of James Callaghan as his successor in Downing Street only made the government more determined to row back from the high public spending of its first year.

Between the two general elections of 1974, the Labour Party had defied the international trend towards economic deflation in the wake of the oil price rise. After October 1974, when this risky strategy had failed to win the government a secure parliamentary majority, it was quickly ditched. In a famous speech to the 1976 party conference, Callaghan signalled that, far from making an unequivocal commitment to socialism as many members hoped, the government would now even turn its back on the new liberal economics of J.M Keynes. Skilfully implying that the government was not responsible for the economic crisis, Callaghan told the conference that the Keynesian approach had failed instead; the strategy of increasing government spending to reduce unemployment during a recession had simply led to higher unemployment in the long run. It was now time to try something different. Since Keynesian economics had been an essential element of social democratic thinking, this speech is often regarded as marking the end of a post-war social democratic 'consensus'.

Callaghan's speech had been written by his son-in-law, Peter Jay, a convert to the 'monetarist' doctrine that inflation rises only when governments allow the growth in the amount of money in the economy to outstrip increases in production. In the circumstances of 1976, monetarist theory dictated a severe reduction in government spending. Like all good converts, Jay over-simplified the situation to discredit his former beliefs. Since Keynes had been well aware of the dangers represented by excessive inflation, his own reaction to the recession caused by the oil price explosion would surely have been more cautious than that of the Wilson government. In fact, Labour had actually increased public expenditure in obedience to its electoral needs rather than to Keynes' theories; but it was safer for Jay to blame a dead economist than to stigmatise living politicians. As early as 1970, in fact, it had been claimed that the style of politics needed to put Keynes' ideas into practice was 'beyond the comprehension of the Labour Party' (Bogdanor, 1970, 113). If anything, the economic crisis of the mid-1970s proved that governments of both parties had misused Keynes' theories, to the detriment of the economy.

The cuts proposed by the Chancellor did not pass through the Cabinet unchallenged. For the social democrats, Anthony Crosland had already been grumbling in private about the `illiterate and reactionary attitude to public expenditure' now being followed at the Treasury (Crosland, S, 1982, 355). From the socialist wing, Tribunites such as Michael Foot campaigned hard, and Tony Benn put the case for the AES, with import and credit controls. However, despite his friendship with Callaghan, Crosland was sidelined from economic policy at the Foreign Office, while Benn now carried less weight with his colleagues. Chancellor Healey, firmly backed by Callaghan, got his way. The precarious parliamentary position of the party meant that a determined rebellion in the House of Commons could only help the Conservatives, now led by Margaret Thatcher. Since Thatcher refused to distinguish between socialists and social democrats (loathing them both equally) this was not a tempting prospect. The Tribune group in particular staged protests against the IMF measures, but when it came to parliamentary votes of confidence they were forced to direct their resentment into different channels. By 1978 supporters of the AES had formed the Labour Co-ordinating Committee (LCC), which produced an alternative manifesto for the party in 1979 (Seyd, 1987, 91–5). However, the full impact of such factions was not to affect the Labour Party until it had fallen from office.

By the autumn of 1976 unemployment exceeded 1.5 million, although it later fell back slightly. The government's freedom of manoeuvre was even further constricted when a pact was forged with the Liberal Party, without which it would have lost a vote of confidence in March 1977 (see

Chapter 3). Callaghan also had to devote precious parliamentary time to devolution legislation for Wales and Scotland, in a bid to secure the support of nationalist parties. The
Labour Party presented an increasingly unreal appearance,
as socialists passed conference motions for radical policies
(including the abolition of the House of Lords), while the
government stuck to no principle more elevated than a
hand-to-mouth struggle for survival. The party's standing
in the opinion polls recovered during the run up to the Winter of Discontent, and it might have scraped a third successive victory if a poll had been called in the Autumn of 1978.
But Callaghan's decision to delay the election looks in hindsight like a merciful one; sufficient damage had been done
to morale without the prospect of another period of Labour
government with an insufficient majority.

What went wrong—this time?

Socialists had no hesitation in allocating blame for the mis-
adventures of the 1974–79 Labour governments. They had
not been socialist enough. This time the verdict could not be
delivered by Reg Prentice, who had joined the Conservative
Party in 1976 after a long battle in his constituency with people whom he could never accuse of insufficient loyalty to
socialism.[1] Others were on hand to identify the culprits.
According to Tony Benn, the 1979 defeat 'followed thirty
years of anti-socialist revisionism preached from the top of
the Labour Party' (Benn, 1980, 213). In a contribution to the
Institute for Workers' Control volume *What Went Wrong?*,
Ken Coates stigmatised the same foe (Coates, K, 1979, 7–33).
Social democracy, or 'revisionism', had failed; socialism
had never been given a chance. In the decade since 1970,
socialist hopes had been raised only to be cruelly dashed.
The logical conclusion seemed to be that if the Labour Party
would not act to transform society, then socialists should act
to transform the Labour Party. After Harold Wilson had
vetoed the commitment to nationalise the twenty-five com-

---

[1]   Prentice was later appointed to a junior ministry by Margaret
      Thatcher.

panies in 1973, a group of activists set up the Campaign for Labour Party Democracy (CLPD), committed to making MPs accountable to constituency activists for their parliamentary actions. Conference decisions should also be binding on the leadership at all times, instead of being ignored when the party was in office. Significantly, in 1973 the ban on 'prescribed organisations' (which usually meant Marxist ones) within the party was lifted, and the following year a Trotskyite, Andy Bevan, was named as the Labour Party's Youth Officer. It was during the IMF crisis that Tony Benn first read Marx's Communist Manifesto. He also consulted the Cabinet minutes from the MacDonald crisis of 1931, and detected some ominous parallels (Benn, 1990, 634–94).

Whether or not a full-blooded socialist programme would have fared better, the idea that social democracy should be exclusively blamed for Labour's plight is untenable. As we have seen, Labour gained office in 1974 armed with socialist policies; when crisis struck, socialism was replaced not by social democracy but by what David Coates has called 'unbridled managerialism' (Coates, D, 1980, 33). Of the leading social democrats from 1964–70, Anthony Crosland died early in 1977, while Roy Jenkins resigned from the Cabinet in September 1976 after being offered the presidency of the European Commission. None of the major Labour figures of this time — Wilson, Callaghan and Healey — was a socialist, but although Healey in particular was strongly attracted by continental social democracy it would be stretching a point too far to claim that any of these party leaders acted in accordance with Croslandite principles.

Social democracy certainly faced a crisis during the mid-1970s, and the problems were not confined to the United Kingdom. Under Helmut Schmidt, the German SPD also had to postpone ambitious reforms during this difficult period (Padgett and Paterson, 1991, 149–50). As David Marquand has pointed out, social democracy was always vulnerable because of its liberal ancestry, which burdened it with a built-in contradiction between its collectivist economic strategy and an acceptance of individualism in its ethics (Marquand, 1987, 323). Yet this was not the primary reason for its problems during the 1970s. The same forces within the world economy, along with the continuing failure of British industrialists to invest — factors which Anthony Crosland had largely overlooked when writing *The Future of Socialism* — knocked both social democrats and the government from their preferred courses. This is not to say that these preferences were identical. Social democratic elements within the party such as the 'Manifesto' group of MPs and readers of the journal *Socialist Commentary* had more reason to support the government than to oppose it, but their attitude was hardly one of positive enthusiasm. It arose partly because they feared letting Mrs Thatcher into Downing Street, and partly because possible successors to Jenkins and Crosland, such as David Owen and Roy Hattersley, were still making their way through the Cabinet ranks, hopefully to positions from where they could exercise more effective influence over policy. In any case, while Crosland had been angry enough to stand out against the IMF terms, other social democrats were not prepared to create a common front with their most hated political opponents.

To compound their misery, these tactical choices left the social democrats vulnerable to their socialist critics when the blame for 1974–79 was shared out. In presenting their analysis, the socialists pulled off a masterful stroke; the defeat was turned into an opportunity to settle ideological scores with their revisionist foes. With the campaign for 'democracy' within the Labour Party gathering momentum, the 1972 deselection of Dick Taverne from his Lincoln seat by socialists in his constituency party stood as a warning to any social democrats who refused to repent for their failings. Some of them concluded after 1979 that they could hope to restore their position only by forming a separate party. This, of course, laid them open to the most destructive of Labour Party insults — 'MacDonaldism'.

Conclusion

In terms of either socialist or social democratic priorities, the record of the 1964–70 and 1974–79 Labour governments cannot be seriously defended. At best, both sides might choose to assert that the governments were beaten by unfortunate circumstances — that Labour seems to be elected only when the Conservatives have left an impossible situation for anyone with consistent principles to deal with (Castle, 1993, 501). For the socialists, however, there was a certain degree of compensation; with Wilsonian 'managerialism' and social democracy wholly discredited, the predictable result of the 1979 defeat was a new shift of Labour towards a more socialist outlook (see Chapter 5).

The IMF loan of 1976, and the cuts in government spending which preceded and followed it, is often taken as the death blow to a post-war consensus which is usually defined as 'social democratic'. While this subject will also be pursued in later chapters, it can already be seen that this picture is a serious distortion of reality. The reasons for social democratic dissatisfaction with the 1964–70 governments have already been explored; Roy Jenkins claims that Labour deserved to have won the 1970 election, but as Chancellor during 1967–70 he was constrained to carry out deflationary policies which did little for the cause of social justice. The 1974–79 government has even fewer claims on social democratic respect. All one can say is that the major decisions of these years were taken by leaders who preferred social democracy to socialism, but, as Anthony Crosland bitterly remarked towards the end of his life, 'Even if the Government survives, does it make such a difference if Labour measures can't be implemented? . . . this is the most right-wing Labour Government we've had for years' (Crosland, S, 1982, 376). Thirteen years after Callaghan's fall, David Marquand was not inclined to be nostalgic; he still rated the 1974–79 government as 'one of the worst of the century' (Marquand, 1992, 158).

Whatever the self-conscious pursuit of ideology in office may do to the well-being of a country, the experience of Labour during these years points to two important political advantages. First, ideology can dictate policy choice, and thus prevent prolonged agonising over decisions. It helpfully provides an authority to leaders which is independent of their own personalities, but in many cases this insurance is unnecessary because ideology can transform ordinary politicians into charismatic figures. Tony Benn was hardly 'ordinary' at any time, but he was regarded as a technocratic follower of Harold Wilson for most of the 1960s. Just before the time of Labour's 1970 defeat he was reinvigorated by speaking to radical audiences; his discovery of new socialist thinking made him a far more formidable operator, with a devoted following among a public which already had little respect for its politicians. Benn identified the revitalizing role of firm convictions when he watched Margaret Thatcher in the House of Commons on the day of her fall from office. 'Thatcher was brilliant', Benn noted. 'She always has her ideology to fall back on' (Benn, 1994, 614).

Secondly, ideology allows scope for the creation of myths. The principles which drive decision-making can also create a ready-made history, showing how good intentions were overborne by enemies or unlooked-for events. As long as the ideology has been correctly followed, something (or someone) else must have been at fault if the policies did not work. These advantages apply to any firmly-held ideological position, and not just to those which are categorised as 'extreme'. Socialists attributed the failure of the 1974–79 governments to the deliberate betrayal of mischievous leaders, while social democrats tended to blame the trade unions. Like all effective ideological myths, these rival explanations contain elements of truth as well as distortions; if most people in Britain sided with the social democratic 'myth', this merely suggests that people were generally more sympathetic to the ideology of social democrats.

By refusing to devalue in 1964, and accepting the IMF cuts in 1976, both James Callaghan and Harold Wilson showed themselves willing to adopt policies which undermined any realistic hopes among their progressive followers. It would be a mistake to dismiss them as mere 'pragmatists', who put personal survival above principle. They clearly hoped to improve living standards for ordinary working people. However, their ideological commitments were insufficiently strong to overcome the difficulties that beset them — Britain's economic plight, and the internal party feuds between colleagues who could offer more distinctive visions of social change. In their eyes, Wilson and Callaghan were no more than well-meaning figures who delivered spending cuts with a sympathetic shrug instead of a joyful grin.

Thus, instead of proving the bankruptcy of social democratic ideology, the Wilson-Callaghan record suggests that Labour could only have hoped to meet the challenges of these years by conveying a clear sense of principled conviction to the electorate. Of course, a Labour government led by social democrats or socialists might still have failed to resolve the many difficulties facing the UK. But it is unlikely that the legacy of failure would have been any more damaging to the country or the party; and at least such a government could have clarified the issues in dispute between the contending Labour factions. As it was, the repercussions of Labour's failure during the 1974–9 period deprived Britain of an effective parliamentary opposition for the ensuing decade.

List of works cited

Benn, Tony (1980), *Arguments for Socialism*, Penguin.

Benn, Tony (1990), *Against the Tide: Diaries 1973-76*, Arrow.

Benn, Tony (1994), *The End of an Era: Diaries 1980-90*, Arrow.

Bogdanor, Vernon (1970), 'The Labour Party in Opposition, 1951-1964', in Vernon Bogdanor and Robert Skidelsky (eds) *The Age of Affluence 1951-1964*, Macmillan.

Castle, Barbara (1993), *Fighting All the Way*, Macmillan.

Coates, David (1975), *The Labour Party and the Struggle for Socialism*, Cambridge University Press.

Coates, David (1980), *Labour in Power? A Study of the Labour Government, 1974-1979*, Longman.

Coates, Ken (eds) (1979), *What Went Wrong?*, Spokesman.

Crosland, Anthony (1964), *The Future of Socialism*, Jonathan Cape.

Crosland, Anthony (1974), *Socialism Now*, Jonathan Cape.

Crosland, Susan (1982), *Tony Crosland*, Jonathan Cape.

Dorril, Stephen, and Ramsay, Robin (1992), *Smear! Wilson and the Secret State*, Grafton.

Drucker, Henry (1979), *Doctrine and Ethos in the Labour Party*, Allen and Unwin.

Ferris, Paul (1972), *The New Militants: Crisis in the Trade Unions*, Penguin.

Greenleaf, W. H. (1983), *The British Political Tradition*: Volume II, *The Ideological Heritage*, Methuen.

Holland, Stuart (1975), *The Socialist Challenge*, Quartet.

Jenkins, Roy (1972), *What Matters Now*, Fontana.

Jenkins, Roy (1994), *A Life at the Centre*, Macmillan.

Marquand, David (1987), 'British Politics, 1945-1987', in Peter Hennessy and Anthony Seldon (eds) *Ruling Performance: British Governments from Attlee to Thatcher*, Blackwell.

Marquand, David (1992), *The Progressive Dilemma: From Lloyd George to Kinnock, Heinemann*, 2nd edition.

Padgett, Stephen, and Paterson, William, (1991), *A History of Social Democracy in Postwar Europe*, Longman.

Prentice, Reginald (1970), 'Not Socialist Enough', *Political Quarterly*, volume 41.

Seyd, Patrick (1987), *The Rise and Fall of the Labour Left*, Macmillan.

Warde, Alan (1982), *Consensus and Beyond: The Development of Labour Party Strategy since the Second World War*, Manchester University Press.

Whitehead, Philip (1985), *The Writing on the Wall: Britain in the Seventies*, Michael Joseph.

Williams, Raymond (ed.) (1968), *May Day Manifesto 1968*, Penguin.

Wilson, Harold (1974), *The Labour Government 1964-70*, Penguin.

Further reading (see also Chapters 3 and 5)

The best primary sources for this period are the diaries of Tony Benn (*Office Without Power: Diaries 1968-72* (1989); *Against the Tide: Diaries 1973-77* (1990); and *Conflicts of Interest: Diaries 1977-79* (1991) (all published by Arrow paperbacks). Another invaluable contribution from a Labour diarist is Barbara Castle, *The Castle Diaries 1964-76* (Macmillan, 1990). For the 1960s, Richard Crossman's *Diaries* remain an incomparable source. It was published in a condensed form (edited by Anthony Howard) by Magnum in 1980.

For an excellent overview of the whole period, see Eric Shaw, *Discipline and Discord: The Politics of Managerial Control in the Labour Party 1951-1986* (Manchester University Press, 1988). For background, students can also consult Clive Ponting, *Breach of Promise: Labour in Power 1964-70* (Hamish Hamilton, 1989. Martin Holmes, *The Labour Government, 1974-79: Political Aims and Economic Reality*

(Macmillan, 1985) has a more specific chronological focus, although the author is much more hostile. A brief summary is Phillip Whitehead, 'The Labour Governments, 1974-79', in Peter Hennessy and Anthony Seldon (eds) *Ruling Performance: British Governments from Attlee to Thatcher* (Blackwell, 1987).

Geoffrey Foote, *The Labour Party's Political Thought: A History*, (3rd edition, Palgrave Macmillan, 1997), is the most authoritative survey of ideas within the party in these years. Students can trace the historical development of Labour's disputes in Patrick Diamond (ed) *New Labour's Old Roots: Revisionist thinkers in Labour's History 1931-1997* (Imprint Academic, 2004); Elizabeth Durbin, *New Jerusalems: The Labour Party and the Economics of Democratic Socialism* (Routledge, 1985); Stephen Haseler, *The Gaitskellites* (Macmillan, 1969); Mark Jenkins, *Bevanism: Labour's High Tide* (Spokesman, 1979); and John Callaghan, 'The Left: The Ideology of the Labour Party', in Leonard Tivey and Anthony Wright (eds) *Party Ideology in Britain* (Routledge, 1989).

Michael Barratt Brown, *From Labourism to Socialism: The Political Economy of Labour in the 1970s* (Spokesman, 1979), and Ralph Miliband, *Parliamentary Socialism: A Study in the Politics of Labour*, Allen and Unwin (1961), are still relevant as critical accounts of Labour's performance in government between 1945 and 1979.

CHAPTER 2

From Selsdon Man to Grantham Woman: The Conservative Party, 1970–79

Background

The Conservative Party has traditionally regarded unity and loyalty to its leader as important assets. This ethos has not meant that the party is immune from internal controversy; indeed, it suffered significant splits in the nineteenth century (over repeal of the Corn Laws) and early in the twentieth century (concerning Tariff Reform). While some might attribute the ethos of loyalty to the aristocratic roots of the party, it undoubtedly owes much to the fact that British politicians who have identified themselves with conservative principles over the years have broadly agreed on the meaning of these ideas. The paper wars which have enlivened the history of other ideologies have rarely distracted conservatives. At least, this was true until the early 1970s. Since then, the nature of conservatism has been as warmly disputed as any other variety of political belief. As a result, describing the impact of conservatism on British politics has become remarkably complicated, and equally sensitive.

Not the least of these complications is the fact that established usage demands that the same word 'conservative' is taken to denote both the ideology and the party. Some commentators try to solve this problem by simply merging the two things, so that whatever the Conservative Party does *is* conservatism at any given time. This is no more helpful than Herbert Morrison's claim that socialism is what the Labour Party does. One does not have to argue that ideologies should remain constant over time to take this view; a more conclusive objection is that modern British political parties tend to be coalitions of people with very different ideas. In the case of the Conservative Party, it is clear that when Margaret Thatcher became leader in 1975 the majority of her MPs disagreed with many of her views, and that this was still true when she resigned in 1990 (Norton, 1990). Given the fundamental nature of these disputes, it cannot be helpful simply to describe the respective positions as different 'strands' of conservative thought. While investigating this awkward problem in the course of this chapter, a capital C will be used to designate the actions and beliefs of members of the Conservative Party, and a lower-case *c* whenever the ideology is meant.

It is easier to give examples of this confusion than to sort it out to everyone's satisfaction. For instance, when Herbert Spencer attempted to warn fellow liberals against excessive state interference in his book *The Man versus the State* (1884), he chose 'The New Toryism' as the title for his opening chapter. Spencer bitterly regretted that the Liberal Party of his time had 'lost sight of the truth that in past times Liberalism habitually stood for individual freedom versus State-coercion'. Tories could be excused for preferring the interests of the state to those of the individual, because this was what Tories had always done. Liberals, in Spencer's view, should have known better. So great was the new liberal propensity to use state power against the individual that 'it may by and by really happen that the Tories will be defenders of liberties which the Liberals, in pursuit of what they think the popular welfare, trample under foot' (Spencer, 1969, 67, 81).[1]

---

[1]   Spencer's use of the capital L to denote liberalism is instructive here. Although one must beware of reading too much into a very different context, it seems to reflect an assumption that liberal thinking and

Spencer's message was very serious, although many of his readers must have thought that he was exaggerating his point for added effect. Whatever the Liberal Party might be up to at any particular time, the Conservatives would never be reliable friends of liberty in Spencer's individualist sense — that is, they would never accept that freedom should be regarded as the most important goal of political action. One hundred years later, however, his words seemed to have come literally true. In 1984, Margaret Thatcher's Conservative Party posed as the liberators of the individual, while the Liberal Party (in alliance with the SDP) consistently rejected Thatcher's rhetoric about rolling back the overmighty state. So who was right about conservatism — nineteenth-century liberals who thought of it as an anti-individualistic creed, or the Thatcherites who presented themselves as enemies of the state? Perhaps they were both right, or perhaps words such as right and wrong are misplaced in this kind of argument? The latter conclusion would be tempting, and some people remain convinced by it. However, it seems too convenient, and the question deserves more investigation.

Although controversy over the nature of conservatism came to a head after Mrs Thatcher's election as party leader in February 1975, the question had been addressed from time to time in the earlier post-war period. In 1947, Quintin Hogg (the future Lord Hailsham) published *The Case for Conservatism*, a book which has escaped criticism during the squabbles of recent years. In his book, Hogg distinguished carefully between British conservatism and a blind resistance to reform. If conservatives tend to fear change, it is because they think that human nature is, and will remain, imperfect and unpredictable. Attempts to mould society into some untried form would court disaster. While socialists and other radicals seek to create a perfect environment for human beings, conservatives are more concerned to combat existing

---

Liberal Party actions are always the same thing, yet *The Man versus the State* would not have been written if Spencer was confident about this continuing to be the case.

evils. Hogg, a deeply religious man, traced the human propensity for evil to the Fall, but he recognised that other conservatives could share his conclusions without adopting his Christian premises.

Hogg, like most British conservatives, tried to distinguish between his world-view and the approach of believers in 'new religions' such as socialism. For him, conservatives were different because they accepted human nature as it was, and were content to grapple with its consequences. In fact, conservatism was a philosophy of government, which had been developed over centuries by the accumulated wisdom of politicians who had readily accepted the responsibilities of power in an imperfect world. Unlike their opponents, conservatives rejected programmatic politics on the basis of their experiences; indeed, for them politics was far from being the most important aspect of life. Conservatism, in fact, was simply the exercise of common sense by practical people (Hogg, 1947).

Hogg's eloquent advocacy certainly highlights some important differences between conservatism and other ideologies. However, he could not establish that these differences are sufficient to outweigh the underlying similarities. *The Case for Conservatism* will be persuasive only for those who share Hogg's view of human nature. It might be true that most people presently think that 'common sense' dictates the defence of private property, for example, but this would be a poor argument against those who believe that human nature can be fulfilled only if all forms of individual ownership are destroyed. The majority might think of themselves as more 'practical', but in the end this is a matter of opinion, because what they regard as practical is itself defined by their view of what human beings really are. If there is a structural difference between the conservative and other ideologies, it concerns the political *strategies* which arise from it rather than its theoretical basis. Other ideologues can be flexible when events force them to be; but conservatives are flexible by choice. In some circumstances this gives conservatives a decided political advantage, but, as we shall see, in recent years it has acted as a crippling handicap.

Post-war conservatism

When the Second World War ended in 1945, the Conservative Party ought to have been well placed for electoral victory. After all, in Winston Churchill it possessed a leader who was Britain's most popular politician. Yet when the election came the party suffered a humiliating defeat, and was out of office for the next six years.

The reasons for this unexpected reverse are crucial to an understanding of post-war conservatism. Perhaps most important was the popular memory of the 1930s, when unemployment soared and Conservative-dominated governments seemed powerless to stop it. This experience convinced many Conservatives that they should always try to prevent such a human tragedy from recurring; unfortunately for them, it convinced a majority of the electorate that they should vote Labour in 1945. A second reason was the dilemma which confronted Conservatives when they presented their case against Labour. Although Labour's programme advocated a radical departure from previous peacetime experience, including extensive nationalisation and economic planning, some of Labour's plans had been worked out while the two parties co-operated in the wartime government. Proposals to extend welfare benefits and to ensure full employment received official approval while Churchill remained Prime Minister. It was also undeniable that economic planning had made a significant contribution to Britain's war effort.

With hindsight, Churchill's reluctance to call a new general election at the end of the war seems understandable. Active opposition to Labour's programme would expose the Conservative Party to the charge that promises made in wartime might be broken as soon as peace returned. More importantly, while the scope of Labour's plans worried many conservatives, the principles underlying them could not be rejected out of hand. As Herbert Spencer had said, an active role for the state was fully in line with the previous approach of the Conservative Party. In this respect, Spencer's 'Toryism' had a great deal in common with conservative ideology. If the state could be used to help ensure social stability, conservative objectives would be satisfied. The capacity for evil might remain within people who were sure of either a job or a generous level of benefit, but such improved security might easily prevent decent people from turning to crime in desperation. It would also encourage people to feel that they were part of 'One Nation' — the goal of Disraelian conservatism in the previous century.

For Churchill himself, the dilemma was particularly acute. Having first been elected as a Conservative, he had quickly defected to the Liberals. As a minister in Herbert Asquith's Liberal Cabinet, he had helped to lay the foundations of the welfare state. In short, he had been a representative of the trend within the *Liberal* Party which Spencer had denounced as 'New *Toryism*'. Since that time, as we have seen, new liberals such as Beveridge and Keynes had developed this tradition further, producing ideas which demanded an even greater role for the state. In 1945, it was difficult for Churchill to present a persuasive argument for rejecting Labour's limited nationalization programme, while accepting more extensive state intervention in the field of welfare policy. His attempt to resolve this personal dilemma produced the most serious electoral misjudgement of his career. In a broadcast he implied that Clement Attlee, the leader of the Labour Party and, until recently, his trusted coalition partner, threatened Britain with the introduction of a 'Gestapo'-style regime. Even the young Margaret Hilda Roberts, listening in her Oxford college, initially thought that this was going too far. It certainly failed to win the election for Churchill. What it did do, however, was to give the Churchillian seal of approval to arguments being advanced at that time by the Austrian liberal, Friedrich von Hayek, who denounced any form of state activity beyond a bare minimum as the beginning of a 'Road to Serfdom' (Hayek, 1962). By a strange twist of historical events, the most outspoken living advocate of Herbert Spencer's views on freedom, and a leading exponent of the 'New Toryism', found a superficial unity in their protestations about the dangers of socialism.

At first, it looked as if this ideological misalliance was a product of unusual circumstances which would not recur. While classical liberals like Hayek remained convinced that freedom was in danger, conservatives could appreciate that in practice Labour was far more flexible than its programme had suggested. Wartime restrictions on economic activity, such as rationing, remained in force for some years. But by March 1949 Harold Wilson, Labour's young President of the Board of Trade, was able to announce a 'bonfire of controls'. When the Conservative Party Conference of 1947 endorsed an *Industrial Charter*, it accepted that the state needed to act in partnership with industry in order to ensure prosperity and full employment. In *The Case for Conservatism*, published the same year, Quintin Hogg outlined the reasons why conservatives should oppose nationalisation, while arguing that when his party returned to office it should do no more than call a halt to further state ownership (Hogg, 1947, 284–95). In practice only road haulage and iron and steel were denationalised by the next Conservative government.

The Conservatives held power for more than half of the period between 1945 and 1970 without finding it necessary to force a radical departure from the approach laid down by the Attlee government. Since successful politicians have to operate within the same framework of events, it often happens that people holding different ideological viewpoints can reach broadly similar policy decisions. This was the experience of leading Labour and Conservative policy-makers during these years. Pragmatic considerations undoubtedly played a part in the Conservative Party's acceptance of the welfare state and more active government involvement in the economy. But, as Hogg demonstrated, there were no significant reasons why conservatives should stand out against these developments on principled grounds. The Labour Party might have provided the initial legislative impetus for post-war British politics, but the

Conservative Party's acceptance of this framework was not just the result of a tendency to acquiesce in the established facts of political life. If there was a 'consensus' after the Second World War, Conservatives could claim that it was just as compatible with their ideas as it was with social democracy.

True to Hailsham's approach, Conservative governments between the end of the war and the advent of Mrs Thatcher varied their emphasis from time to time. The brief period during which Peter Thorneycroft was Chancellor (1957-58), for example, is often identified as a precursor to the monetarist experiment after 1979. According to one distinguished commentator, 'the post-war objectives of full employment and economic expansion ... seemed for a time to have been abandoned' (Brittan, 1971, 209). Yet under the same Prime Minister, Harold Macmillan, the Conservative Party established the National Economic Development Council (NEDC), where ministers, trade unionists and employers met to discuss economic performance. This 'corporatist' framework was intended to ensure that the priorities of both workers and bosses could be considered together; indeed, it is doubtful whether the Council would have been set up in the absence of general agreement on the goals of full employment and economic growth (originally projected to be a healthy 4 per cent annually). Alan Budd has argued that this initiative 'was by no means alien to the tradition of the Conservative Party' (Budd, 1978, 80). In 1962, when the NEDC was set up, the party still contained dissidents like Enoch Powell, who thought that state activity in the economic sphere was counter-productive. But although Powell resigned with Thorneycroft over what they saw as financial irresponsibility in 1958, both of them were back in the government by 1960. The Tory Party debate about the role of the state seemed to be settled in favour of the interventionists.

In opposition, 1964–70

Scandals such as the Profumo affair marred the early 1960s, yet the Conservative election defeat of 1964 was still a shock to the party after thirteen years in power. Like most setbacks of this kind, returning to opposition at least offered a chance for reflection. The Conservatives embarked on an far-reaching policy review, which was barely interrupted when Harold Wilson called a new election in 1966. The new Conservative leader, Edward Heath, had been elected in 1965 as an appropriate challenger to Harold Wilson. Like Wilson, Heath had risen through his own abilities, thus symbolising the 'meritocratic' mood of the times. He also resembled Wilson in presenting an efficient, business-like image. Heath certainly translated this image into action as Leader of the Opposition; according to one of his aides, he ensured that the party 'was equipped with policies more elaborate and better researched than any opposition had ever attempted' in preparation for the 1970 general election (Hurd, 1979, 7).

With Labour back in power, the Conservative Party's attitude towards state intervention in the economy was revised. It was one thing for a Conservative government to provide subsidies and to run the nationalised industries, but could Labour be trusted to operate the system responsibly? During the 1960s young and ambitious Tories, such as Geoffrey Howe, began to study pamphlets produced by the Institute of Economic Affairs (IEA), which had kept alive the laissez-faire liberal tradition of Herbert Spencer and Friedrich Hayek. Although Enoch Powell was sacked from the Shadow Cabinet in 1968 because of his provocative views on immigration, his 'Morecambe Programme' of sweeping tax cuts and denationalisation provided a rallying point for members who thought that state intervention had gone too far (Powell, 1970). These ideas could not be ignored by Heath, who needed to keep his party united and realised the complexity of this task from his experiences as a former Chief Whip.

Heath's exact position in 1970 has been fiercely debated (Russel, 1978, 11). Thatcherites tend to argue that he was committed to a platform very similar to the one adopted in 1979: the only difference was that Heath, unlike Margaret Thatcher, lacked the courage to carry it through (Holmes, 1982). Some versions of the story are self-contradictory, but the most coherent one explains Heath's subsequent opposition to Thatcherite policies as the product of personal bitterness, rather than any serious difference of principle (Tebbit, 1989, 134–5). At the centre of the controversy is the well-publicised meeting of Heath and the Shadow Cabinet, held at the Selsdon Park Hotel in January 1970. Actually, the meeting produced very little of substance, and showed that the ambitious Conservative policy exercise was far from complete. But Harold Wilson claimed that there had been a significant shift towards classical liberalism. He coined the phrase `Selsdon Man', to emphasise what he regarded as the reactionary nature of Heath's developing programme.

The 1970 Conservative manifesto was forcefully worded, and provided plenty of hostages to fortune. In his foreword, Heath asserted that 'once a policy is established, the Prime Minister and his colleagues should have the courage to stick to it'. The manifesto promised a reduction in direct taxation and public spending, reform of the trade unions, and more efficient use of public funds in the areas of economic intervention and welfare payments. Unlike the Wilson government, a new Conservative administration would not attempt to control prices and wages through legislative action. After the indecision and waste of the Wilson years, Britain would become strong again under tough and principled leadership. Restored to economic and social health, it could finally join the EEC and play a central role in the development of European institutions.

One suspects that if the Conservatives had won the February 1974 general election — which they very nearly did — then the controversy over Selsdon Man would not have been so loud and lasting. Defeat then, and a similar result in October, gave Heath's ideological opponents the chance to get their own version of events accepted. Yet this interpretation was seriously exaggerated. The proposals contained in the 1970 manifesto certainly represented a change from recent policies in some areas, and there would be no continuation of the interventionist momentum established by the Macmillan government. Yet the detail of the proposals represented a shift to more discriminating intervention by the state, rather than a concerted attack on the whole idea of big government (Middlemas, 1990, 319). Nicholas Ridley's subsequent claim that Heath had 'promised to stop subsidising industry' was quite untrue (Ridley, 1991, 13). In any case, Ridley was a prejudiced witness, having become one of the few ministers to be sacked from the Heath Government. As Secretary of State for Industry under Margaret Thatcher, Ridley himself subsidized industry (albeit in a more subtle fashion).

Still, the tone of the 1970 manifesto was open to such misinterpretations. A study of the election campaign concluded that in drawing up the document, the party leadership 'compensated for rejecting the views of *laissez-faire* radicals by using their language' (Butler and Pinto-Duschinsky, 1970, 91). Possibly Margaret Thatcher's later verdict that 'our rethinking of policy had not been as fundamental as it should have been' will mark the end of the myth that Heath really intended to push through a free-market revolution (Thatcher, 1995, 160–1).[2]

In office, 1970–74

The first few months of the Heath government suggested that election promises would be honoured. A mini-budget in October 1970 matched tax cuts with public expenditure reductions. Margaret Thatcher, in the Cabinet for the first time as Education Secretary, fought hard to maintain her large departmental budget, but had to accept the abolition of free milk for primary school children over 7, and an increase in the cost of school meals. The travel firm Thomas

---

[2]   When assisting Heath with the composition of his memoirs, the present author extracted an admission that the tone of the 1970 manifesto had been a bad mistake. However, Heath removed the relevant passage prior to the publication of his book. This was a typical gesture from a man who never felt the need to address the arguments of his critics — to the detriment of his own reputation.

Cook was denationalised, and the Industrial Reorganisation Corporation, which had encouraged mergers under Labour, was abolished. John Davies, the former director-general of the Confederation of British Industry (CBI), was brought into the government to head the new Department of Trade and Industry (DTI); one of his first pronouncements was to deny that he would intervene to save any of British industry's 'lame ducks'. Heath also took up the challenge which had proved too much for Harold Wilson, and introduced an Industrial Relations Act before the end of the year. Like Labour's ill-fated *In Place of Strife* proposals, the Act mixed concessions to the trade unions with stricter conditions for strike action; it set up an Industrial Relations Court to deal with union non-compliance. Just after the first anniversary of the government had passed, Heath secured the aim which he considered the most important, by negotiating the UK's entry into the EEC.

Unfortunately, these steps towards fulfilment of the 1970 manifesto pledges could not disguise the impression that this was to be an unlucky government. Within a few weeks of taking the office of Chancellor, the popular and able Iain Macleod was killed by a heart attack. Macleod's value as a force for unity is ironically attested by the fact that both sides of the ideological divide within the party still claim that he agreed with their views (Tebbit, 1989, 94–5). The 'lame ducks' policy of refusing to rescue failing companies soon came under strain; Rolls-Royce was nationalised in February 1971 in order to avert bankruptcy. Rolls-Royce's importance in terms of both international prestige and technological research made it something more than a 'duck', and state ownership was only intended to be temporary. But the contradiction with previous rhetoric did not pass unnoticed among the government's critics. It was not the last time that front-bench speakers would have to fight off accusations of policy reversals.

When the Conservatives took office, inflation was identified by the electorate as the most pressing domestic problem (Wybrow, 1989, 95). Yet the government had rejected both monetarism and prices and incomes policy as possible remedies, while the plan to switch some of the tax burden from income to consumption (through the introduction of VAT) was likely to add to existing inflationary tendencies. There was clearly an expectation that sustained economic growth would help to curb inflation, but by the end of 1971 this hope had not been fulfilled. Even without the continuing headache of inflation, the government also had to contend with rising unemployment, which topped 1 million in January 1972. This phenomenon was new; previously policy-makers had believed that there was a 'trade-off' between inflation and unemployment. With no sign of a revival in industrial investment, the economy seemed to be stuck in an inevitable cycle of decline.

In response to this uninviting prospect, the new Chancellor Anthony Barber introduced what has been called 'the most expansionary Budget ever' (Stewart, 1978, 142). In pursuit of a 5 per cent annual growth target, Barber reduced income tax by more than £1 billion, and restored regional grants to industry which had earlier been withdrawn as part of the government's drive for more selective intervention. The Budget was quickly followed by the passage of an Industry Act which gave the government unprecedented scope for investment. In combination with lower interest rates which sparked off a steep rise in consumer borrowing, this was certainly a spectacular dash for growth.

Even though public spending was on an upward trend, the government could claim that it was broadly following its original plan; it was certainly cutting taxes, and although the Industry Act was a blunt instrument, it could still be used 'selectively' by a prudent minister. Not surprisingly, however, the Budget did nothing to stem the rise in prices, and wages soared as employees struggled to keep up. Even before the Budget, the miners had received a 30 per cent pay increase after calling their first national strike for more than forty years. By September the government had decided on a move which really could not be squared with the rhetoric of the 1970 manifesto; it opted for a prices and incomes policy, the tactic which it had derided when Labour were in power. At least Labour entered into the spirit, and now attacked

Heath for bringing in a policy which they had used themselves. Even so, this was a difficult time for Conservative back-benchers.

The severity of the blow would have been reduced if other measures had worked. But this was not the case, particularly with the industrial relations legislation. It was always likely to be a hazardous operation. The trade unions had refused to accept similar proposals from Labour, despite their ties of friendship, so why should they now co-operate with the Conservative enemy? Although the legislation was not repealed until Labour returned to office, it was clearly unworkable from the time that the unions hit on the idea of refusing to register under the Act. Unless unions pursued their grievances in line with the terms laid down by the Act, they would be acting illegally and thus become liable to potentially ruinous fines. But the system threatened to collapse under its own weight unless at least the great majority of unions signed up. For the government, it was more embarrassing to have prosecutions brought under the Act that it was to have the legislation ignored, especially after the Court of Appeal ruled that unions should not be held responsible for the actions of local shop stewards. This led to the creation of individual 'martyrs' such as the 'Pentonville Five', dockers who were arrested while on picket duty.

By outfacing the government over the Industrial Relations Act, the trade unions showed that they had the muscle to humiliate any party in power. However, they had not finished with Heath. Despite the Prime Minister's best efforts, the TUC refused to cooperate with the second stage of the prices and incomes policy, due to take effect in April 1973. Stage III, which was announced in October of that year, included a flexible (if complicated) formula which would allow pay rises to take automatic account of inflation. In this way it was at least hoped that unions would not make excessive pay claims in anticipation of future increases in the cost of living, a process which itself pushed prices up. Unfortunately for the government, this plan coincided with the outbreak of the 'Yom Kippur' Arab-Israeli War. In order to punish Israel's western sympathisers, Middle Eastern oil producers increased prices and restricted supplies. This was disastrous enough in itself, to add to a general increase in world commodity prices over the year. What made it fatal for the Heath government was that it greatly increased the bargaining power of the miners, who had already put in a substantial pay claim. The government was prepared to treat the miners as a special case under Stage III of the pay policy, but was unwilling to accommodate their demands in full. As a result of the second miners' dispute, starting with an overtime ban in November, Heath called a three-day working week, with other restrictions which included a fifty mile-per-hour speed limit and a 10.30 p.m. shutdown for television broadcasts. Before Christmas Anthony Barber also cut public expenditure by more than £1 billion. The government had effectively abandoned its first economic strategy after a year in office; now a host of unfriendly events were driving it away from its revised course. Heath was advised to call a snap general election to provide the government with a mandate for further strong action, and eventually the country went to the polls on 28 February 1974 (Campbell, 1993, 585–97).

Defeats and recrimination, 1974–75

Many commentators believe that if Edward Heath had called a general election earlier, perhaps in January rather than February 1974, the Conservatives would have won. Delay could not stop speculation, giving the opposition parties ample time to organise (Hurd, 1979, 133). Heath was reluctant to give the appearance of forcing voters to choose between the democratically-elected government and the miners. Even so, he earned himself wounding criticism only from Enoch Powell, who avenged himself for his 1968 sacking by protesting against an election called by a Prime Minister who still enjoyed a working parliamentary majority. Powell, who had once supported EEC membership but was now vehemently opposed, urged his supporters to vote Labour, apparently, in some areas at least, to good effect.

Although the Conservatives won more votes than Labour in the election, they could not form a government without support from elsewhere, and after negotiations the Liberals refused to offer this. Labour returned to office, and started to deliver the promises made to the trade unions under the Social Contract (See Chapter 1).

As Andrew Gamble has noted, 'the Conservatives entered the election campaign with one of the least promising records any British Government has ever offered to the British electorate' (Gamble, 1974, 228). Apart from the successful EEC negotiations (which were fiercely opposed in many quarters), Conservative achievements were as limited as those of Labour in 1964–70 and 1974–79. In all these cases, it was difficult to decide whether errors or ill-luck had been deciding factors; certainly the Heath Government fell victim to both. Perhaps the confrontational message of the 1970 manifesto was the worst mistake it made, because it raised unjustified fears amongst trade unionists and corresponding hopes in the hard-line minority of the Conservative Party.

Even before the 1970 election, commentators were questioning the nature of Heath's political thinking (McKie and Cook, 1970, 148–50). He gave the impression of being more interested in action than ideas. Yet while his opponent Harold Wilson deliberately tried to avoid identification with any ideological faction within his party, Heath enjoyed personal friendship and loyalty with a distinct Cabinet grouping. The 'Heathmen' were all in broad agreement with mainstream thinking within the post-war party. For them, the welfare state and the mixed economy were wholly in line with conservative principles. Once this framework was accepted, the balance of policy might differ from time to time; although free enterprise was the system most likely to produce prosperity for all, at times of crisis more significant state intervention would be necessary. Unlike the social democrats, they rejected equality as even a vague long-term goal; this anti-egalitarian stance accorded with a distinctive conservative view of human nature. If action was necessary to prevent serious poverty (and, in particular, unemployment) then it should be taken for the sake of social harmony. Differences in wealth could never truly reflect individual merit, so those who had been fortunate in life owed a moral duty to give the poor at least the opportunity of a worthwhile existence.

Heath and his supporters, then, were not mere 'pragmatists' (or 'technocrats' as their critics alleged). Their views were in keeping with the postwar settlement as it worked out in practice. As such, they were opposed by a relatively small number of MPs within the party, whose ideas led to very different conclusions. The critics were not a coherent grouping: true to their belief in individualism, many were prickly characters for whom co-operation did not come easily. During the 1970–74 government some of them were known as 'Powellites', indicating support for Enoch Powell's economic ideas rather than his views on race. These ideas are variously described as 'monetarist', 'neoliberal' or laissez-faire; for convenience, it is best to use the term 'classical liberalism' (see Introduction) to denote the ideology that inspires them.

Between 1970 and 1974, as the Heath government changed tack in response to the stagnation of the economy, Conservative MPs such as Nicholas Ridley, John Biffen and Powell himself regularly spoke and voted against what they regarded as an irresponsible move towards wider state intervention (Norton, 1978, 93–7, 120–4). They had little success in changing government policies, but when Heath was defeated in February 1974 their activities could serve as an inspiration to others who had swallowed their doubts while the party remained in office. The return of a Labour government was a signal to former Cabinet ministers who sympathised with classical liberalism to express views which had never been voiced while they remained in office. Keith Joseph, who had been a high-spending Minister of Health and Social Services in the Heath government, was the most prominent of these ministers. In June 1974 he announced that he was setting up the privately-funded Centre for Policy Studies (CPS) with another former minister, Margaret Thatcher, as a director. Although both of these ministers were well known to a long-established free-market think-tank, the IEA, forming a new body was a useful way to publicise the direction of their thinking; it also mimicked Heath's earlier decision to set up a governmental think-tank, the Central Policy Review Staff (CPRS) under Lord Rothschild. The re- education that Joseph received from the most dynamic member of the CPS—the former communist, Alfred Sherman—led him to deliver a speech at Preston in September 1974 which marked him as the intellectual successor to Powell, who had now left the Conservative Party. He might easily have become a candidate for the party leadership if he had not implied in a later speech that the 'human stock' of Britain was threatened because the poor bred too quickly (Denham and Garnett, 2001, 265–76).

Joseph was more interested in the cause of truth (as he saw it) than in his own leadership ambitions. He later proudly announced that he had experienced a conversion: 'I had thought that I was a Conservative (before 1974) but now I see that I was not one at all.' This statement was not calculated to make life easier for the student of ideology. Even Joseph's allies were quick to assure him that he had discovered classical liberalism rather than conservatism, and a close study of his views over the years shows remarkably little change (Denham and Garnett, 2001, 250). The significance of the remark lies in the fact that Joseph *thought* that his views had changed radically; this goes some way towards illustrating the ideological gulf within the Conservative Party at that time.

'Thatcherism', the somewhat indiscriminate label which now embraces British classical liberals, does share a few broad characteristics with conservatism. Yet even where they seem to coincide, there remain significant differences of emphasis. Thatcherites reject the idea of equality, but for them inequality takes on the appearance of a desirable goal, rather than an inevitable feature of human society (Joseph and Sumption, 1979). Ideological conservatives do not rejoice that human beings are capable of selfishness; they also acknowledge that on rare occasions people can be motivated to act unselfishly. Thatcherites, by contrast, tend to attribute all conduct to selfishness. On their view of human nature, altruism is impossible; those who claim to act from this motive are either fooling themselves or trying to hood-wink others. Luckily there is no reason to feel guilty about selfishness, because this 'natural' impulse can be turned to the good of all members of society. Conservatives are sceptical of any theory which suggests that people can act 'rationally' in any meaningful sense, but the Thatcherite belief in the superiority of the free market is based on the premise that individuals can be trusted to act in accordance with their own rational self-interest in economic matters. This 'rational individualism' lies at the heart of Thatcherism and is even less palatable to conservatives than the socialist vision, which at least recognises that society is interdepen-dent. Thatcherites place great emphasis on freedom, defin-ing this as the absence of deliberately fashioned constraints (such as state intervention). They do not advocate freedom without responsibility, but they are much more likely than conservatives to regard freedom as a virtue in itself. This notion of freedom leads Thatcherites to reject the idea of 'dependency', which they see as one of the great evils of a system of welfare payments. For conservatives, however, society cannot function without dependency in some form. This list of disagreements, which could be greatly expanded, includes almost all the central questions of domestic policy. More importantly, the contrast between the underlying premises of conservatism and Thatcherism is so marked that it is difficult to imagine circumstances in which they could *ever* be made to agree.

This account of Thatcherism necessarily misses the full complexity of the creed, but it suffices to prove that the split between Thatcherites and conservatives in the 1970s and 1980s was no less serious than that between socialists and social democrats. It can be claimed that the division is as old as the Conservative Party itself, dating from the time when Sir Robert Peel adopted the liberal proposal to abolish the Corn Laws in 1846, against a majority in his own party which was quite happy with interference in the free market (especially when, as in this instance, it benefited the aristocracy). Yet the gulf between the two ideologies has never been more apparent than since 1979. There are several reasons for this, some of which have been in operation for many decades but have exercised a decisive effect only in combination. These include the deterioration in Britain's economic performance, the apparently relentless growth in the activities of the state, and a definite change in the ethos of the party, reflecting the gradual eclipse of aristocratic dominance (Ramsden, 1978). In some respects, the `Thatcherisation' of the party can be interpreted as a logical outcome once Britain moved towards full democracy. This system encourages party strategists to focus on the perceived demands of 'rational', 'self-interested' voters. It also reflects the decline of the Liberal Party as an alternative to the developing Labour Party, in both electoral and ideological terms. The party which boasted Keynes and Beveridge among its supporters could not be a comfortable home for those who wanted to roll back the frontiers of the state; their only remaining option was to join the Conservative Party.

After February 1974 Edward Heath was in an unenviable position as Conservative leader, having lost two out of the three elections he had contested. The momentum within the party passed to the classical liberals, who could claim with distorted hindsight that the `Selsdon' programme would have been a triumph if Heath had stuck to it. The leader responded by calling for a Government of National Unity. Opponents naturally interpreted this as a confession that Heath's conservatism had no distinctive answers; more accurately, it was an invitation for politicians of all parties to reject the very distinctive answers provided by socialism and classical liberalism, which Heath regarded as equally divisive. In the end, the October 1974 election was not a disaster for the Conservative Party, as it held Labour's majority to single figures. But Heath was now widely regarded as a serial election-loser, and had also made personal enemies through his lack of social skills.

The crusade begins, 1975–79

Margaret Thatcher's election to the Conservative Party leadership in February 1975 was unexpected, and certainly did not represent a Joseph-like 'conversion' of the whole party. Although recent research has suggested that the new leader did not lack ideological support among Conservative MPs, an authoritative study conducted closer to the time estimated that the overwhelming majority was opposed to 'Thatcherism'. Specific ideas did not decide the result, although Mrs Thatcher used a *Daily Telegraph* article to imply that the Conservative Party had surrendered to 'socialism' (Thatcher, 1995, 274–5). William Whitelaw, the chairman of the Conservative Party and favourite to succeed Heath, refused to stand against his leader on the first ballot. Mrs Thatcher had no such scruples, and by establishing a lead over Heath enjoyed a bandwagon effect which could not be reversed when Whitelaw joined in the second ballot.

The skills which Thatcher had deployed in her leadership campaign served her equally well when deciding on her Shadow Cabinet. Although many of Heath's supporters were kept on, the post of Shadow Chancellor went to Sir Geoffrey Howe, and Peter Walker was dropped because he had been an outspoken opponent of Thatcher and Joseph. Realising the importance of controlling the party machine, Thatcher appointed the veteran Lord Thorneycroft as party chairman; the sympathetic Angus Maude replaced Ian Gilmour at the Conservative Research Department (CRD) (Thatcher, 1995, 290–2). The sense of loyalty which had prevented William Whitelaw from becoming leader now ensured that he was a compliant deputy. The overall balance of the Shadow Cabinet remained 'Heathite'. But Thatcher ensured that the key economic posts went to her supporters. This sure touch did not desert her until after the 1987 election, when she presumably believed herself to be beyond challenge.

In opposition, Thatcher's main purpose was to win what she saw as 'the battle of ideas' against socialism. One major development in preparation for the coming conflict with 'socialism' in all its forms was the establishment of a Conservative Philosophy Group of academics and MPs; at one of their meetings, Mrs Thatcher reportedly announced 'We must have an ideology. The other side has got an ideology they can test their policies against. We must have one as well' (Ranelagh, 1991, 187; Young, 1990, 406). If Mrs Thatcher ever made this statement, it shows her imperfect understanding of the Labour Party of the time. Labour had more than one 'ideology'; and when tested against the current policies of the government the ideas of both camps caused nothing but trouble (see Chapter One).

Another important milestone was the publication of *The Right Approach*, a statement of the Conservative position which cleverly patched over continuing internal disputes (Conservative Central Office, 1976). Identifying the 'ethos of modern Conservatism' as 'balance and moderation', the pamphlet pointed out the decay of social democracy and attacked *Labour's Programme for Britain, 1976* as a sign of Labour's drift towards Marxism. The difference between Labour and the Conservatives, however, was that Labour's radicals were being ignored, while the Conservative radicals were in charge. The chief radicals, Joseph and Thatcher, revealed their intentions in speeches inspired mainly by the work of the classical liberal think-tanks (Thatcher, 1977; Joseph, 1976). Joseph warned that Keynesian ideas had merely paved the way for socialism; as the intervention of one government failed, its successor would intervene further in an attempt to clear up the mess. This effort would fail in its turn, and this 'ratchet' would continue until freedom had been destroyed. For classical liberals, the obvious answer was to ditch Keynes. As we have seen, Keynes had never been a socialist, and neither was the Labour government. But Joseph and Thatcher had no time for what they regarded as ideological hair-splitting. They were more troubled by Callaghan's renunciation of Keynes in 1976, which threatened to obscure the ideological differences between the two main parties. But the Prime Minister had opposed *In Place of Strife* back in 1969, and unlike the Thatcherites he had no intention of acknowledging the growing public feeling that the trade unions needed to be reformed (Crewe and Searing, 1988, 375–6).

In 1977 the Conservatives issued *The Right Approach to the Economy*, which announced that the next Conservative government would be mainly concerned with setting a framework for economic activity by acting against inflation through control of the money supply (Maude, 1977). Lower taxation was also promised. Mrs Thatcher did not entirely approve of this document, which was insufficiently radical in the area of Conservative policy which she considered to be most important. The document even acknowledged the potential value of 'corporatist' consultations between government, employers and unions. Heath's allies within the Shadow Cabinet were also becoming restless. Ian Gilmour, whose book *Inside Right* appeared in the same year as *The Right Approach to the Economy*, insisted that conservatism was not an ideology (Gilmour, 1978). The very thinly veiled implication of his book was that Mrs Thatcher was an ideologue, and as such neither a conservative nor electable unless she changed her thinking. Lord Hailsham did not seem so anxious; his 1978 book *The Dilemma of Democracy* contained a plea for limited government, and his warnings about a possible 'Elective Dictatorship' was an attack on Labour's current practices rather than an accurate prediction of his own leader's intentions (Hogg, 1978). In the pre-election dash into print, one rising star of the party who might have been expected to support Gilmour produced a similar attack on the overmighty state (Waldegrave, 1979). Other senior Conservatives who shared Gilmour's views were content with the (mistaken) hope that the experience of office would mellow Mrs Thatcher.

The 1979 Conservative manifesto, in fact, was a relatively moderate-sounding document. It promised tax cuts, better value for public expenditure, very limited denationalisation, lower inflation, union reform and the sale of council houses. Most of this was compatible with other post-war Conservative manifestos. The content reflected concerns that Labour intended to portray Mrs Thatcher as a dangerous extremist, in contrast to James

Callaghan, who was widely perceived as a good-natured moderate. In an effort to combat this, the very first line of Mrs Thatcher's foreword downplayed the importance of political theorising. This was a direct reversal of the 1970 ('Selsdon') manifesto, which had *exaggerated* Heath's radicalism. Perhaps the most worrying aspect of the 1979 manifesto from the point of view of conservatives was the promise `to work with the grain of human nature'; if conservatives did not know already, the following years were to show that their interpretation of human nature was very different from Mrs Thatcher's belief in the 'rational' individual.

Conclusion

By the end of the 1970s, both the Conservative and Labour parties seemed to have fallen under the control of ideological factions which advocated a clean break from post-war politics. Obviously both the socialists and the classical liberals believed that their remedies would work, but their solutions gained added attraction from the apparent failure of alternative positions within the respective parties. The argument that unlooked-for events had beaten Wilson, Callaghan and Heath cut no ice with these factions; as they saw it, the determined implementation of their beliefs in government would transform society in such a fashion that mere events would be transcended.

Both of these internal revolutions – the 'peasants' revolt' which toppled Edward Heath from the Conservative Party leadership, and the campaign for party democracy which seemed to place sitting Labour MPs at the mercy of their constituency activists – were essentially incomplete in 1979. Their subsequent fortunes will be traced in later chapters. Contrary to the view propagated by sections of the media, however, the supporters of Tony Benn within the Labour Party were far more vulnerable than their Thatcherite counterparts. Mrs Thatcher, after all, led her party; once Jim Callaghan had resigned from the Labour leadership, the poisoned chalice passed to Michael Foot, whose radical sympathies clashed with a consistent desire to maintain party unity which had led him to support uncongenial policies in recent years. Foot beat Denis Healey to the leadership because of the split in his party; Margaret Thatcher's defeat of Heath and Whitelaw largely created the internal problems of the Conservative Party. The fact that the national press was far more sympathetic to the Conservatives than to Labour helped to create a public perception which reversed the true state of both parties in 1979.

The social democrats were defeated within the Labour Party because they seemed to have run out of new ideas in a situation which their greatest thinkers had not foreseen. It would be a mistake to say the same of conservatism. After all, this is a world-view which prides itself on flexibility. If Enoch Powell had been Conservative Party leader in 1970 – not an entirely far-fetched idea – it would have been interesting to see whether he would have fared any better than Heath in the face of a buoyant labour movement and the oil price rise.

In fact, the problems for conservatives began much earlier. Michael Oakeshott once wrote that conservatism thrives best when there is much to be enjoyed in life (Oakeshott, 1962, 169). Post-war Britain has generally failed to fit that description, contrary to the views of nostalgia-mongers. If the problems associated with Britain's decline were not grave enough, the technological advances of the post-war period mean that ministers now get to know about far more problems in much greater detail; in addition to the problems which have actually arisen, they are also bombarded with predictions about hazards to come. Media pundits encourage the electorate to demand immediate solutions to all of these difficulties, both real, distorted or imagined. After the war, conservatives agreed that big problems demanded big governmental solutions – but could big government be wholly justified in terms of a creed which is sceptical about human nature? Conservatism originally provided a solid justification for the rule of a gifted elite, but it needed to be adapted in the age of bureaucratic armies. Despite the work of Hogg and others, this problem was never tackled in sufficient depth.

Modern government seems ill-suited to the gentle conservative scepticism of a Halifax or a Hume (or even the angrier vision of Burke). The writings of Michael Oakeshott, the twentieth-century legatee of these thinkers, symbolises a general loss of confidence among conservatives who are forced to operate in an unwelcoming world. In a famous essay, Oakeshott argued that conservatism is a disposition rather than an ideology (Oakeshott, 1962). His account of this disposition is alluring, but it remains ambiguous; it fits the characteristics of Lenin as well as those of Churchill. In fact, although it is easy to detect the developments which Oakeshott opposed, his work offers very few positive remedies (Crick, 1973). It is tempting to attribute this reticence to a sense that things had gone irretrievably wrong, and it was now impossible to do more than 'chart the route to disaster' (Gilmour, 1978, 99). Some of Oakeshott's admirers, unable to sustain this mood of resignation, gravitated towards Thatcherism — although it is difficult to imagine a disposition as far removed from Oakeshott's description as Mrs Thatcher's.

We saw earlier that conservatives claim to express nothing more than common sense, but that their conclusions will be shared only by those who agree with their sceptical view of human nature. Burke wrote his *Reflections* to reassert his own idea of common sense at a time when the French Revolutionaries were questioning all that he cherished. With only one or two exceptions, conservatives failed to copy Burke's example when their approach to government was being assaulted on all sides after the fall of Edward Heath. Their failure to do so shows how seriously they took their own cliché that conservatism was not an ideology — and that setting out an impassioned defence of their beliefs was somehow bad form, and contrary to the conservative tradition. This self-denying ordinance, and the genteel style of politics associated with it, could not have been better suited to Mrs Thatcher's purpose if it had been dreamed up by the

IEA. If William Whitelaw was an ideological opponent of Mrs Thatcher, she had no need of ideological allies.

The revival of classical liberalism after 1975 was an odd twist of ideological history. In part, its success with certain politicians can be attributed to the promising solution it offered to the problem of 'overloaded' government. The influence of classical liberalism did little to reduce the role of the public sector — contrary to Thatcherite claims. But it did make it easier for ministers to avoid accountability, since many functions of government were passed on to semi-autonomous agencies. Classical liberalism also thrived because its followers transformed the intellectual weaknesses of the doctrine into practical strengths. Its greatest popularity had coincided with Britain's industrial supremacy in the nineteenth century. Even at that time, the doctrine of free trade was an odd way of describing a system in which Britain controlled vast overseas possessions. If classical liberalism was best suited to the time when Britannia ruled the waves, its central figure, the rugged, rational entrepreneur, was an unlikely hero for a post-war world of huge monopolistic concerns. In order to overlook the real reasons for the growing economic involvement of the state, Thatcherites had to engage in a historical rewriting campaign, using Hayek's *Road to Serfdom* in much the same way that the unsophisticated 'leftist' might use Marx. Yet this systematic programme of simplification provided Thatcherism with a potent weapon. Mass democracy is the enemy of complex messages, and Mrs Thatcher's opponents in all parties found it difficult to translate their thoughts into an idiom which could convince the electorate. Even when Mrs Thatcher's speech writers proved unequal to this task, elements of the popular press such as the *Sun* newspaper were very happy to supply the deficiency.

Within the Conservative Party as in Labour, the 1970s were not easy years for those who were unprotected by firm ideological principles. Those who had not defended their beliefs with sufficient passion now found themselves either applauding views they detested, or seeking employment elsewhere. On the argument advanced in this book, the supposed failure of the post-war 'consensus' was at least in part the product of a mismatch between ideologies and institutions. The social democrats were hampered by the fact that they were almost invariably middle-class intellectuals, operating within a working class party. When the economic crisis erupted in the mid-1970s, they tended to keep silent for fear of offending vested interests within the party; it was no accident that people like Shirley Williams and David Owen only began to expound their beliefs in books *after* they had left Labour. A similar judgement could be applied to Edward Heath, who stated his principles with much greater eloquence after he had been superseded by Mrs Thatcher. On close examination, it can be argued that Heath's principles were not distinctively conservative, in the ideological sense. Keynes, rather than Burke, was his chief intellectual influence; although he kept a portrait of the Tory William Pitt the Younger in his study, it was hung alongside a picture of the liberal icon Charles James Fox. If the Liberal Party had still been in a healthy condition after the Second World War, when Heath began his rise in the Conservative Party, there is a good chance that his allegiance would have been different. Indeed, in those circumstances Heath and Harold Wilson could easily have become colleagues within the Liberal Party. If either can be categorized in ideological terms, new liberalism provides the closest match. Although this judgement supports the claim of Heath's Thatcherite critics that he was not a true conservative, there is no doubt that his ideas inspired policies which were broadly compatible with the conservative tradition; and this is not something that can be said for the majority of Mrs Thatcher's reforms.

Whatever the reason for their shortcomings, the failure of social democrats, new liberals and conservatives to rise to the challenge presented the prize of North Sea oil to others. This development was another ironic twist. Politicians who believed in the post-war settlement thought that the possession of oil might save the British economy, but its full benefits arrived under a Prime Minister who thought she could perform an economic miracle whether there was oil or not.

Whatever the fate of the Thatcherite crusade, the zeal of both the leader and her supporters meant that someone would always be willing to proclaim that she had really made the miracle happen.

List of works cited

Brittan, Samuel (1971), *Steering the Economy: The Role of the Treasury*, Pelican.

Budd, Alan (1978), *The Politics of Economic Planning*, Fontana.

Butler, David, and Pinto-Duschinsky, Michael (1970), *The British General Election of 1970*, Macmillan.

Campbell, John (1993), *Edward Heath: A Biography*, Jonathan Cape.

Conservative Central Office (1976), *The Right Approach: A Statement of Conservative Aims*, Conservative Central Office.

Cowley, Philip, and Bailey, Matthew (2000), 'Peasants' uprising or religious war? Re-examining the 1975 Conservative leadership contest', *British Journal of Political Science*, 599-629.

Crewe, Ivor, and Searing, Donald (1988), 'Ideological Change in the British Conservative Party', *American Political Science Review*, volume 82, number 2.

Crick, Bernard (1973), *Political Theory and Practice*, Allen Lane.

Gamble, Andrew (1974), *The Conservative Nation*, Routledge and Kegan Paul.

Gilmour, Ian (1978), *Inside Right: A Study of Conservatism*, Quartet.

Hayek, Friedrich A. (1962 ed), *The Road to Serfdom*, Routledge.

Hogg, Quintin (1947), *The Case for Conservatism*, Penguin.

Hogg, Quintin (Lord Hailsham) (1978), *The Dilemma of Democracy: Diagnosis and Prescription*, Collins.

Holmes, Martin (1982), *Political Pressure and Economic Policy: British Government 1970-74*, Butterworth.

Hurd, Douglas (1979), *An End to Promises: Sketch of a Government 1970-1974*, Collins.

Joseph, Keith (1976), *Stranded in the Middle Ground? Reflections on Circumstances and Politics*, Centre for Policy Studies.

Joseph, Keith, and Sumption, Jonathan (1979), *Equality*, John Murray.

Maude, Angus (1977), *The Right Approach to the Economy: Outline of an Economic Strategy for the Next Conservative Government*, Conservative Central Office.

McKie, David, and Cook, Chris (1970), *Election '70*, Panther.

Middlemas, Keith (1990), *Power, Competition and the State*, Volume II: *Threats to the Post-War Settlement: Britain, 1961-74*, Macmillan.

Norton, Philip (1978), *Conservative Dissidents: Dissent within the Parliamentary Conservative Party 1970-74*, Temple Smith.

Norton, Philip (1990), ' "The Lady's Not for Turning", But What About the Rest?', *Parliamentary Affairs*, volume 43, number 1.

Oakeshott, Michael (1962), *Rationalism in Politics and Other Essays*, Methuen.

Powell, Enoch (1970), *Income Tax at 4/3 in the £*, Tom Stacey.

Ramsden, John (1978), 'The Changing Base of British Conservatism', in Chris Cook and John Ramsden (eds) *Trends in British Politics since 1945*, St Martin's.

Ranelagh, John (1991), *Thatcher's People*, HarperCollins.

Ridley, Nicholas (1991), *My Style of Government: The Thatcher Years*, Hutchinson.

Russel, Trevor (1978), *The Tory Party: Its Policies, Divisions and Future*, Penguin.

Spencer, Herbert (1969 edn), *The Man Versus the State*, Pelican.

Stewart, Michael (1978), *Politics and Economic Policy in the UK since 1964: The Jekyll and Hyde Years*, Pergamon.

Tebbit, Norman (1989), *Upwardly Mobile*, Futura.

Thatcher, Margaret (1977), *Let Our Children Grow Tall: Selected Speeches 1975-1977*, Centre for Policy Studies.

Thatcher, Margaret (1995), *The Path to Power*, HarperCollins.

Waldegrave, William (1979), *The Binding of Leviathan: Conservatism and the Future*, Hamish Hamilton.

Wybrow, Robert (1989), *Britain Speaks Out, 1937-87: A Social History as Seen through the Gallup Data*, Macmillan.

Young, Hugo (1990), *One of Us: A Biography of Margaret Thatcher*, Pan.

Further reading (see also Chapter 4)

For views on Conservative policy development in the 1960s, see Rhodes Boyson (ed.) *Right Turn* (Churchill, 1970); *The Conservative Opportunity: Fifteen Bow Group Essays on Tomorrow's Toryism*, Conservative Political Centre (1965); W.H Greenleaf, 'The Character of Modern British Conservatism', in Robert Benewick, Robert Berki and Bhiku Parekh (eds) *Knowledge and Belief in Politics: The Problems of Ideology*, (Allen and Unwin, 1973); Richard Hornby, 'Conservative Principles', *Political Quarterly*, volume 32, number 3 (1961); Robert Rhodes James, *Ambitions and Realities: British Politics 1964-70* (Weidenfeld and Nicolson, 1972); and Andrew Roth, *Heath and the Heathmen* (Routledge, 1972).

On the 1970s, see Stuart Ball and Anthony Seldon (eds), *The Heath Government 1970-74: A Reappraisal* (Longman, 1996); Robert Behrens, *The Conservative Party from Heath to Thatcher: Policies and Politics 1974-79*, (Saxon House, 1980); Robert Blake and John Patten, *The Conservative Opportunity* (Macmillan, 1976); Richard Clutterbuck, *Britain in Agony: The Growth of Political Violence* (Faber and Faber, 1978); Maurice Cowling, 'The Sources of the New Right', preface to *Mill and Liberalism*, (Cambridge University Press, 2nd edition, 1990); Patrick Hutber, *The Decline and Fall of the Middle*

Class (Penguin, 1977); Denis Kavanagh, 'The Heath Government, 1970-1974', in Peter Hennessy and Anthony Seldon (eds) *Ruling Performance: British Governments from Attlee to Thatcher* (Blackwell, 1987); and Zig Layton-Henry, *Conservative Party Politics*, (Macmillan, 1980).

CHAPTER 3

The Liberals and their Allies, 1970–2006

Background

The British general election of 1906 produced an overall majority of eighty-eight seats for the Liberal Party. After years of internal arguments, notably over Irish Home Rule and the Boer War, the Liberals now seemed far more stable than the Conservatives, who were bitterly divided over Tariff Reform. Apparently the Liberal Party could look forward to a bright future. It formed a talented government, which in time would produce some of the century's most important legislation. In addition to its own MPs it could normally count on the support of eighty-eight Irish Nationalists, along with fifty-one representatives of the newly-formed Labour Party. Many of the latter group owed their seats to the Liberals, who had agreed not to oppose thirty-one Labour candidates in a bargain struck three years earlier. Perhaps in future the Labour Party might be a helpful junior partner in an anti-Conservative coalition; for now the scale of the Liberal landslide meant that no assistance was required.

Sixteen years later the last Liberal Prime Minister was hounded out of office by very different coalition partners. Instead of a handful of friendly Labour MPs, a suspicious and resurgent Conservative Party sustained David Lloyd George in power from December 1918 until it decided to discard him in October 1922. Since that time, only coalition governments have provided the Liberals with ministerial office. On occasion (notably during the Lib-Lab Pact of

1977–78) they have exercised some power, but this has depended on the position of the two main parties rather than Liberal strength in the House of Commons.

The reasons for the decline of the Liberal Party have been thoroughly investigated (eg, Wilson, T., 1966). The personal rift between Lloyd George and his predecessor as Liberal Prime Minister, Herbert Asquith, was fatal to the party's electoral prospects. Six years after Lloyd George's death in 1945 the Liberals were able to field only 109 candidates in a general election; of these, more than half lost their deposits. The party which had once nurtured the Labour Party now depended upon Conservative charity to keep up its parliamentary numbers. It seemed only a matter of time before it disappeared altogether (Wallace, 1983, 43). When Robert McKenzie wrote *British Political Parties* in 1955, he apologised for the apparent cruelty of simply relegating the Liberal Party to an appendix—but then, the Liberals had received less than 3 per cent of the vote at the preceding general election (McKenzie, 1964, v).

The poor electoral performance of the party did not mean that individual Liberals were wholly without influence. It is difficult to exaggerate the contribution to post-war economic and social policy made by John Maynard Keynes and Sir William Beveridge. Keynes' commitment to the party lasted for most of his life, although his interest fluctuated; when he was awarded a peerage in 1942 he agreed to sit as a Liberal (Harrod, 1972, 636). Beveridge became a Liberal MP at the end of the Second World War. The work of Keynes and Beveridge built on the reforms of the Asquith government, which had laid the foundations for the British welfare state in the years before the First World War. Between the wars, the Liberal Party seemed to produce all the promising ideas while the Conservatives and Labour shared political power; it was almost as if the future Liberal role would be to act as an involuntary think-tank for political opponents.

While individual Liberals have exerted more influence over twentieth-century Britain (and beyond) than their party as a whole, the ideology of liberalism has also prospered. It survived a crisis at the end of the nineteenth century, when liberal thinkers such as T. H. Green and L. T. Hobhouse recognised that the classical liberalism which had flourished during Britain's industrial supremacy would not suffice now that the economy had begun to stagnate and most workers could express their grievances in elections. Retaining the liberal focus on the individual, these 'new' liberals argued that the state must intervene to ensure that at least a minimum level of income was available for unemployed, elderly and sick people. Provided that the necessary increase in taxation fell mainly on the well-off, the balance of meaningful freedom in society would increase. Previous liberals had defined 'freedom' as the absence of restraints; in arguing that such freedom was pointless for those who lacked resources, the New liberals caused offence among advocates of classical liberalism such as Herbert Spencer. Yet their ideas represented no significant breach of the central elements of liberalism; the quarrel was bitter (and remains unresolved), but this is typical of disagreements within any ideological family.

Despite the activities of New liberals such as Keynes and Beveridge, classical liberalism retained a foothold within the Liberal Party after the Second World War. A prominent advocate of 'rolling back the state' was Major Oliver Smedley, a founder of the Institute of Economic Affairs (IEA), which later provided intellectual support for classical liberalism within the Conservative Party. In 1956 some of Smedley's allies left the Liberal Party to form the People's League for the Defence of Freedom, while Smedley himself set up a Free Trade Liberal Party in 1962 (Cockett, 1994, 127). These defections marked the gradual victory within the Liberal Party of the Radical Reform group, which accepted the post-war mixed economy on New liberal grounds. In 1956 Jo Grimond, whose sympathies lay with the Radical Reformers, was elected as leader of the party. It was a doubtful inheritance, but Grimond was a popular figure who promised to restore Liberal fortunes at last.

Under Grimond's leadership, the Liberals lived up to their bold-thinking reputation. They responded positively to the formation of the EEC while the other major parties hesitated, and advocated withdrawal of British forces from bases East of Suez (with the exception of Singapore). Parliamentary reform was also a distinctive Liberal policy; it was argued that the UK's 'winner-takes-all' electoral system was grossly unfair because it devalued the votes of those who opposed the Labour and Conservative parties. This argument was obviously convenient for Liberals, but it was also compatible with their belief that the opinions of all individuals should carry equal weight. The Liberals also accepted nationalisation, but rejected the bureaucratic form in which it had been carried out by the Attlee government. Their preference for worker participation would become a consistent theme.

At a time when official policy differences between the Labour and Conservative parties seemed to be diminishing, the Liberals could present a distinctive alternative. The main Liberal disadvantage was that unlike their main party rivals they did not enjoy the backing of a significant social group. The support which workers gave to the Labour Party and industrialists provided for the Conservatives brought them both votes and money; like the electoral system, this link between parties and interests could be denounced by Liberals as anti-democratic. The 1950s, however, brought encouraging symptoms of change. The social democratic ideas of Anthony Crosland, and the Conservative acceptance of nationalization, could both be interpreted as signs that the major parties were less inclined to pay undue attention to their client interests. Crosland's ideas in particular pointed to a decline in the importance of class divisions. Grimond believed that values, rather than interests, would be the key to winning elections in a classless society. In these circumstances the Liberal Party would thrive, and there was likely to be a radical realignment of political forces in Britain.

On occasions between 1956 and 1966, the Liberals seemed to be on the verge of a conclusive breakthrough. They enjoyed some notable by-election successes, the most sensational of which was the victory at Orpington in March 1962. Membership boomed, and was estimated to have risen from

150,000 in 1959 to 350,000 in 1963 (Wallace, 1983, 52). New members meant extra revenue, and a research department was set up to look at future policy developments. The party's success promised to be self-perpetuating, as innovative ideas enticed still more recruits, which would have a further beneficial effect on finance. As the Labour Party argued over nationalisation and membership of the EEC, and the Conservative government suffered from scandals and a feeling that it had been in power too long, the Liberals looked poised to draw support from both sources, as well as from young idealists who had no sympathy with either of the main parties.

These hopes went unrealised. The succession of Harold Wilson to the Labour leadership after the death of Hugh Gaitskell in 1963 was probably the main reason for this. Wilson presented a dynamic, classless image; having once been Beveridge's research assistant (and, briefly, a member of the Liberal Party) there could not have been a more appropriate choice to see off the Liberal threat. According to William Wallace, the 1964 general election brought 'the worst possible outcome for the Liberals' (Wallace, 1983, 57). The Labour Party had a tiny majority, but still did not need Liberal support. When a new general election was called in 1966 Liberal representation increased, but only to 12 MPs. With the momentum of the early 1960s running out and a major party realignment now unlikely, Grimond resigned from the Liberal leadership in January 1967.

The electoral prospects of the party might have seemed gloomy when Jeremy Thorpe replaced Grimond as leader, but the Liberals were impossible to ignore in the late 1960s. The membership now included a high proportion of young (predominantly middle-class) activists, who found inspiration in the student activism and civil rights movements of these years. Parliamentary Liberals reflected this new impetus in their support for social reforms affecting abortion, race relations and homosexuality, and the increasingly vocal Young Liberal section of the party was particularly prominent in the attack on racism at home and abroad. Activists such as Peter Hain opposed the South African cricket tour of 1970, and the energetic Young Liberals began to advocate 'Community Politics', which raised the profile of the party by focusing on specific grievances within different constituencies. For many senior Liberals, this was the unacceptable face of individualism; without encouragement from the top, many of these enthusiastic recruits drifted away in later years. When Peter Hain was eventually elected to Parliament in 1990 it was as a member of the Labour Party.

Looking for allies, 1970–81

By 1970 the Liberals had relatively settled principles, which formed the basis of a distinctive programme. True to the core liberal belief in the rational individual, they opposed the growth of a paternalistic state bureaucracy, and concentrated on the establishment of equal civil rights. Their acceptance of the welfare state followed the principles of Keynes and Beveridge. For them, it was nonsensical to speak of freedom in the context of absolute poverty; and even if the poor could survive in reasonable comfort, if social inequalities passed beyond a certain point there could be no 'equality of opportunity'. The state should provide a framework of benefits to enable individuals to plan their lives with a reasonable degree of security, and a free education system was necessary to give young people something like an equal chance of leading a productive and fulfilling life. The compulsory taxation which funded these state activities was a necessary evil; used properly, the receipts from taxation would result in greater benefits for all.

The problem for the Liberal Party was not the lack of ideas, but communicating them to the electorate. Even when the Young Liberals were the most controversial political activists in the country, it remained difficult to convince voters that the party stood for anything more than a middle course between Conservative and Labour. This perception was fostered by the unhelpful view of politics as essentially a clash between 'left' and 'right', a one-dimensional map which left Liberals with only unpalatable positional choices. Regular poll findings that the majority of voters thought of themselves as standing close to this elusive 'middle ground' only made things more maddening for the party; the failure to capitalise on this potential support meant that the Liberals could not even reap the advantages of being misrepresented as incurably moderate. They were ideally placed to pick up the support of protesters against the two major parties, but the British electoral system seemed to ensure that even when governments were unpopular the main opposition party was usually the chief beneficiary.

Of course there is no political law which dictates that third parties can never prosper; for Liberals, the Labour Party was an all-too-real example of a party which had succeeded in 'breaking the mould', in the early part of the twentieth century. For most of the post-war period, though, the Liberals were handicapped not just by a low level of overall support, but by its distribution. Invariably, under the first-past-the-post electoral system the Liberal share of the popular vote was greater than its share of seats. Understandably, this situation promoted a tendency for Liberal leaders to pay excessive attention to tactics. Their realistic hopes lay in either a close election which would enable them to secure electoral reform as the price of their support, or the disintegration of the Labour Party, which would bring about the long-desired realignment. For members of a third party, however, political realism is not always conducive to success. When such a party spends too much time stressing the novelty of its views, it can leave the impression that it is trying to create differences for their own sake. This is just another example of the kind of Catch-22 situation faced by a third party under the British electoral system.

The Liberal manifesto for the 1970 general election reflected the developments of the 1960s, with particular emphasis on civil liberties. Superficially, the result of the election looked bad for the party, which was left with only six Members of Parliament. However, the aftermath proved more hopeful; Labour's internal divisions began to re-emerge, and the Conservative Party soon ran into trouble with what many perceived to be a divisive programme. Between 1970 and 1974 the Liberals gained five seats in spectacular by-elections, and Dick Taverne's defection from Labour over Europe could be interpreted as the beginning of major political changes. The February 1974 general election brought over 6 million votes for the Liberals; even though this produced only fourteen seats the injustice of the outcome could hardly have been a better illustration of the case for proportional representation.

Unfortunately for the party, the overall national picture was even worse than it had been in 1964. With no single party able to form a majority government, Jeremy Thorpe was called to Downing Street for negotiations with Edward Heath. These talks failed to produce an offer of electoral reform, and in any case Liberal activists were outraged at the prospect of sustaining the Conservatives in office. The Labour Party might have disintegrated in the face of another defeat; the former minister Christopher Mayhew gave a tantalising glimpse of what could have happened when he joined the Liberals from Labour between the two 1974 elections. Instead, Wilson scraped back into office, and his minority administration pushed through policies which were popular enough to help him win a second contest in October. The Liberal vote declined by 1 million compared with February, and the parliamentary party was reduced to thirteen MPs.

Events seemed to be conspiring against Thorpe, particularly since the new government's fragile majority gave its leadership the perfect excuse to turn its back on the kind of full-blooded socialism which might have encouraged non-believers to defect. Thorpe himself was soon in worse personal trouble, as a former male model produced allegations against him which eventually forced his resignation as party leader in May 1976. Additional revelations about financial improprieties within the party did nothing to improve matters. Despite the attempts of Liberals to offer the electorate distinctive ideas, which now included a guarantee of minimum income levels through radical reforms of the taxation and benefit systems, they were still widely seen as little more than a receptacle for the disillusioned supporters of other parties. Now it was the turn of Liberal Party members to register their own dissatisfaction.

Amidst these difficulties, however, there was one significant positive development. The 1975 referendum over UK membership of the EEC was fought on cross-party lines, and was unusual in the extent to which it gave politicians from different backgrounds the opportunity to emphasise areas of agreement. In particular, it brought the consistently pro-European Liberal leadership into contact with Labour politicians who had been angered by Harold Wilson's tactical gymnastics over the European issue. Foremost among this group was the former Chancellor and current Home Secretary, Roy Jenkins. Jenkins had co-operated with David Steel, the Liberal Chief Whip, over social legislation during the 1960s. This association would develop further.

In the summer of 1976 Steel succeeded Jeremy Thorpe as Liberal leader. Almost immediately he was presented with the situation which so many of his predecessors had dreamed of. The Labour government lost its parliamentary majority when two MPs left to form the Scottish Labour Party. Faced with imminent defeat in a confidence vote, it turned to the Liberals for help in March 1977. The Prime Minister James Callaghan offered Steel a consultative committee, which would give the Liberals a chance to influence the government's proposals before they reached the House of Commons. There would also be ministerial meetings, which would involve not only Steel and Callaghan but also the Chancellor, Denis Healey, and the Liberal economic spokesman John Pardoe. Short of actual membership of the Cabinet, it seemed that Steel had secured some important concessions; in particular, Callaghan promised to introduce a Bill to hold elections to the European Parliament on the basis of proportional representation (Cook, 1993, 163–4). If this Bill could be passed, the habit of electoral reform might spread.

The long-sought opportunity to exercise real political power turned out to be another headache for the Liberals. In part,this was evident before the 'Lib-Lab Pact' was forged, because the last thing the Liberal Party needed was another general election with the Thorpe affair still rumbling on. Thus Steel was as much the prisoner of events as Callaghan. Without this weakness in his position, Steel might have satisfied demands from inside his party for a tougher bargain. As it was, Callaghan decided not to upset his back-benchers by forcing them to vote for proportional representation in European elections: many of them did not want to see elections to a European Parliament under *any* system. Thus the European legislation failed. Another ironic problem for the Liberals was that at this time Labour was following the deflationary policies imposed by the IMF — measures which normally both parties would vigorously have opposed. While most Liberals grumbled about this, the irony was increased by the fact that Jo Grimond, who was moving towards the classical liberalism he had once denounced, disagreed with the pact because he opposed the way Labour had run the economy *before* the IMF loan (Grimond, 1979, 249–51). The Liberals did win some victories while the pact lasted (notably over taxation), but co-operation was unpopular in the constituency parties and relations between Healey and Pardoe soon deteriorated. The situation became farcical at the time of the 1978 Budget, when the Liberals joined the Conservatives in forcing the Chancellor to cut income tax by a penny in the pound; one of the party's most significant post-war parliamentary victories was thus achieved at the cost of a government strategy which they were supposed to be assisting (Healey, 1990, 403). Meanwhile the Liberal vote in by-elections was dropping sharply. When the pact ended in May 1978 there was little lamentation from either of the partners.

The May 1979 general election was never likely to be easy for the Liberals, and in the circumstances their retention of eleven seats was a creditable performance. As usual, the party fought the election on a distinctive platform, which mixed demands for a Bill of Rights and government decentralisation with a call for a long-term prices and incomes policy and proposals for energy conservation. It was natural for the Liberals to show concern for the environment, an issue which fitted well with their established Community Politics approach. Yet in the 1979 election it brought few rewards, and served mainly to fuel the division between activists, who saw the party as a vehicle for local campaigning, and the party leadership, which was increasingly preoccupied with the tactical manoeuvres necessary to achieve realignment (Behrens, 1989, 85–6).

David Steel had good reason to hope for dramatic changes among opponents of the new Conservative government. On 22 November 1979 Roy Jenkins delivered the BBC's Dimbleby Lecture, and made it 'an unashamed plea for the strengthening of the political centre' (Jenkins, 1982, 21). It looked as if a major political realignment was really taking place at last. Jenkins and Steel met in January 1980, and reached an understanding that, although Jenkins would not be joining the Liberals himself, the new party he intended to set up would first work closely with Steel, then 'consider an amalgamation after a general election' (Jenkins, 1989, 553).

While the 1970s had been another decade of dashed Liberal hopes, the 1980s began with almost unmixed good news for the party. The Conservative government of Margaret Thatcher had quickly run through its honeymoon with the electorate; Mrs Thatcher's refusal to contemplate a U-turn despite soaring unemployment might have been popular with her hard-line supporters, but it was an open invitation for moderates to look for alternatives. Normally Labour might have been expected to exploit this opportunity by ditching any policy which could be portrayed as 'extreme', but the experience of the previous twenty years had left the socialists as the only faction within the party which retained a healthy sense of political mission. To those who rejected both socialism and Mrs Thatcher's classical liberalism, it looked as though the Liberals were on the verge of a significant breakthrough; if they could work in tandem with a new party which excited the public, then the road to Downing Street might be opened. The reaction of some Liberals was less than enthusiastic; Cyril Smith, for example, thought that the SDP should be 'strangled at birth' (Steel, 1989, 223). Steel's negotiating skills proved sufficient to quell the doubters, at least temporarily. Amid the ensuing euphoria, he told delegates at the 1981 Liberal Party Assembly to 'Go back to your constituencies and prepare for government'. Subsequently the statement was ridiculed, but at the time it did not seem to be an unwarranted precaution for a party which was unaccustomed to the prospect of power.

Realignment, 1981

Roy Jenkins' Dimbleby Lecture was a crucial catalyst for the development of a new political party, but it can also be seen as the logical result of a much earlier incident. In October 1971 seventy Labour MPs voted against a three-line whip on the principle of UK entry into the EEC. For social democrats like Jenkins, membership of the Community was essential if Britain was to remain prosperous, and to exercise significant influence over world events (Jenkins, 1972, 74–80). Harold Wilson had attempted to negotiate entry in 1967; by choosing to oppose Edward Heath's resumption of talks, Jenkins believed that Wilson was exploiting the European question for purely party-political reasons. When Wilson allowed Tony Benn to convince him that the next Labour government should hold a referendum on membership, Jenkins resigned from his position as deputy leader of the party.

Jenkins and his supporters had other reasons for unhappiness. In opposition, Labour had drifted towards more socialist policies, including a renewed programme of nationalisation. The social democrats saw nationalisation as an irrelevance at best. Harold Wilson (and the state of the economy) ensured that socialist hopes were eventually disappointed, and social democrats did serve in the 1974–79 governments. After the IMF agreement of December 1976, however, these ministers were left in positions of responsibility without exercising significant power. The usual reward for people in this predicament is to be blamed by everyone; apart from the predictable socialist criticisms, social democrats were pilloried in *The Future that Doesn't Work*, a collection of essays by Anglo-American commentators including the future Ambassador to the USA, Peter Jay (Tyrrell, 1977). Jenkins' departure to take up the post of President of the European Commission was quite consistent with his views, but it also implied a deepening and understandable disillusionment with domestic politics.

From his post in Brussels, Jenkins kept in touch with the British political scene, but his perspective was bound to be more detached than that of the social democrats who still held senior posts within the Labour Party. The response to his Dimbleby lecture was therefore crucial. His concern was focused mainly on two close friends and former ministers, William Rodgers and Shirley Williams; another potential recruit was an ally from the early 1970s, Dr David Owen, who had succeeded Anthony Crosland as Foreign Secretary in the Callaghan government. Rodgers, Williams and Owen all opposed Labour's European policy, and were worried by moves to increase trade union and constituency power within the party at the expense of MPs. Unlike Jenkins, all three had good reasons to stay in the Labour Party provided that its present course could be changed. There were hopes, for example, that the grass-roots Campaign for Labour Victory (set up in 1977) could reverse the trend towards socialism in the constituency parties. Much also depended upon the party's choice of a successor to Callaghan, whose retirement was seen as inevitable after the 1979 defeat. For the moment, the reaction of Jenkins' friends was lukewarm; David Owen, whose personal relations with Jenkins were not so close, actually denounced what he called 'siren voices from outside, from those who have given up the fight from within' (Owen, 1992, 426). Jenkins would remain in Brussels for a further year, so for now he could be happy that at least press reaction to the speech was favourable, and a public debate had begun.

In some parties this public threat of a split would have effectively prevented one; both sides to the dispute would have thrashed out a compromise. For the Labour Party, however, any hint of 'treachery' could only inflame the situation. At a special conference in May 1980 David Owen was heckled when he opposed unilateral nuclear disarmament; in the following month he met Rodgers and Williams to issue a joint statement on Europe. Roy Jenkins chose this moment to remind the public of his support for a new party. Owen, Rodgers and Williams, now popularly known as 'The Gang of Three', were pushed further towards Jenkins in September when Labour's annual conference voted for unconditional withdrawal from the EEC and the abandonment of nuclear weapons. Michael Foot's defeat of Denis Healey in the November leadership election was a further blow, and when another special conference decided that in future the party leader would be elected jointly by MPs, constituencies and trade unions (with the unions enjoying the greatest influence), the Gang of Three were ready to abandon their struggle. On Sunday 25 January 1981, soon after Jenkins' return from Brussels, the membership of the Gang increased to four. The group issued the Limehouse Declaration' setting up a Council for Social Democracy which was the basis for a new Social Democratic Party (SDP). The formation of the party was announced on 26 March.

A partnership of principle or a marriage of convenience? 1981–92

The Limehouse Declaration explicitly rejected the notion that the new party would follow 'the politics of an inert centre merely representing the lowest common denominator between two extremes' (Stephenson, 1982, 186). Despite this disavowal, the two main parties knew that the best way of attacking the SDP was to deny that it had any principled basis (Owen, 1992, 504). Whatever its future relationship with the Liberal Party turned out to be, the SDP already shared the Liberal problem of establishing an identity as more than just a colourless alternative for disgruntled voters. The media attention which the Limehouse Declaration sparked off might have helped to generate initial public interest, but it also increased the necessity of establishing firm principles, and a policy programme to attract mass support. By June a working party of Liberals and Social

Democrats had established a statement of principles entitled 'A Fresh Start for Britain', yet this took on the appearance of a generalised wish-list rather than a detailed programme (Stephenson, 1982, 187–9).

The immediate fulfilment of the agreement between Steel and Jenkins about inter-party co-operation led to difficulties within the Gang of Four. The most reluctant member, David Owen, thought that too close an association with the Liberals would prevent the SDP from establishing itself as a principled party. Even if the SDP's new members had previously voted Liberal, they had not felt motivated enough actually to join the party. Why disappoint these recruits by allowing the SDP to get bogged down with the Liberals in the political middle ground? Owen was particularly worried about the division of seats to be fought by each party in a future election. By contrast, Roy Jenkins appreciated the value of alliance with the experienced grassroots activists which the Liberals could provide; in addition, he denied that the ideas of social democrats and liberals were very different. In short, while Owen wanted to build a distinct, radical party, which could even compete with the Liberals in future if circumstances changed, Jenkins saw no reason why there should not be a merger at the appropriate time — perhaps after the two parties had governed in coalition.

The disagreement between Jenkins and Owen covered both tactics and principles, and provides an interesting case-study in the interplay of ideas with other political considerations. The task of isolating one factor from the other would be fascinating but ultimately fruitless; it can be concluded only by producing an inaccurately simplistic interpretation of political action. For example, in his memoirs David Owen portrays Roy Jenkins as an elderly politician 'in a hurry', who intended to use the SDP as 'a disposable vehicle for his ambition to be Prime Minister' (Owen, 1992, 531). As the most experienced leader in either party, Jenkins would be the likely Prime Minister of any coalition government, provided that victory was achieved without excessive delay. In the mean time, any radical thinking which might scare off both the Liberals and the electorate should be avoided. In other words, on Owen's account, Jenkins was driven almost exclusively by his desperation to become Prime Minister. On the other hand, it is equally possible to interpret Owen's opposition to eventual merger as the product of his own ambition. There was every chance that David Steel would succeed Jenkins as leader of a merged party, and this would probably put an end to Owen's chances, since he was only three months younger than Steel.

It would be naive to suppose that these calculations were wholly absent on either side, but they should not obscure the underlying divisions of principle which helped to destroy the dreams of 1981. By this time Jenkins had long ceased to call himself a socialist; true to the ideas of his old friend and rival Anthony Crosland, he believed that the mixed economy could provide the basis for greater social and economic equality, and acknowledged that this was not socialism as understood within the Labour Party. By contrast, when Owen published *Face the Future* in 1981, the word `socialism' featured prominently (at least in the first edition). Unlike Jenkins, Owen was unhappy with post-war thinking and constantly sought fresh solutions. This attitude produced some sympathy for Mrs Thatcher's crusading style of politics, which was matched by agreement with at least some of her reforms. Neither William Rodgers nor Shirley Williams, who also published books before the 1983 election, felt this ambivalence about Thatcherism (Williams, 1981; Rodgers, 1982). They agreed with Jenkins (and Steel) in finding little to applaud in Conservative Party policies.

Before establishing an agreement with the Liberals, the SDP leaders needed to sort out their own differences. Yet the divisions were too deep, and could never be resolved. When the SDP's membership (which then stood at 68,000) voted for the party's new leader, Jenkins narrowly defeated Owen, despite the fact that the latter seemed to be more popular with the electorate as a whole. By this time (June 1982), the party had twenty-nine MPs, thanks to further defections from Labour; and both Jenkins and Williams had achieved spectacular by-election victories (at Glasgow Hillhead and Crosby respectively). For the first year of the

SDP's existence, the allied parties achieved a steady 40 per cent in most opinion polls; in December 1981 their support was recorded at 50.5 per cent (Wybrow, 1989, 126). The success of the party was not an unmixed blessing, however; as Ivor Crewe and Anthony King have shown, the differences within the SDP were not confined to the leadership (Crewe and King, 1995, 61–83). A more obvious blow was the Argentine invasion of the Falkland Islands in April 1982, and their subsequent recapture by British forces. These developments removed the attention of the media from the new party, which depended heavily on consistent publicity. Only one Conservative MP (Christopher Brocklebank-Fowler) had defected to the SDP, and after the Falklands campaign the government received a boost in opinion polls which were already registering a recovery as economic problems eased.

Despite underlying disagreements, the SDP and the Liberals fought the 1983 elections as allies, with Roy Jenkins as 'Prime Minister Designate'. Joint policy committees produced a manifesto, *Working Together for Britain*, which reaffirmed the liberal and social democrat commitment to the mixed economy in the face of attacks from Thatcherites and socialists. The European Convention on Human Rights would be incorporated into British law, and Britain would remain a member of the North Atlantic Treaty Organisation (NATO) and the EC. Electoral reform, democracy in the workplace and environmental protection were other survivals from previous Liberal manifestos; indeed, the programme would have looked very similar had the SDP never existed. For Roy Jenkins, broad agreement was only to be expected, but David Owen and his supporters took this as further evidence of the Liberals' ability to get their own way.

In the words of the Prime Minister Designate, the 1983 Alliance campaign was 'a brilliant success', but the result did not tally with this judgement (Jenkins, 1994, 574). Although the Alliance achieved over a quarter of the vote, narrowly failing to overtake Labour, Liberal activists found that their preparations for government had been premature. The outcome of the election disappointed Jenkins, but the fact that he could take some comfort from a contest which saw the SDP's representation in the House of Commons reduced to six is perhaps a measure of the extent to which his expectations had been guided by the previous record of the Liberals. In Parliament, the original Gang had been reduced to two – both Shirley Williams and William Rodgers lost their seats.

After the general election Owen told Jenkins that unless he resigned from the SDP leadership immediately there would be a contest between them. Jenkins regarded this behaviour as 'somewhat incontinent', but acquiesced (Jenkins, 1994, 578). Owen was elected unopposed, and continued his theoretical musings with greater urgency. In 1984 he published *A Future that Will Work: Competitiveness and Compassion*. This book revealed the effect of Thatcherism on Owen's thinking. He introduced the concept of a Social Market, a phrase which had been used by Keith Joseph in the 1970s. Denouncing an over-extended and bureaucratic state, Owen argued that market forces should be introduced within the public sector, and that welfare benefits ought to be targeted more narrowly on the worst-off in society (Owen, 1984, 1–29, 104–31). The need to reduce class divisions in society was forcefully reiterated, but critics saw this as a rhetorical gloss on a programme which embraced too many Thatcherite premises. By mid-1985 Owen was being warned by David Steel and William Rodgers that his flirtation with Thatcherism was going too far; Roy Jenkins made a barely-coded allusion to Owen's 'sub-Thatcherism'.

Economic and social policies were not the only sources of disagreement. In the following year the latent subject of nuclear weapons added to the tension. A joint commission of the parties agreed that in view of current moves towards superpower disarmament, no immediate decision about a replacement for Britain's existing Polaris missile system was necessary. Owen, whose opposition to unilateral disarmament had not diminished, saw this as a compromise to appease the opponents of nuclear weapons within the Liberal Party. As both Shirley Williams and William Rodgers pointed out, the commission's findings were carefully worded to avoid fomenting any differences of principle (Steel, 1989, 265). Owen could not agree, declaring that 'Conviction politics must not become a monopoly of Mrs Thatcher' (Wilson, D., 1987, 28). The situation was not helped when the 1986 Liberal Party Assembly passed a resolution in support of non-nuclear European defence co-operation (Steel, 1989, 270-1). This was a major setback to chances of cooperation between the parties after an election victory. Owen felt so strongly about defence that during the 1987 election campaign he announced that Labour would not be fit to govern until it changed its unilateralist position (Owen, 1992, 693). At this time, the Conservatives were benefitting from Labour's defence policy, but Owen's repeated outbursts only publicised an internal difficulty which the Liberal leadership was anxious to smooth over.

For the election, the Alliance produced a manifesto based on a book published under the joint names of Owen and Steel: *The Time has Come: Partnership for Progress* (Owen and Steel, 1987). The attempt to disguise differences led to what Owen regarded as a 'rather bland' manifesto, but skillful presentation on paper could not prevent the splits from re-emerging when the two leaders were subjected to the interrogations of an election campaign (Owen, 1992, 679). The confusion caused by the divided leadership meant that the 'Two Davids' could not capitalise on poll findings which suggested that whatever their voting intentions most people felt that the Alliance best represented their views (Heath et al., 1991, 217). The result reduced SDP strength in the House of Commons to five; it was natural for the Liberals, with seventeen seats, to see themselves as the senior partner in the Alliance. In the aftermath of defeat, Steel announced plans for a merger. Owen had opposed this from the outset; his opinion of the typical Liberal Party member had never been high, and it was not improved by the controversy over nuclear weapons. Despite his opposition, the SDP membership voted for merger talks on 6 August 1987, and the party finally agreed to the terms on 2 March 1988.

David Owen resigned from the SDP leadership after the vote of 6 August. He took no part in the negotiations, and decided to lead those who opposed the merger in a new, much reduced, SDP. Only two MPs, John Cartwright and Rosie Barnes, decided to follow him, and after some disastrous by-election results the national party was wound up in June 1990.

For a while, it looked as though the merged party would suffer the same fate. Not all Liberals had approved the merger, and a faction led by Michael Meadowcroft subsequently set up a new party, retaining the name of Liberal. Finding that 'Social and Liberal Democrats' only produced the nickname of 'The Salads', their former colleagues finally settled on 'Liberal Democrats' for themselves in October 1989. Paddy Ashdown took over the leadership as the party hovered close to bankruptcy. In the May 1989 elections to the European Parliament it lost third place in the popular vote to the Green Party; support had dropped to only 6 per cent. Ashdown, a dynamic ex-serviceman who had once annoyed the Liberal leadership (and David Owen) by advocating the withdrawal of US cruise missiles from Britain, gradually emerged as a popular figure, and in the run up to the 1992 general election the party enjoyed a revival. The Liberal Democrats scored a notable by-election victory at Eastbourne in 1990, and two further gains followed in 1991. Their 1992 manifesto was acclaimed by the Guardian as 'the best show in town'; apart from the familiar proposals for electoral reform, decentralisation and state intervention to secure economic recovery, it included a promise to raise income tax by a penny to improve education (Cook, 1993, 208–9). The party polled just under 6 million votes, although the tally of MPs dropped from twenty-two to twenty. The recent by-election gains were wiped out. Given the difficulties of 1987–89, however, the Liberal Democrats could be reasonably satisfied with their performance. They were back in the habitual post-war position of hoping for a hung Parliament after the next election, which might bring them a promise of electoral reform in return for their support. This time, though, with Labour apparently looking more sympathetically at proportional representation, there was still a reasonable hope that this long-cherished measure would soon be realised, even without a close result at the next election.

'Owenism' and the SDP

For Liberal Democrats, the frustration of the period between 1970 and the end of the 1980s was aggravated by the occasional signs of imminent breakthrough. By 1988 many must have felt that they had spent a decade running very hard to stand still; all the Alliance seemed to have done was to show how difficult it was for a third party to win seats, and Liberal Democrats did not need any more lessons in the injustices of the winner-takes-all electoral system. At a time when the two major parties were widely perceived as too extreme, the Liberal share of the vote might have risen steeply without all the heartaches of the Alliance years.

Outwardly the period was one of dramatic changes for the Liberals, perhaps more so than for any other party. Yet while the two main parties rethought their principles the Liberals remained relatively consistent. The legacy of new liberals such as Keynes and Beveridge might be denounced by Labour's socialists and Thatcherites within the Conservative Party, but the Liberal Party stayed loyal. Its members regarded the state as too bureaucratic and centralised, but denied that there was an acceptable alternative to economic intervention and a well-funded welfare system.

Members of the Liberal Party could share these conclusions with social democrats. Differences did exist, but they concerned nuances rather than fundamentals. In practice both Liberals and social democrats wanted to prevent social inequality from growing too wide, but the extent to which that should go was not spelled out precisely by either group. In the past social democrats might have been less critical of state bureaucracy than the Liberals, but compromise on this issue was not difficult to contemplate. A genuine 'partnership of principle' was perfectly conceivable; the problem remained one of convincing the electorate that these principles amounted to more than splitting the difference between Conservative and Labour.

For David Owen, though, the dilemma was about more than principles. The failure of centre parties to break the political mould could also be traced to personalities; indeed, the two factors were inseparable. He came to believe that 'Moderates make bad militants' (Owen, 1992, 482). This view implied that unless the Alliance changed its principles it would never discover a successful electoral idiom; in turn, a philosophical rethink might produce the dynamism which had previously been absent from third party politics. Previous third parties had lacked a social basis, but the goal of Owen's rethink was to wrest the middle classes and skilled workers away from the Conservative Party. *A Future that Will Work* presented the most promising means to this end – the Social Market, or Thatcherism with a conscience. In order to make social democracy popular, Owen ceased to be a social democrat; he had become a 'militant', but was no longer a 'moderate' in the context of the 1980s. It was his misfortune that neither his SDP colleagues nor their Liberal Party allies were interested in the prospect of winning power at that price; ironically, the only prominent Liberal who could broadly agree with Owen's new principles was Jo Grimond, who had worked to reduce the power of similar ideas within his party during the 1950s.

Owen's abandonment of Croslandite social democracy was based on a faulty analysis. Jenkins, Rodgers and Williams were determined not to attribute the failures of recent Labour governments to the limitations of social democratic thought. For them, the real cause of Labour's plight was its connection with an irresponsible trade union movement. The SDP, liberated from this distasteful partnership, would set the record straight. Crosland's 'revisionism' was itself capable of being revised and updated, as David Marquand proved later in the decade with his *The Unprincipled Society* (1988). By the time that this book had appeared, however, something had gone wrong. Perhaps Jenkins and his allies thought that they would win elections just by not being either the Labour Party or Mrs Thatcher. Whatever the reason, in the early days of the SDP no one came forward with the necessary rethink.

A Future that Will Work could have changed all this. Instead, it showed that Owen actually agreed with the opponents of social democracy. Like Mrs Thatcher and the socialists, he thought that the poor record of the 1960s and 1970s was the result of woolly 'consensual' thinking. Social democracy had seemed to be a romantic fighting creed during the Labour Party's battles; now that the social democrats had a party to themselves, their ideas just looked dull in comparison to Thatcherism. 'Conviction politics' were back in fashion, and Owen wanted a piece of the action. He did not notice that the convictions of the Liberal Party had inspired its membership to survive against the odds throughout the post-war period, and that the ideas of New liberalism had once inspired the impassioned oratory of Lloyd George. In fact, he despised the modern Liberals for the manner in which they fought, particularly during by-elections. In combination with this fighting force, Owen's charisma might have brought him the power he craved. Instead he decided to translate his impatience with Roy Jenkins into an issue of principle.

Owen subsequently claimed that he did not regret his time with the SDP. If this was true, it shows him in a charitable light. Some believe that he might have become leader of the Labour Party if he had not left before 1983. Alternatively, instead of letting his market value fall as a result of his association with the SDP, he might have been making his way within the Conservative Party (after a token period of fighting within the Labour Party to bolster his dynamic image). In time, he would have made an ideal successor to Margaret Thatcher as leader of the party. By 1991, when negotiations were finally opened to bring him into a Conservative Cabinet, it was far too late. It might be unfair to accuse the Conservatives of pulling off a cynical publicity stunt in this instance, but John Major offered a deal from which only he could truly benefit. Even if the old SDP vote was not substantial enough to ensure a Conservative victory in the forthcoming election, Major was unlikely to experience a sudden conversion to the principle of proportional representation which Owen could not renounce. The offer of a place in Major's Cabinet came to nothing, but Owen's willingness to negotiate presents a stark contrast to his obstructive attitude when the Liberal-SDP merger was being discussed. It signalled his belief that the two-party mould had triumphed after all.

Equidistance? 1992–99

For the Liberal Democrats, the period between the general elections of 1992 and 1997 was dominated by tactical considerations. The overall Conservative majority was down to just 21 seats, and almost immediately this figure was reduced by by-election defeats. In May and July 1993, the Liberal Democrats won Newbury and Christchurch from the Conservatives; in the following June they took Eastleigh. The government was also embroiled in bitter disputes over Europe. Although the Liberal Democrats had no illusions about winning the next election, there was a realistic chance that they could end up holding the balance of power.

In such circumstances, the party would be faced with a crucial choice. If neither of the two major parties could command an overall majority, which one should it support? To an objective outsider, there could only be one answer. The Liberal Democrats had been arguing since 1979 that the Conservatives were unfit to govern. Admittedly, they had said much the same about Labour. But that party had been transformed since the mid-1980s, and after John Smith took over the leadership in 1992 it was unequivocally committed to the important Liberal Democrat goal of devolution to Scotland and Wales. Smith was also an advocate of more open government, and a supporter of the EU. By contrast, the Conservatives were opposed to constitutional change, and taking an increasingly eurosceptical line. The substitution of Tony Blair for Smith in 1994 made Labour even more attractive, since Blair had persuaded his party to drop its long-standing commitment to nationalisation.

However, many Liberal Democrat members wanted to retain a policy of 'equidistance' from their rivals; and several senior colleagues shared that view. In part, this approach was based on principle. Former members of the Liberal Party were suspicious of Labour's apparent 'conversion' to civil liberties and open government. But they also exhibited a tribal animosity towards Labour, created by a long history of conflict between the institutions, particularly at local level.

Ashdown eventually secured the abandonment of equidistance, but only after a long and exhausting battle. As his published diary shows, he was emboldened by secret talks with Tony Blair and Gordon Brown, which held out the promise that Labour would deliver the ultimate Liberal Democrat prize of proportional representation in future UK general elections. There was also talk of cabinet positions for senior Liberal Democrats, even if Labour gained an overall victory (Ashdown, 2000). Ashdown did not undertake similar negotiations with the Tories, for the very good reason that they could never have offered so much.

Ashdown was attracted by Blair's view that the division between Labour and the Liberals had been a disastrous historical blunder. Now that Labour was distancing itself from the trade unions, there was a possibility that the two parties could merge at some point in the future. But in the short term, Ashdown had every reason to fight the next election on a distinctive policy programme and to hope for a marked improvement in Liberal Democrat representation in parliament. The 1997 party manifesto included a proposal to raise income tax by a penny in the pound, for the specific purpose of boosting government spending on education. Emboldened by Labour's commitment to constitutional reform, the Liberal Democrats suggested that the number of MPs could be cut by 200. In keeping with recent tradition, the manifesto was also strong on environmental protection.

On the surface, the 1997 general election was a great success for the Liberal Democrats. Their tally of MPs was more than doubled, compared to the situation in 1992; 46 of their candidates were elected. However, this was achieved on a smaller proportion of the UK vote – 16.8 per cent, compared to 17.8 in 1992; many of its victories were the result of 'tactical voting' by supporters of other parties who wanted to displace sitting Conservative MPs. At least Ashdown had more colleagues beside him in what was often a hostile House of Commons. But there were now 419 Labour MPs, with an overall majority of 179. Blair had no need for Liberal Democrat support, and the half-promises he had given to Ashdown had been rendered irrelevant. Liberal Democrats did attend a cabinet committee on constitutional reform, but had little or no effect on the government's own plans. Lord Jenkins was asked to consider options for a change in the voting system, but the findings of this 'Independent Commission' were ignored despite a Labour manifesto commitment to a referendum on the subject. Labour was no longer interested in proportional representation, since the first-past-the-post system had given it a majority beyond its most sanguine expectations.

Another false dawn? 1999–2006

Recognising that his hopes had been dashed, Ashdown announced in January 1999 that he would leave his post six months later. His successor, chosen in August 1999 after a ballot of party members, was Charles Kennedy, who defeated Simon Hughes by a margin of 57:43 per cent. Kennedy who had first been elected to parliament as a representative of the SDP, was unconvinced by Ashdown's *rapprochement* with Labour. Although Liberal Democrats joined coalitions with Labour in Scotland, and (initially) in Wales, the prospect of a merger between the parties at UK level rapidly receded.

Whatever the reasons for Kennedy's antipathy towards Labour, he had taken the leadership at a time when the Liberal Democrats could be more distinctive than ever in their policy proposals. In 2001, the party advocated a new 50 per cent rate of income tax on people who earned more than £100,000 a year. As the manifesto emphasised, this was still less than high earners had paid for most of the Thatcher years; but it represented an increase in income tax when the two main parties had no desire to frighten the rich with similar proposals. The previous proposal to increase the basic rate by 1 per cent was retained. The Liberal Democrats also emphasised their environmental credentials by adding a 'green' element to all of their key proposals.

The result of the 2001 general election was a triumph for Kennedy. His party now held 52 seats, and his personal majority in Ross, Skye and Inverness West was trebled. However, the Liberal Democrats had only edged up slightly in terms of vote-share, to 18.3 per cent. This was the same percentage it had won in October 1974, when only 13 of its candidates had been returned; by contrast, in 1983 it had won only 23 seats on more than a quarter of the popular vote.

Between 2001 and 2005 politics was dominated by the war against terror, which allowed the Liberal Democrats to take another distinctive stance. From the outset, they were opposed to UK involvement in the war on Iraq. The unity of the party on this crucial issue overshadowed continuing doubts about Kennedy's leadership. However, apart from gossip about a drink problem, there was also disquiet within the party about Kennedy's supposed failure to give a strong lead on domestic issues. In September 2004 *The Orange Book: Reclaiming Liberalism* was published, including essays by several Liberal Democrat MPs. Among other things, the book proposed a tough approach to crime, a more sceptical view of the EU, and stronger support for the free market.

The emergence of a fervent free-market faction within the Liberal Democrats was not a major surprise. As we have seen, the nineteenth century party had been strongly influenced by classical liberals. Although New liberals had been dominant since 1900, suspicion of an over-mighty state had persisted, particularly in policies to defend civil liberties. New liberals might accept that the state should intervene to ensure that poverty and sickness did not prevent people from fulfilling their potential; but the 'rational' individual remained the focus of their concern. Ashdown had echoed this view in his foreword to the 1992 Liberal Democrat manifesto, when he argued for the creation of 'a nation of self-reliant individuals'.

Thus the authors of the *Orange Book* had good reasons to claim that their ideas were compatible with the traditional outlook of their party. Kennedy duly welcomed their contribution, while noting that their suggestions did not necessarily coincide with official party policy. However, from one liberal perspective the timing of the book was unfortunate. Liberals believe in political *pluralism*; that is, they argue that voters should be presented with a wide range of distinctive policy ideas. Yet the *Orange Book* appeared when 'New' Labour and the Conservatives were both committed to extending the free market into public service provision. If the contributors to the volume had their way, all three major parties would come closer together, at a time when it was already difficult to make a clear distinction between them on ideological grounds.

The 2005 Liberal Democrat manifesto reflected some of the new thinking, particularly in the proposal to abolish the Department of Trade and Industry which had been the source of much detailed economic intervention by the state. The proposal to raise the basic rate of income tax was dropped, and although the party was still committed to increasing the higher rate to 50 per cent it stressed that this would only affect a tiny minority of taxpayers. As a result of this single tax increase, and savings in existing state spending, the Liberal Democrats promised to introduce free care for the elderly and to abolish tuition fees for students.

In their manifesto, the Liberal Democrats presented themselves as 'The Real Alternative'. This was still true, since Labour and the Conservatives had no intention of making a case for tax increases. Even so, the war on Iraq was the issue which made the Liberal Democrats most distinctive. The popularity of the party's stance meant that it entered the election with expectations of a strong showing, although a hung parliament was an unlikely prospect. As it was, the Liberal Democrat performance in 2005 was easily the best since the merger in terms of vote share. But 22.1 per cent of the vote was still less than the Alliance had received in 1987, when it was facing a popular government and a reviving Labour Party. The party now had 62 MPs, which was more than the Liberals had won since the early 1930s when they were part of a national government. However, the figure marked an increase of only 1 seat compared to the position when parliament was dissolved.

In normal circumstances, Liberal Democrats would have been fairly satisfied with this result. At first, indeed, Kennedy's position seemed secure, and he went through the formality of re-election as leader without a challenge. However, within a few months rumours were circulating that senior colleagues were losing patience with him, and were preparing to organise a vote of no confidence in his leadership. Kennedy hoped that he could cling on, despite admitting that he had sought treatment for his drink problem. But the momentum for a change was now unstoppable, and Kennedy resigned on 7 January 2006. After a somewhat undignified leadership battle, Sir Menzies Campbell was chosen as the new leader in March 2006.

Conclusion

Although Kennedy's downfall could be attributed solely to his health problem, several other factors were involved. Despite the initial hopes surrounding the Alliance, and the gradual increase in Liberal Democrat representation since 1992, the party was still widely regarded as a vehicle for protest votes in Westminster elections. The dedicated members, who had kept the organisation going through many dark days, were seen as woolly-minded eccentrics. If people thought seriously about the party, they would probably acknowledge that Liberal Democrats must see themselves as fighting for distinctive principles: otherwise they would have given up the struggle long ago. However, a cynical observer could reflect that it was easy for Liberal Democrats to stick to their principles since they had no chance of forming a government; and it was notable that when the party was a realistic contender in by-elections it tended to adapt its message to the needs of the occasion.

The (relatively) ruthless deposition of Charles Kennedy proved that this popular image of the Liberal Democrats was outdated. The main cause of the change was a renewed hope that the party could be on the verge of an electoral breakthrough. Even those members who had discounted the possibility of a coalition government after the 2005 general election could reasonably hope for a very close contest at the next one, in which the Liberal Democrats might hold the balance of power as they did in Scotland (and had briefly done in Wales). The prospect of at least a share of power—leading to a change in the voting system which might make the party a permanent fixture in future coalition governments—was enough to evoke a different attitude among Liberal Democrat candidates who were anything but 'woolly-minded'. As well as being the largest contingent of third-party MPs for more than 70 years, they were certainly the most ambitious. They would only serve under a leader who was primarily focused on the pursuit of power, and Charles Kennedy did not fit that description.

But Charles Kennedy was not just pushed out because his party's prospects had improved. As usual, ideology also played an important role. Kennedy was not the only recent leader to face divisions. But during his battles with the party, Paddy Ashdown was at least fairly confident that his view of the world was broadly shared by his critics. Ashdown's party, in short, was generally united in opposition to 'Thatcherite' classical liberalism. By 2006 this was no longer true. The *Orange Book* showed that classical liberals had established a strong foothold in the senior ranks of the party, and were confident enough to initiate a re-examination of fundamental policies. Whatever his personal sympathies, Kennedy showed no appetite for this debate; and the lack of ideological allies deprived him of solid support when his personal qualities came under attack.

The initial public response to Kennedy's departure was a plunge in the opinion polls, as voters registered a change in the Liberal Democrat ethos. As the best-known and most widely respected leadership candidate, it was easy to present Sir Menzies Campbell as the 'unity candidate' in 2006. In his acceptance speech, Campbell gave notice that his party would continue to offer distinctive policies, including a specific attack on poverty. However, in the context of the time the dictates of party unity suggested that Campbell would have to pay close attention to the *Orange Book* radicals. If it adopts their approach, the party may look more business-like; but the scope to offer truly distinctive policies will be greatly reduced. In both of its aspects, this strategy is much more risky than the hard-headed careerists in the senior ranks seem to realise. There is no reason why people should not vote for a third party; but there is little incentive to back such an organisation when it presents the same ideas and image as its more powerful rivals.

List of works cited

Behrens, Robert (1989), 'The Centre: Social Democracy and Liberalism', in Leonard Tivey and Anthony Wright (eds) *Party Ideology in Britain*, Routledge.

Cockett, Richard (1994), *Thinking the Unthinkable: Think-Tanks and the Economic Counter-Revolution 1931-1983*, HarperCollins.

Cook, Chris (1993), *A Short History of the Liberal Party 1900-92*, Macmillan, 4th edition.

Crewe, Ivor, and King, Anthony (1995), 'Loyalists and Defectors: the SDP Breakaway from the Parliamentary Labour Party 1981-2', in Peter Jones (ed.) *Party, Parliament and Personality: Essays Presented to Hugh Berrington*, Routledge.

Grimond, Jo (1979), *Memoirs*, Heinemann.

Harrod, Roy (1972) *The Life of John Maynard Keynes*, Penguin.

Healey, Denis (1990), *The Time of My Life*, Penguin.

Jenkins, Roy (1972), *What Matters Now*, Fontana.

Jenkins, Roy (1982), 'Home Thoughts from Abroad', in Wayland Kennet (ed.) *The Rebirth of Britain*, Weidenfeld and Nicolson.

Jenkins, Roy (1989) *European Diary 1977-1981*, Collins.

Jenkins, Roy (1994), *A Life at the Centre*, Macmillan.

McKenzie, Robert (1964), *British Political Parties*, Heinemann, reprint of 2nd edition.

Marquand, David (1988), *The Unprincipled Society: New Demands and Old Politics*, Fontana.

Owen, David (1981), *Face the Future*, Oxford University Press.

Owen, David (1984), *A Future that Will Work: Competitiveness and Compassion*, Penguin.

Owen, David (1992), *Time to Declare*, Penguin.

Owen, David, and Steel, David (1987), *The Time has Come: Partnership for Progress*, Weidenfeld and Nicolson.

Rodgers, William (1982), *The Politics of Change*, Seeker and Warburg.
Steel, David (1989), *Against Goliath: David Steel's Story*, Weidenfeld and Nicolson.
Stephenson, Hugh (1982), *Claret and Chips: The Rise of the SDP*, Michael Joseph.
Tyrrell, R. Emmett (ed.) (1977), *The Future that Doesn't Work: Social Democracy's Failures in Britain*, Doubleday.
Wallace, William (1983), 'Survival and Revival', in Vernon Bogdanor (ed.) *Liberal Party Politics*, Oxford University Press.
Williams, Shirley (1981), *Politics is for People*, Penguin.
Wilson, Des (1987), *Battle for Power*, Sphere.
Wilson, Trevor (1966), *The Downfall of the Liberal Party*, Collins.
Wybrow, Robert (1989), *Britain Speaks Out, 1937-87: A Social History as Seen through the Gallop Data*, Macmillan.

Further reading (see also Chapters 1 and 5)

On developments within British liberalism, see Peter Clarke, *The Keynesian Revolution in the Making* (Oxford University Press, 1988); Robert Eccleshall, *British Liberalism: Liberal Thought from the 1640s to the 1980s* (Longman, 1986); Michael Freeden, *The New Liberalism: An Ideology of Social Reform* (Clarendon Press, 1978); Thomas Hill Green, *Lectures on the Principles of Political Obligation* (Longman, 1941 edition); Jo Grimond, *The Liberal Challenge* (Hollis and Carter, 1963); and James Meadowcroft (ed.), *L. T. Hobhouse: Liberalism and Other Writings* (Cambridge University Press, 1994).

On the Liberals and the SDP, see Ian Bradley, *Breaking the Mould? The Birth and Prospects of the Social Democratic Party* (Martin Robertson, 1981); Ken Coates, *The Social Democrats: Those Who Went and Those Who Stayed* (Spokesman, 1983); Ian Gilmour, 'Tories, Social Democracy and the Centre', *Political Quarterly*, Volume 54, number 3 (1983); Roy Jenkins, *Partnership of Principle: Writings and Speeches on the Making of the Alliance* (Secker and Warburg, 1985); and David Steel and Richard Holme (eds), *Partners in One Nation: A New Vision of Britain 2000* (Bodley Head, 1985).

The best historical sources for the Liberal Democrats between the merger and the end of the twentieth century are the two-volume Ashdown *Diaries* (Volume I, 1988–1997 (2000), and Volume II, 1997–99 (2001), both published by Allen Lane). Despite the party's improving electoral performance in recent years, it has yet to attract adequate scholarly attention.

CHAPTER 4

Thatcherism and its Legacy, 1979–90

Opening shots, 1979–83

On 4 May 1979, Margaret Thatcher became Britain's first woman Prime Minister, as the Conservatives won a majority of forty-three over all other parties. The feeling that this had been an unusually significant general election was marked by the fact that the Conservatives achieved the biggest swing since 1945. Even before the election, James Callaghan had detected 'a sea-change in politics' (Whitehead, 1985, 366). Evidence from opinion polls did not clarify whether the electorate had voted for this change because of a positive response to Mrs Thatcher's vigorous leadership, or as a reaction against the Labour government. Since 1975, Thatcher had been on trial as Conservative leader; despite passing her first electoral test, it was recognised that she remained to some extent on probation.

The uncertainty of Thatcher's position stemmed largely from the fact that her admirers still constituted a minority of senior Conservatives. Possibly in deference to her opponents, before entering 10 Downing Street she quoted a prayer (attributed to St Francis of Assisi) which promised to replace discord with harmony. St Francis's genuine teaching about giving up worldly goods went unmentioned. Following up her conciliatory Shadow Cabinet appointments, Thatcher's first administration was a fair reflection of the balance of forces within the party. Of Edward Heath's allies, Lord Carrington went to the Foreign Office, the recalled Peter Walker was given Agriculture, and James Prior was entrusted with trade union reform at Employment. Francis Pym, another known opponent of classical liberalism, became Secretary of State for Defence, and even Ian Gilmour, the most vocal opponent of Mrs Thatcher's ideas, took Cabinet rank as Lord Privy Seal. The precise views of Michael Heseltine (Environment) were less certain, and at least Thatcher already knew that she could depend upon the loyalty of William Whitelaw (Home Secretary). According to one very sympathetic observer, Thatcher had been 'fair to the point of being generous to her potential opponents' (Holmes, 1985a, 20).

These appointments were important concessions: they might even have been taken as a sign that Mrs Thatcher would prove to be a consensual Prime Minister after all. Yet this impression was misleading. Economic policy was by far Mrs Thatcher's highest priority, and she ensured that fellow-believers were installed in the key offices. Sir Geoffrey Howe became Chancellor of the Exchequer, with the economic Powellite John Biffen also entering the Cabinet as Chief Secretary to the Treasury. Sir Keith Joseph, Thatcher's first choice for the Treasury, took a post of almost equal importance at Industry. With John Nott at Trade and David Howell at Energy, economic liberals could feel that they had a very fair representation in the departments that mattered. The new junior-ranking ministers showed an even greater tilt towards the Thatcherite tendency, with such figures as Nicholas Ridley, Norman Tebbit, Nigel Lawson and Cecil Parkinson winning preferment. For these rising stars, radical economic reform could not proceed quickly enough. Before long, the opponents of Thatcherism within the Conservative Party had been dubbed 'the wets' by enemies of compromise.

The economic situation bequeathed by Labour looked unpromising on paper, but in three respects at least it was helpful to the Thatcherite project. First, North Sea oil was about to make Britain a net exporter of this invaluable commodity, which had done so much to destroy Mrs Thatcher's Conservative predecessor. Second, the trade unions had incurred a loss of public goodwill after the Winter of

Discontent, which promised to make reforms more easy to implement. Finally, in the last years of the Callaghan government unemployment had fallen, but inflation stood at over 10 per cent in June 1979. Mrs Thatcher would have chosen the control of inflation as her priority in any case, but the problem obviously required urgent attention.

By the end of this Parliament in 1983, the government could boast of important achievements in the fight against inflation. Although the rate increased to 21.9 per cent by April 1980, it fell to around 5 per cent in January 1983. While this result was highly satisfactory for the government, it had not been secured in the intended fashion. True to the monetarist approach forced on Labour after 1976, Sir Geoffrey Howe published targets for future growth of the money supply. According to the theory, once the quantity of money was under control the rate of inflation would start to fall. Unfortunately for the theory, the quantity of money proved difficult to define, and when the government chose sterling M3 (notes and coins in circulation plus current and deposit accounts) as its preferred measure, this proved to have little predictive value. Inflation fell, even though the government's targets for growth of M3 were massively exceeded. Although the government was reluctant to admit anything which smacked of a U-turn, the monetarist experiment was effectively dead by January 1985 (Smith, 1987, 123).

Another success which could not have entirely satisfied Mrs Thatcher's supporters was trade union legislation. Overcoming criticism and a back-bench revolt, James Prior embarked on a gradualist strategy with the Employment Act 1980, which outlawed secondary picketing and laid down that union 'closed shops' would be legal only if a ballot gave overwhelming support. Prior's successful approach was rewarded in a reshuffle which sent him into harm's way at the Northern Ireland Office. But Prior's successor at Employment, Norman Tebbit, continued his cautious approach in 1982 with an Act which clamped down further on closed shops and made unions liable for damages incurred during unlawful strikes. Supplementary benefits were reduced for the families of strikers to concentrate the minds of anyone contemplating industrial action. Although industrial disruption continued, and the government actually settled with the miners to avert a strike in 1981, the number of lost working days sharply declined, as did union membership.

The manifesto pledge on income tax was also adequately fulfilled. The top rates of tax on both 'earned' and 'unearned' incomes were slashed by more than 20 per cent, and the basic rate was reduced from 33 to 30 per cent. Personal tax allowances were also raised by more than the rate of inflation. However, these reforms were controversial; even in 1979 Gallup polls were already finding that most people thought of this as a rich person's government, and the overall balance of the tax cuts could only reinforce this view (Wybrow, 1989, 121). The government was unabashed, claiming that high earners needed incentives, although the psychological theory behind this view was problematic. According to later survey evidence, high earners were not gracious enough to support it by working any harder after they had pocketed their tax cuts (Riddell, 1991, 226). Meanwhile the poor were certainly given a powerful disincentive against the purchase of VAT-rated goods when the level of this tax on consumption was raised from 8 to 15 per cent in Howe's first Budget. Prescription charges were also increased.

The Thatcher government was intent on reducing public spending, which would provide scope for further tax cuts as well as limiting the size of the state. Sir Derek Rayner was seconded from Marks and Spencer (a favourite firm of Mrs Thatcher's) to look for savings within the civil service, while the amiable radical John Hoskyns went to the Downing Street Policy Unit to provide ideas for other cut-backs. Unfortunately, the record on spending was not as good as the government had hoped. As an electoral gambit Mrs Thatcher had accepted the Clegg Commission recommendations on public sector pay, which caused the government's wage bill to rise by a quarter (Young, 1990, 151). Mrs Thatcher's tough line did not deter the usual clamour from spending ministers; an unlikely offender was Keith Joseph, who implicitly reconverted to his sinful ways by pouring money into nationalised industries such as British Steel and British Leyland. Admittedly, these concerns needed cash injections to finance redundancy payments; in December 1979 the chairman of British Steel announced that 53,000 jobs were to go over nine months (Holmes, 1985a, 43).

The extra financial burden of redundancy pay and unemployment benefits surprised the government's policy-makers. Even their guru, the American economist Milton Friedman, claimed to be taken aback by the rate of job-destruction. Having made the most of Labour's poor record on employment (notably through the notorious 1978 'Labour Isn't Working' poster campaign), Mrs Thatcher watched the dole queues grow from 1.2 million in May 1979 to over 3 million by late 1982. The Conservatives could claim that much of the increase simply showed how inefficient British industry had been during the 1970s: these jobs had not been economically justified in the first place. Yet as Geoffrey Howe's high interest rate policy deterred investment (which had been too low in the first place), manufacturing output fell by 17.5 per cent between 1979 and 1982. Many well-run businesses collapsed. While Keith Joseph agonised over propping up nationalised 'lame ducks' such as British Leyland, the private sector which the government had promised to boost was still struggling to regain lost markets when the next recession arrived in 1989.

Apart from the practical difficulties associated with the rising social security budget, unemployment proved to be a serious theoretical blind spot for Thatcherites. It called into question the individualist premise which crucially underpinned their theories. In 1981, as if to show his contempt for Edward Heath's example, Geoffrey Howe introduced a Budget which further reduced demand during a recession. In the words of a former Cabinet minister, this was 'inverted Keynesianism', which inevitably delayed economic recovery and increased unemployment (Gilmour, 1992, 33). How could such measures be explained to those who had accepted Thatcherite rhetoric about the need for hard work and thrift, but now found themselves out of work or bank-rupt? Perhaps it was fortunate for the government that an outbreak of inner-city rioting during the summer of 1981 allowed ministers to deflect attention from those who were suffering more silently. Yet the philosophical problem remained, and since a policy 'U-turn' was ruled out the only alternative was to blame unemployed people for their own problems. The most notable example of this was Norman Tebbit's 1981 party conference speech, when he remarked that his father had 'got on his bike and looked for work' dur-ing the 1930s (Tebbit, 1989, 236). Once unemployed people became reliant on social security benefits, they were open to further attack as the allegedly voluntary products of a 'dependency culture'. The worst effects of the recession were geographically localised, in areas such as the north-east of England and the Midlands. Michael Heseltine, the Secretary of State for the Environment, launched an initiative to bring new investment to Merseyside. But this only increased the Prime Minister's suspicion of Heseltine.

One reason why the government could remain relatively inactive during this recession was that it chiefly affected areas in which Labour was already strong. Much of the South-East of England escaped unscathed; and government strategists knew that the Conservative Party could still win general elections on the basis of support in this densely-populated area. Mrs Thatcher's decisive election victory of June 1983 is often attributed to the 'Falklands Factor'. The recapture of the Falkland Islands after the Argentine invasion of April 1982 certainly helped to raise Mrs Thatcher's approval rating way above her record-breaking low of 23 per cent—if only for a while. Her inflexi-bility, which had received a mixed public reception when applied to domestic matters, now seemed to be a national asset. The performance of the 'Iron Lady' effectively obscured the fact that government defence cuts had played a vital role in encouraging the invasion in the first place. It also switched media attention from the SDP, for whom Roy Jenkins had just won the Glasgow Hillhead by-election. Even without the war, however, the Conservatives probably would have secured a second term. The opposition was divided, and the inevitable economic upturn had begun, creating a genuine 'feel-good' factor in the government's electoral strongholds. The Falklands undoubtedly did have an impact on the scale of the Conservative victory, which gave them a majority of 144 seats. Even then, the party attracted fewer votes than in 1979. This was short of being a ringing endorsement for the far-reaching changes that Mrs Thatcher had already introduced.

Up to 1983, the verdict of a critique of economic policy entitled *Could do Better* seems, if anything, to be an under-statement (Beenstock et al., 1982). The judgement was the more hurtful to Thatcherites since it came from their ideo-logical allies in the IEA. The UK was coming out of reces-sion, but government policy had made this a more painful process than it ought to have been. The government's great-est successes, in fact, had come with trade union reform and the sale of council houses; one of these policies had been fol-lowed with un-Thatcherite caution, while the other had been a Conservative Party aspiration at least since the 1950s. Another policy which could be described as a success was denationalisation (or privatisation, as it was now usu-ally called), but this had hardly featured in the 1979 mani-festo. Instead of securing the commanding heights of the economy for the state, as socialists had hoped, the National Enterprise Board was now acting as the government's sales showroom; British Aerospace, Britoil and the National Freight Company were all disposed of during this Parlia-ment.

Ironically, the government was also in danger of demon-strating that nationalised industries such as British Leyland (BL) could be made to yield a profit to the taxpayer – albeit at a cost, in BL's case, of over 100,000 jobs since 1978. To demonstrate the changed attitude from the days when Edward Heath and his Cabinet agonised over a possible return to the conditions of the 1930s, the Conservative Research Department's 1983 summary of the government's activities turned the decimation of jobs in the public sector into a boast that 'State monopolies have been exposed to the disciplines of competition' (Conservative Research Department, 1983). This was a refreshing outbreak of honesty, because the abandonment of the post-war goal of full employment was the key factor in achieving the government's major goals of lower inflation and trade union reform.

Second innings, 1983–87

During the 1983 general election campaign, the new Foreign Secretary Francis Pym suggested that a landslide victory would not be helpful to the Conservatives. As a speculative remark this was impeccable; the example of the last Labour government had shown that a precarious majority is a good way to ensure parliamentary discipline. Under the circumstances, though, Pym would have been wiser to keep his thoughts private. Mrs Thatcher saw him as the most dangerous of the wets, and could interpret his views only as an invitation for the electorate to give the Prime Minister something less than a vote of confidence. Thatcher's response was to withdraw her confidence from Pym. After his sacking he launched the 'Centre Forward' group to argue for less divisive policies; this body attracted some publicity, especially after the publication of Pym's book *The Politics of Consent* (1985). Yet if Pym had raised the flag of rebellion, he was still disinclined to wave it with much enthusiasm: his book was an attack on extremism, but for tactical reasons he exempted the government and the Prime Minister from that charge (Pym, 1985, 211–12). In the mean time, the vacancy at the Foreign Office allowed Mrs Thatcher to move Geoffrey Howe from the Treasury. His replacement, Nigel Lawson, seemed to be even closer to the Prime Minister's thinking. The Prime Minister no doubt calculated that Howe's growing ability to irritate her would be less of a problem if he went to the Foreign Office, which she already distrusted.

With the wets now largely rinsed out of their threatening outposts, and the opposition parties regrouping after their defeat, the Thatcher revolution moved on to fresh territory.

Room for manoeuvre was increased by the revival in the economy, helped by a world upturn associated with the US budget deficit. Since 1980 Ronald Reagan had acted as a powerful ideological ally for Mrs Thatcher, although the emphasis of his policies had been on tax cuts rather than sound money. This personal version of the `special relationship' certainly helped Britain during the Falklands War, and Reagan's presence gave Thatcher reassurance that she was not alone in her battle against 'socialism'. As relations with the exhausted Soviet Union thawed, the Prime Minister was in need of new enemies to showcase her combative qualities.

Fortunately for Mrs Thatcher, fresh challengers were soon forthcoming. The 1983 manifesto had promised to abolish the Greater London Council (GLC), along with other metropolitan councils. This was part of the campaign to reduce public spending, which also included proposals to cap the amount of money which local councils could raise through their own system of taxation, the rates, which were related to property values. In the case of the GLC, at least, a potent motive was a desire to destroy a symbol of opposition to the government; Ken Livingstone, the charismatic leader of the ruling Labour Group, had described the Council as `a bastion of power for the Labour movement', which could carry through socialist policies while the nation as a whole awaited the final Tory defeat (Baker, 1993, 99).

Despite Mrs Thatcher's claim that the abolition of the GLC enjoyed 'the generalised approval of the silent majority', the issue provoked serious party revolts in both the House of Commons and the Lords (Thatcher, 1993, 305). Heath, Gilmour and Pym were prominent in these campaigns, citing the importance of preserving local democracy. This was not an issue for a government U-turn, however, and the GLC was replaced at the end of March 1986 by centrally-appointed quangos. By that time Mrs Thatcher had fought and defeated a more serious threat – the National Union of Mineworkers (NUM), led by the communist Arthur Scargill. The miners' strike, which lasted a year from March 1984, was called over planned pit closures. Whereas the 1981 miners' dispute had caught the government under- prepared, this time, in accordance with a plan laid down by Nicholas Ridley in opposition, coal stocks were plentiful and Scargill mistakenly called the strike in the spring, when demand was low (Young, 1990, 358–9, 368). The government was also able to overcome the traditional independence of Britain's police-forces, and coordinated the response to the strike on a national basis. Scargill's fatal error, however, was to proceed without holding a ballot, giving the government a propaganda triumph and leaving the NUM open to prosecution. Scargill hoped that the dispute would lead to a repeat of 1974, and the fall of another Conservative government; for Mrs Thatcher, revenge for that humiliation was particularly sweet. Ironically, the Energy Secretary directly responsible for handling the strike was Edward Heath's old ally, Peter Walker.

These events might have left Mrs Thatcher safe from external foes for the moment, but there were still some 'enemies within' ready to challenge her authority. In the last months of 1985 her new Chancellor, Nigel Lawson, urged her to let Britain join the Exchange Rate Mechanism (ERM) of the European Monetary System (EMS). Having tacitly abandoned the attempt to find an appropriate measurement of money, Lawson had concluded that the exchange rate stability promised by membership of the ERM would have the same virtuous effect on inflation; it also tied the UK to the successful low-inflation West German economy. While this issue remained unresolved, Thatcher agreed to the Single European Act (SEA), which was to set up a European Single Market by January 1993, but at a cost of extending the use of qualified majority voting within the EC.

These developments would have significant long-term consequences for the Thatcher premiership. A more immediate problem, also connected to Europe, arrived when Michael Heseltine, now Secretary of State for Defence, resigned from the Cabinet on 9 January 1986. For several months Heseltine had been locked in an argument with the Secretary of State for Trade and Industry, Leon Brittan, about the fate of the ailing Westland company, Britain's only manufacturer of helicopters. Heseltine, a strong supporter of the Community, wanted a European consortium to take over the firm, while Brittan favoured a bid from the USA. At first the public bickering between the ministers gave the impression that Thatcher could not control her Cabinet; after Heseltine resigned, he claimed that Thatcher's control was too strong. Ideology played a part in the dispute, since Brittan was in broad sympathy with the Prime Minister while Heseltine had been regarded as a critic (though not exactly a wet) since advocating extra state help to depressed areas in the aftermath of the 1981 riots. The affair nearly brought about the downfall of Mrs Thatcher, who was widely suspected of having conspired against Heseltine. Instead, Leon Brittan was selected as an adequate scapegoat, and followed Heseltine out of the cabinet (Linklater and Leigh, 1986).

The European issue was an additional complication to the ideological debates in the UK during these years. Both major parties were divided, between determined advocates of closer union, people generally in favour but wary of developments, and the so-called `Euro-sceptics', who were rarely very sceptical in practice and sought to take the UK out of the EC. The impression left by the 1975 referendum campaign might suggest that opposition to Europe was shared by Labour's socialists and the classical liberals within the Conservative Party; the most prominent advocates of withdrawal were Tony Benn and Enoch Powell (now the Ulster Unionist MP for South Down). The 'Yes' campaign, by contrast, had been led by Edward Heath and Roy Jenkins. At that time Margaret Thatcher favoured continued membership, but over the years her position hardened. In office, she adopted a tough negotiating stance to reduce the UK's budgetary contributions, and her hostility to 'Brussels bureaucrats' became more apparent. Her speech delivered at Bruges on 20 September 1988 explicitly linked the case for classical liberalism to Euro-scepticism, since she claimed that a European 'superstate' would endanger her domestic achievements.

The straightforward equation of socialist and Thatcherite = Euro-sceptic is an oversimplification, however. Not only did European institutions develop over the years, but also politicians changed their views when they took on different responsibilities. For example, after the Thatcherite Lord Cockfield was appointed to the European Commission in 1985 he became an enthusiast for deeper European economic integration — much to Mrs Thatcher's chagrin. Leon Brittan, who took a Commission post as compensation for acting as the Westland scapegoat, underwent a similar transformation. By contrast, the social democrat David Owen grew more sceptical during his tenure of the Foreign Office (Owen, 1992, 245–6).

Mrs Thatcher's suspicion of Europe grew as she came to think that the UK's partners wished to impose 'socialist' laws on the British people. During the 1980s this was an eccentric fear; the only notable attempt to pursue a socialist policy in western Europe was made by the French President Mitterrand, but was abandoned in 1982 after only one year. Mrs Thatcher's definition of socialism could embrace a wide variety of ideas. Even so, it was strange that the Prime Minister denounced the intentions of European figures such as the President of the European Commission Jacques Delors, while simultaneously boasting that she had won the battle of ideas throughout the developed world. One of the most telling pieces of evidence for this claim was the extent to which other nations had adopted her most characteristic policy — privatisation.

From being a subsidiary element of the 1979 manifesto, the privatisation programme attained the status of a Thatcherite flagship after the 1983 election. The sales of British Gas and British Telecom were probably the most important, since they combined many attractive features for the party. Privatisation satisfied the ideological requirement that the government should withdraw from direct economic management. The revenue raised from the flotations provided useful funds, and by creating the opportunity for small investors to buy a stake in the companies the Conservatives could pose as the advocates of 'popular capitalism'.

This chimed in with their existing successful policy of council house sales. There was an obvious danger of simply replacing public with private monopolies, and the supply of suitable candidates for privatisation was limited. Yet the programme, nurtured by John Redwood in the Downing Street Policy Unit, undoubtedly helped to create the impression that the Conservative Party, rather than Labour, was the source of new thinking in the 1980s.

Mrs Thatcher's decision to call an early general election, on 11 June 1987, was not regarded as a great risk. The Conservative manifesto was designed to show that the party had not run out of ideas; it promised a cut in the basic rate of income tax to 25 per cent, further reforms of the trade unions, the introduction of a National Curriculum to raise education standards, and the replacement of local government rates with a 'fairer' Community Charge. As in 1983, the state of the opposition was a crucial factor in ensuring a third consecutive victory. Neil Kinnock's efforts to exert control over the Labour Party served only to redistribute the opposition vote; cracks were appearing in the SDP-Liberal Alliance, and Labour recovered sufficiently to secure a comfortable second place. There were some strange last-minute panics within the Conservative campaign, but the party's share of the vote was almost unchanged, and its majority was 102 seats. This was more than adequate to carry the revolution still further.

Hubris, 1987–90

Mrs Thatcher was now the first twentieth-century Prime Minister to win three general elections in a row. All of her opponents, both domestic and foreign, were apparently humiliated. This even applied to the BBC, which wrongly forecast a Parliament with no overall majority. The Prime Minister seemed uncomfortable in the absence of foes, and on the day after the election she sacked her ideological ally John Biffen, who had made the mistake of speculating on television about the virtues of a 'balanced ticket'. To outsiders, at least, Norman Tebbit's decision to leave the government was even more surprising, despite the serious injuries he had suffered in the IRA bomb attack on the Grand Hotel in Brighton during the 1984 Conservative Party Conference. As Andrew Gamble has remarked, Thatcher 'appeared to exhaust and then alienate even some of the colleagues closest to her' (Gamble, 1994, 129). In fact, although the careers of both Biffen and Tebbit had been advanced by Mrs Thatcher, they were suspect because they now enjoyed independent reputations. The Prime Minister did not want her own creations to become rivals. The fate of Tebbit in particular was a worrying precedent for future dealings with Nigel Lawson and Geoffrey Howe, who were proud men of independent stature, despite their devotion to Thatcherism.

After the 1987 election, the absence of dangerous enemies outside the Conservative Party meant that the government was able to focus on consolidating its revolution by re-designing the institutions of the welfare state. However, it was agreed that this could not be carried beyond certain limits. In 1981 the government's think-tank (the CPRS) had proposed the privatisation of the NHS; the outcry caused by the leak of this idea suggested that it would lead to electoral disaster. Mrs Thatcher responded by abolishing the CPRS, although she had mixed feelings about its findings (Blackstone and Plowden, 1990, 179–90; Young, 1990, 300–1). The fate of this advisory body did not deter private free-market groups (including Mrs Thatcher's own joint creation, the CPS), from offering their thoughts on the subject of state-funded provision in all areas. Ministers hoping to impress the Prime Minister with their passion for reform had a full stock of ideas to sift through.

The process had begun during the previous Parliament, when Norman Fowler (assisted by John Major) pushed through some ambitious (and ill-fated) reforms of the pension system (Marr, 1995, 143–8). Privatisation was an important element of the overall strategy, and after the 1987 election this notably embraced the electricity and water industries, with the promise of more to come. As usual, critics claimed that these national assets were undervalued for sale to the private sector, but such objections were brushed aside. Meanwhile, radical reforms of education and the NHS were being devised with some help from the think-tanks. The advertised theme of these reforms was the widening of choice, although they actually involved a strange mix of democracy and central dictation. In education, for example, Kenneth Baker allowed parents to vote on whether or not schools should remain under local authority control. Whatever the decision, however, individual schools were forced to take responsibility for their own budgets. A uniform national curriculum would be decided by the government's appointed experts. The main targets of these reforms were clearly those favourite ogres of Conservative conferences — non-Thatcherite councils and 'trendy' teachers.

The NHS presented different challenges. While a dwindling birth-rate would affect education spending in future, potential costs in the health service seemed to be unlimited. New techniques available to prolong life cost more in themselves, and they would also produce an imbalance within the population. Elderly people were more likely to need medical care, and there would be more of them in future. The government tried to meet this challenge by encouraging private health insurance, but this was unavailable to low-paid and unemployed people. Its immediate solution was to retain the state-funded system, but to introduce changes which created an 'internal market'; hospitals would now compete against each other for patients, and, as in the case of schools, spending was decentralised. These measures were intended to increase efficiency, and it was hoped that bureaucracy would be reduced. However, the complexities of the system meant that the latter goal was always unrealistic; in addition, the government was criticised for appointing its own supporters to the boards of the new administrative trusts (thus adding to the scandal of quangos). The government's obsession with setting targets for services which could not be quantified did nothing to reduce bureaucracy, and doctors (like teachers) found themselves increasingly diverted from their main work by the need to fill in forms. Critics who claimed that these changes were inspired by ideology rather than the needs of the health service had their task made much easier by the government's inadequate attempts at consultation. Even the presentational skills of Kenneth Clarke could not reassure the public on this matter; between 1983 and 1990, the percentage of those who were dissatisfied with the NHS almost doubled (Taylor-Gooby, 1991, 37).

The need for good presentation was a key theme of the third Thatcher government, particularly after Kenneth Baker was appointed chairman of the party in July 1989. Thatcherite assumptions about human nature decrees that votes are decided by economic factors; on this view, provided that a significant minority of people were content with their bank accounts and the opposition parties were divided, the government could afford to be careless in other respects. It would be helpful, nevertheless, if mishaps could be explained by a skillful communicator. In the USA, Ronald Reagan had shown that an affable public image could make voters overlook even dangerous economic indicators, like his record state budget deficit. This was just one respect in which UK politics (like the rest of life) was 'Americanised' during the Thatcher years. The Prime Minister herself seemed to act like a presidential head of state (although she was well advised not to copy Reagan's 'fireside chats' to the nation).

In the 1987 election the Conservatives had benefited from a general feeling of economic well-being, at least among those who were in well-paid jobs. Despite the insecurity of a large section of the community, consumers took advantage of the deregulated credit markets to indulge in unprecedented borrowing. The most spectacular example of this took place in the housing sector. In spite of the additional supply created by council house sales, prices rose steeply, particularly in the south-east of England. The stock market crash of October 1987 did nothing to shake this 'feel-good factor'. Having allowed the money supply to rise prior to the 1987 election, the government now refused to tighten it. With inflation still low and unemployment finally beginning to fall, it seemed as if the austerity of the early 1980s could now be treated as just a bad memory. The Thatcherite 'economic miracle' might not have restored the fortunes of manufacturing industry — and, ominously, North Sea oil would not last forever — but underlying economic realities were easily ignored by consumers at this time.

The buoyant mood reached its height with Nigel Lawson's 1988 Budget. The manifesto pledge to slash the basic rate of income tax to 25 per cent was honoured. However, the rich were the greatest beneficiaries, thanks to a top rate reduction to just 40 per cent. It was argued that this would increase incentives, although it was just as likely to have the opposite effect. Inheritance and corporation taxes were also cut. The yearly effect of the Budget was to reduce taxation by over £6 billion. This Budget was the mirror image of Geoffrey Howe's measures in 1981. Despite having once been an enthusiastic Keynesian, Lawson took delight in contradicting his old master's theory by acting to increase demand when Britain already enjoyed boom conditions. With hindsight, Lawson claimed that 'it was a tight budget in overall terms', but this protestation was not widely believed (Lawson, 1993, 808). The 1988 Budget certainly cheered the government's supporters, but when the good times came to their inevitable end in a new recession the Chancellor had 'retired' to a lucrative City post. Those who had once welcomed his proposals now found him a convenient target for their frustrations, but he could still hit back with a remarkable 1,000-page volume of memoirs.

In response to the excessive demand, inflation began to rise again through 1989, to peak at over 10 per cent in 1990. The consumer boom also sucked in additional imports (UK manufacturing was scarcely in a position to respond), and as the balance of payments deteriorated the Chancellor raised interest rates to 15 per cent by October 1989 in order to protect sterling. By this time Lawson had lost the confidence of the Prime Minister, who preferred to listen to her economic adviser Sir Alan Walters (a veteran free-market propagandist). In March 1989 Lawson and Thatcher had fallen out publicly over the Chancellor's policy of 'shadowing the Deutschmark'; by pegging the value of sterling to the German currency, Lawson hoped to gain the advantages of ERM membership without having to persuade Thatcher actually to join it. Thatcher, bolstered by Walters, thought that the pound should find its own level on the exchange markets without intervention from the state. In late October Lawson decided that he would no longer tolerate the role of Walters; he told the Prime Minister that unless she sacked her economic adviser he would resign. In the end, both of them departed (Lawson, 1993, 960–8; Thatcher, 1993, 715–17).

This incident marked the beginning of the end for Mrs Thatcher. Lawson was not the most clubbable of politicians, but his intellectual strength was widely recognised, even among those who disagreed with his philosophy and loathed the 1988 Budget. Furthermore, his departure occurred soon after another major Cabinet upheaval, when Geoffrey Howe was moved from the Foreign Office to the post of Leader of the House of Commons. He also inherited the role of Deputy Prime Minister, recently vacated by Lord Whitelaw on health grounds. Briefings from the Prime Minister's Press Secretary, Bernard Ingham, drew attention to the fact that this title had no constitutional significance (Harris, 1990, 174–5). This was a gratuitous insult, which showed that despite his lengthy service to the Thatcherite cause Howe did not enjoy much respect in Downing Street. In combination, the joint resentment of Howe and Lawson would be irresistible, but for the moment Howe stayed in his new office.

With Lawson's resignation, the inexperienced John Major found himself shuffled from the Foreign Office, where he had replaced Howe, to the Treasury. In turn, Douglas Hurd moved from the Home Office to become Foreign Secretary, a job which eminently suited his skills. By September 1990 Hurd and Major had convinced Thatcher that the UK must join the ERM. By this time, Britain's economy was weak, and Lawson's high interest rate policy meant that sterling was over-priced when it entered the mechanism. This humiliation for the Prime Minister closely followed the loss of her loyal follower Nicholas Ridley, who was forced to resign as Secretary of State for Trade and Industry because of some injudicious remarks about Germany. Despite three election victories, Mrs Thatcher was now becoming isolated within the Cabinet; even those who might have offered constructive advice tended to owe the Prime Minister too much to tell her distasteful truths. William Waldegrave and Kenneth Baker, once seen as allies of the wets, played significant roles in the development of the Thatcherite 'flagship' policy, the Poll Tax. Later the tax was defended by Christopher Patten. In 1983 Patten had risked his career prospects by writing an elegant attack on Thatcherism, *The Tory Case*. The Prime Minister might have calculated that Patten's dissenting days were over, and indeed his views had changed. But his promotion still shows that she was running out of die-hard ideological supporters who were fit for promotion (Patten, 1983).

Towards the end of Mrs Thatcher's regime events quickly gathered momentum. In November 1989, sixty MPs refused to support Mrs Thatcher in a leadership challenge from the pro-European Sir Anthony Meyer. The Prime Minister now looked vulnerable to attack from a more prominent opponent, and despite consistent denials Michael Heseltine was well prepared for the right moment. Norman Fowler, the Employment Secretary, decided that he would like to spend more time with his family and resigned in January 1990. Peter Walker chose to end his high-spending stint as Welsh Secretary two months later. On the surface, this seemed like delicious timing by someone who had never become even a 'career Thatcherite', but Walker had made his decision some time earlier, and unlike Fowler he stuck to it.

The furore over the Community Charge, or Poll Tax, was a further weakening blow to the Prime Minister. The replacement of domestic rates with a flat-rate levy to fund local services was prepared in haste and implemented without proper consideration (Butler et al., 1994). Just after the Conservatives lost the mid-Staffordshire by-election at the end of March, 1990, a demonstration against the tax in Trafalgar Square turned into a riot. Attempts to explain the violence as an example of 'hooliganism' had less effect than usual, since the tax was clearly regressive and marked a further redistribution of wealth away from the poor. In the wake of the 1988 Budget another bonanza for the rich proved impossible to justify. On 21 October 1990 the Conservatives lost another by-election at Eastbourne; this was particularly telling, because a government victory might have been expected in a contest which occurred only because the IRA had murdered Ian Gow, formerly Mrs Thatcher's Parliamentary Private Secretary.

Economic troubles and the Poll Tax formed the essential background to Mrs Thatcher's fall, although this was ultimately precipitated by the European issue. Senior figures within the party were dismayed when Mrs Thatcher returned from the Rome Inter-Governmental Conference of October 1990 with a message of defiance against Jacques Delors and other supporters of 'Ever Closer Union' amongst European member-states (Thatcher, 1990). The argument that closer economic co-operation with Europe would actually secure the triumph of classical liberalism — an argument accepted by Thatcherites like Howe and Lawson and dreaded by socialist Euro-sceptics — made no impression on the Prime Minister. If there was a choice between national sovereignty and full integration within a free-trade, monetarist Europe, Thatcher would side with the nation; at least that way she could be sure of being able to control politics at home. Realising this after the meeting in Rome, Howe finally lost patience and resigned from the Cabinet after 11 years of reliable service. His ensuing speech in the House of Commons, when he spoke of his agonising 'conflict of loyalties', provided Michael Heseltine with the necessary justification for contesting the leadership of the party (Howe, 1990).

Among many ironies, Thatcher's fall took place just one year after she had felt able to tell the Lord Mayor's Banquet that the recent collapse of communism represented conclusive victory in the battle of ideas to which she had dedicated herself since 1975 (Young, 1990, 561). Some of her allies thought that she should have bowed out in the previous year, after a decade in office. But it was difficult for Mrs Thatcher to accept this view, when her supporters greeted her with chants of 'Ten more years'.

The legacy of the Thatcher project will take many years to work out. From the outset, commentators were divided. Some regarded Mrs Thatcher as perhaps the only whole-hearted ideologue ever to become Prime Minister, yet there were some who denied that her policies were inspired by ideology at all (Riddell, 1983, 1-20; Holmes, 1985a, 51). Often (but not always) this view was held by admirers who felt that she had not gone far enough. In some cases the argument depended upon the notion that Thatcher's ideas arose from 'instincts', as if this somehow prevented them from being classified as ideological. Mrs Thatcher herself was not a great student of political theory; in the words of one personal admirer, 'her feminine mind is seldom diverted by profitless essays into abstract thought' (Wyatt, 1985, 343). However, she had read her Hayek and she con-tinued to listen to liberal think-tanks (the IEA and CPS had been joined by the Adam Smith Institute (ASI) in 1978) (Denham, 1996). Contrary to Wyatt's account, Thatcher's homespun metaphors barely disguised a very abstract mind; unlike political intellectuals, however, she was eager to grasp solutions instead of wrestling with difficulties.

Others, more fruitfully, have characterised Thatcher's success as an exercise in 'statecraft' (Bulpitt, 1986, 19-39). But such critiques, which play down the importance of ideas to Mrs Thatcher, are based on a misinterpretation of British politics – or indeed of most political systems. Politi-cal survival is rarely possible without an element of calcu-lated compromise, or an acknowledgement of the power of circumstances and existing institutions. Lenin was hardly a believer in consensus, but he was forced to tolerate capital-ism in the short term. The fact that Mrs Thatcher had to curb her 'instincts' at times tells us more about the British system of government than it does about her.

Commentators also disagree about the extent to which Mrs Thatcher was able to reshape ideas of what was politi-cally possible in Britain. Socialists are prepared to acknowledge her success in this respect, possibly because they share her impatience with the framework of post-war politics. In fact, Thatcherite ideas thrived in the vacuum left by the decline of the best-known alternatives. The apparent failure of other approaches was exaggerated because the feeling that Britain was a formidable world power lingered long after it had become outdated. When the performance of the economy was compared with what people assumed that it should be, post-war politics fell into disrepute. In particular, the relative prosperity of Germany was a source of disquiet.

Mrs Thatcher's greatest achievement was to talk as if Britain could be made great again while her policies were undermining the basis of that former greatness — manufacturing industry. This rhetoric could be regarded as the indulgence of a harmless dream if the human cost had been smaller. Throughout the post-war period policy-makers had known that certain crucial economic indicators, notably inflation, could be improved if unemployment were allowed to rise. Sometimes this alternative might have been resisted for electoral reasons, but the ethos of the Beveridge report demanded that it should be rejected on principle. The possibility of re-election amidst mass unemployment had already dawned on the Labour Party in the years up to 1979 — Joel Barnett, for instance, could not recall receiving 'a single letter' of protest on the subject — but unlike Mrs Thatcher ministers had mixed feelings about the discovery (Holmes, 1985b, 114). Mrs Thatcher provided conclusive proof that unemployment could be survived — at least by governments. Yet even this would be a short-lived triumph unless the Prime Minister could make voters believe that it was morally tolerable.

For all Mrs Thatcher's talk of a battle of ideas, the record of her government in this respect is doubtful. Among elite opinion, it is significant that most prominent 'conversions' to Thatcherism took place before the 1979 election (Cormack, 1978). The born-again enthusiasm of former Labour supporters such as Woodrow Wyatt and Paul Johnson could not entirely compensate for their lack of numbers.

The general failure of Thatcherism to impress the academic community was demonstrated by Oxford University's refusal to award her an honorary degree in 1985; in the general election two years later, the Conservatives won a greater degree of support from unemployed people than from academics (Willetts, 1992, 21). Outside the opinion-formers the record looks no better. In November 1987, 87 per cent of respondents refused to accept that unemployed people were responsible for their own plight. Ivor Crewe has also shown that while tax cuts and better public services were equally desired in 1979, within months of exposure to Thatcherite rule the majority for better public services was 22 per cent; by October 1987 it stood at 55 per cent (Crewe, 1989, 244–6). This impression of increasing discontent with Thatcherite priorities might be discounted as the product of 'bourgeois guilt', and the evidence of actual voting can be cited against it. But it is still significant that so many people felt ashamed to agree with the Prime Minister.

The nature of Thatcherism

Mrs Thatcher's ideas might not have convinced people in the way she would have hoped, but they were certainly discussed very widely. Some of her supporters were very happy to see her as a representative of the classical liberal tradition, like Herbert Spencer and F.A Hayek. For others, however, it was important to argue that she was a sound conservative who simply had to make radical changes because, in Britain's critical position, there really was 'no alternative' (Willetts, 1992; Lawson, 1993, 1039–54; Tebbit, 1985). On this argument, conservatism had been betrayed by postwar governments, not by Mrs Thatcher. A more subtle analysis, based mainly on the work of Andrew Gamble, portrayed Thatcherism as a strange hybrid of classical liberalism ('The Free Economy') and social conservatism ('The Strong State') (Gamble, 1994). This approach had been heralded at the start of her first premiership in a *Daily Telegraph* leading article, which applauded her mix of 'old-fashioned' liberalism with 'conservatism, patriotism, thrift and hard work'.

An essential aspect of the first argument is the often-repeated claim that Thatcherites, like conservatives, 'work with the grain of human nature', while their collectivist opponents try to make people different. Yet this interpretation of human nature turns out to be highly characteristic of classical liberalism, which assumes that people are competitive, impatient of restraint, and primarily motivated by self-interest. Above all, it is an *individualistic* vision (Kingdom, 1992). According to Mrs Thatcher, British people were different from their European neighbours because of their 'great sense of individuality and initiative' (Thatcher, 1992). Her remark in a famous *Woman's Own* interview that 'There's no such thing as society' is often quoted out of context, but this form of words would never have occurred to a conservative (Rentoul, 1989, 17-20). For conservatives, society is a complex web of interactions without which civilised existence is impossible. The claim of Mrs Thatcher's ally Angus Maude, that `Man is a rational being, capable of making and acting upon rational decisions', is also anathema to conservatives; as a political guide, it points towards anarchy rather than the strong state which conservatives see as a permanent (if unfortunate) necessity (Maude, 1969, 98). Indeed, some of the most enthusiastic supporters of the government (notably those within the Federation of Conservative Students) thought that the logic of Thatcherism suggested a 'libertarian' agenda, including the lifting of prohibitions on mind-altering substances.

Did Mrs Thatcher act on this guidance? Clearly not, if one considers the extra resources allotted to the forces of law and order, and the regular passage of legislation to restrict civil liberties. Stuart Hall and Andrew Gamble have branded Mrs Thatcher as an 'Authoritarian Populist', who exploited widespread fears of a moral and social breakdown in order to enhance the authority of the state (Hall, 1980; Gamble, 1994, 178-84). For example, the writers associated with the *Salisbury Review*, who believed that morality was more important than economics, allowed their distaste for economic liberalism to be overcome by Mrs Thatcher's moral stance. Roger Scruton, editor of the Salisbury Review, joined the Conservative Philosophy Group even though he later correctly identified liberalism 'as the principal enemy of conservatism' (Scruton, 1980, 16). Other social conservatives reacted in a similar fashion (Cowling, 1978). The moral campaigner Mary Whitehouse, for example, related how her 'heart rejoiced' when the Conservative Party won in 1979 (Durham, 1989, 185). Mrs Thatcher could draw on the advice of experts in family policy, such as Ferdinand Mount and David Willetts. Yet all the developments which worried social conservatives continued during the 1980s, and some trends actually accelerated. Between 1979 and 1987, the percentage of births inside marriage declined from 87 to 75 per cent (Letwin, 1992, 94). Divorce and crime rates also rose sharply, and remained a concern mid-way through the second decade of Conservative rule (Riddell, 1991, 169; Greaves and Crosbie, 1995).

In fact, it can be argued that for all her talk of 'Victorian Values', Mrs Thatcher pleased social conservatives only in so far as she provided them with more to complain about. For all their initial hopes, campaigners such as Whitehouse found that the government was content to meet their demands with rhetoric rather than legislative assistance. Much of the 1980s legislation with a moral content arose from back-bench agitation, and on issues such as Sunday trading and divorce laws the government actually worked against the priorities of the social conservatives (Durham, 1991). The fact that the government could promote individualism in these areas, while retaining its reputation as the guardian of tradition moral values, only shows how far the Conservative Party was now driven by Thatcherite ideas about human nature. The junior minister Rhodes Boyson, for example, thought that 'possibly 80 or 90 per cent of my fellow countrymen and women' already shared the party's moral outlook, the implication being that this 'silent majority' would reassert themselves once the nightmare of collectivist politics was ended (Boyson, 1978, 8). This view was later echoed by Shirley Letwin, who acknowledged that

direct government action would not have been an appropriate means of stimulating a moral revival (Letwin, 1992, 41).
Yet the urgency of the problem diagnosed by Thatcherites
implied that the talking needed to be backed up by concerted action; after all, Edmund Burke had warned that
'Manners are of more importance than laws. Upon them, in
a great measure, the laws depend' (Himmelfarb, 1987, 15).

Supporters of Thatcherism will hotly deny that government policies actually increased the problems of social
order, but many commentators thought that they did. Notably, the Church of England issued a report in late 1985 (*Faith
in the City*), which advocated measures to tackle unemployment and to increase welfare payments. These views were
promptly denounced by government spokespeople, who
argued that social malaise was the product of evil (and the
1960s) rather than the effects of Thatcherite policies. Norman Tebbit, for example, blamed 'the valueless values of
the Permissive Society'; the rise in crime could have nothing
to do with unemployment, because there had been no similar trend in the 1930s (Tebbit, 1985, 15, 14). This response
neatly illustrates the difference between Thatcherism and
conservatism; conservatives agree that the potential for evil
is inherent in everyone, but the conclusion they draw is that,
as far as practicable, social conditions should be improved
to reduce the temptation for crime. While Thatcherites
claim that poverty is absolute, not relative, conservatives
accept that when the majority of the population enjoy
unprecedented living standards, those who are excluded
from these benefits will suffer from feelings of deprivation
even if they have enough to scrape a bare existence. In
answer to Tebbit, observers could point out that the governments of the 1930s did not celebrate greed—at least in
public. Some mischievous commentators thought that
Thatcherism itself was a product of the individualism of the
1960s—a fertile suggestion which has not been adequately
investigated (Jenkins, 1988, 66-77).

In the absence of legislation based on distinctive conservative social philosophy, it is only possible to conclude that
the strong Thatcherite state was designed to protect those

who benefited from the classical liberal revolution. The strong state was an *essential feature* of Mrs Thatcher's liberalism, not an addition to it. After all, the government believed that it had to combat attitudes which had prevailed since the war; prosperity for all would not happen immediately, and in the intervening period they could expect a high level of protest, particularly from those who had been indoctrinated by the dependency culture. Hopefully in time unrest would die down, as the poor learned to accept that their unequal status was a reflection of their own shortcomings. In the mean time, hard-line rhetoric at the party conference would serve a useful electoral purpose.

This picture is quite different from the genuine idealism which fuelled Thatcherism before 1979. Some classical liberals, for example, sincerely believed in the 'trickle-down effect', which meant that higher incomes for the rich would stimulate economic activity across the board, to the benefit of the poor. However, over time it became obvious that government's policies were not achieving this goal in any meaningful way. Yet, if anything, Thatcherites became even more vocal in upholding the moral rectitude of their creed, while continuing to pour money into the welfare state which sustained its victims. In this context, it is important to remember that until 1979 classical liberalism had always been regarded as an 'oppositional' viewpoint, from which true believers could criticize the policy of successive governments. The chapter of accidents which propelled Margaret Thatcher to the Conservative Party leadership confronted classical liberals with the brutal test of practice, and it was no surprise that they were found wanting.

Another aspect of Mrs Thatcher's creed which demands explanation is her nationalism (see Chapter 6). In at least one respect this was in keeping with the rest of her thinking, because it was unusually abstract. Thatcherites could claim that it merely followed the conservative tradition of Disraeli, but this was a mistake; Disraeli, after all, had coupled his patriotic rhetoric with a belief that Britain was 'One Nation', in which the state should act to ensure something like equal consideration for rich and poor. Even in the geo-

graphical sense, Thatcherism was not a One Nation movement. Little was done to correct the imbalance of prosperity
between north and south, and the gap between the rich and
the poorest widened considerably. Mrs Thatcher believed
that 'Britain' was synonymous with England; or rather,
with those English people who shared her priorities. As
such, her loyalty to what she conceived to be its interests
was not very surprising.

Towards the end of her premiership Mrs Thatcher's
nationalism was often associated with her opposition to
closer European unity. Her assertion that British people did
not want to be ruled from Brussels coincided with a popular
feeling, even if this arose from a media-manipulated
account of EC decision-making. Behind this lurked concern
that the developing EC threatened at least to modify
Thatcherite policies. As the Prime Minister declared in her
Bruges speech, 'We have not successfully rolled back the
frontiers of the state in Britain, only to see them reimposed
at a European level' (Thatcher, 1988, 48). Mrs Thatcher
might disagree with senior colleagues about the potency of
the European threat, but in this instance at least it would be
wrong to say that her nationalism overrode her belief in the
free market. Instead, the two concerns suggested identical
policies to her, while other classical liberals who looked more
deeply into the issues ended up facing agonising choices.

Conclusion

The immediate legacy of the Thatcher years was deeply
ambiguous. Events in Eastern Europe in 1989 and 1990 suggested that the battle of ideas had indeed been won on an
international scale. The economic liberalism of Reagan and
Thatcher, supported by superior military technology, had
apparently exposed the economic and intellectual bankruptcy of the Soviet Union. In the rest of Europe the signals
were similar; any socialist aspirations of Francois
Mitterrand in France and Spain's Felipe Gonzalez had been
abandoned, and these governments were now accepting
Thatcherite policies such as privatisation. At home, the

Labour Party was looking to Scandinavian social democratic models in its search for an election-winning formula. Mrs Thatcher's fall almost coincided with the disbandment of the British Communist Party, and the closure of the magazine Marxism Today (which in 1989 had correctly predicted her fate)(Hobsbawm, 1989). The dangers of `loony left' councils still had to be exaggerated for electoral reasons, but a sober assessment showed that the movement associated with Tony Benn was unlikely to recover, at least for many years.

In some respects, however, this deluge of good news for Thatcherites was dangerous for them. The feeling that there really was 'no alternative' was bound to induce complacency, and there was an increasing tendency for leading ministers to indulge in damaging quarrels after the 1987 general election. Also, Thatcherism thrived best when it was confronted by enemies, and Mrs Thatcher's style was particularly suited to situations when she was apparently battling against the odds (Denham and Garnett, 1994). After the collapse of communism potent enemies were suddenly scarce. This allowed attention to focus on the actual achievements of Thatcherism, especially around the tenth anniversary of her first electoral victory. Here the record was open to serious question. Reforms in the welfare state encountered serious resistance, and even their sponsoring ministers were forced to tinker with them. If a real economic miracle had occurred, the hardships of the early 1980s would now seem insignificant. Yet the approach of a new recession at the end of the decade revealed that Thatcherite success in this sphere had been superficial at best. Even the much-trumpeted tax cuts were a mirage; the share of national product taken by the state remained relatively constant, and even the richest 5 per cent of the population paid more of their income to the Inland Revenue in 1991 than they had done in 1979 (Norton, 1994). Statistics told only half of the relevant story; with the collapse of communism in Europe attention began to focus on the conduct of governing parties, and scandals broke throughout the capitalist world, in France, Italy and also in Japan. Margaret Thatcher left office before this mood struck the UK, but when it did commentators could reflect that corruption had been encouraged partly by the longevity of the government, but also by the philosophy of Thatcherism itself.

When all the evidence is examined in context, the only plausible interpretation of 'Thatcherism' is that it was a reassertion of classical liberalism. Although the advocates of this ideology were never silent, their impact on policy-making between the mid-Victorian period and the mid-1970s had been limited. Generations of political leaders had rejected the classical liberal view of human nature, mainly because they found the idea of 'rational', self-interested individuals unconvincing in itself. Mrs Thatcher, by contrast, thought that classical liberalism was right on moral and practical grounds, and that her recent predecessors had only rejected it out of fear of the likely electoral consequences. She was determined not to be cowed by such considerations. She was capable of being pragmatic (particularly in foreign affairs), but her failure to enact a thorough-going liberal programme proves only how resistant the British system is to revolutionary change. Even so, her impact was enormous and lasting. The contrast between Thatcherism and earlier policies has seduced commentators into thinking that it was different because it was ideological; in fact, it was just a different ideology, upheld with unusual determination. Part of its power came from the fact that it took opponents by surprise; these ideas, after all, had seemed to be politically dead for almost a century. Even though Mrs Thatcher was drummed out of office amid signs that her ideology was vulnerable to criticism both in theory and practice, it remained to be seen whether her successors would have either the inclination or the will to govern in accordance with alternative principles.

List of works cited

Baker, Kenneth (1993), *The Turbulent Years: My Life in Politics*, Faber and Faber.

Beenstock, Michael, et al. (1982), *Could do Better: Contrasting Assessments of the Economic Progress and Prospects of the Thatcher Government at Mid-Term*, Institute of Economic Affairs.

Blackstone, Tessa, and Plowden, William (1990) *Inside the Think Tank: Advising the Cabinet 1971-1983*, Mandarin.

Boyson, Rhodes (1978), *Centre Forward: A Radical Conservative Programme*, Temple Smith.

Bulpitt, Jim (1986), 'The Discipline of the New Democracy: Mrs Thatcher's Domestic Statecraft', *Political Studies*, volume 34, 19-39.

Butler, David, Adams, Andrew, and Travers, Tony (1994) *Failure in British Government: The Politics of the Poll Tax*, Oxford University Press.

Conservative Research Department (1983), *Four Years' Work: A Summary of the Achievements of the Conservative Government since May 1979*, Conservative Central Office.

Cormack, Peter (1978), *Right Turn: Eight Men who Changed their Minds*, Leo Cooper.

Cowling, Maurice (ed.) (1978), *Conservative Essays*, Cassell.

Crewe, Ivor (1989), 'Values: The Crusade that Failed', in Dennis Kavanagh and Anthony Seldon (eds) *The Thatcher Effect: A Decade of Change*, Oxford University Press.

Denham, Andrew (1996), *Think-Tanks of the New Right*, Dartmouth.

Denham, Andrew, and Garnett, Mark (1994), '"Conflicts of Loyalty": Cohesion and Division in Conservatism, 1975-1990', in Patrick Dunleavy and Jeffrey Stanyer (eds) *Contemporary Political Studies 1994*, volume I, Political Studies Association.

Durham, Martin (1989), 'The Thatcher Government and the Moral Right', *Parliamentary Affairs*, volume 42, number 1.

Durham, Martin (1991), *Moral Crusades: Family and Morality in the Thatcher Years*, New York University Press.

Gamble, Andrew (1994), *The Free Economy and the Strong State*, Macmillan, 2nd edition.

Gilmour, Ian (1992), *Dancing with Dogma; Britain under Thatcherism*, Simon and Schuster.

Greaves, Gerard, and Crosbie, Paul (1995), 'End of Family Life in Britain', *Daily Express*, 23 August.

Hall, Stuart (1980), 'Popular Democratic versus Authoritarian Populism',
in A. Hunt (ed.), *Marxism and Democracy*, Lawrence and Wishart.

Harris, Robert (1990), *Good and Faithful Servant: The Unauthorized Biography of Bernard Ingham*, Faber and Faber.

Himmelfarb, Gertrude (1987), *Victorian Values and Twentieth-Century Conservatism*, Centre for Policy Studies.

Hobsbawm, Eric (1989), 'Another Forward March Halted', *Marxism Today*, October.

Holmes, Martin (1985a), *The First Thatcher Government 1979-1983: Contemporary Conservatism and Economic Change*, Wheatsheaf.

Holmes, Martin (1985b), *The Labour Government, 1974-79: Political Aims and Economic Reality*, Macmillan.

Howe, Geoffrey (1990), Resignation Statement, 13 November 1990, *Parliamentary Debates*, volume 180, cols. 461-5.

Jenkins, Peter (1988), *Mrs Thatcher's Revolution: The Ending of the Socialist Era*, Pan.

Kingdom, John (1992), *No Such Thing As Society? Individualism and Community*, Open University Press.

Lawson, Nigel (1993), *The View from No. 11: Memoirs of a Tory Radical*, Corgi.

Letwin, Shirley (1992), *The Anatomy of Thatcherism*, Fontana.

Linklater, Magnus, and Leigh, David (1986), *Not with Honour: The Inside Story of the Westland Scandal*, Sphere.

Marr, Andrew (1995), *Ruling Britannia: The Failure and Future of British Democracy*, Michael Joseph.

Maude, Angus (1969), *The Common Problem: A Policy for the Future*, Constable.

Norton, Philip (1994), *The British Polity*, Longman, 3rd edition.

Owen, David (1992), *Time to Declare*, Penguin.

Patten, Chris (1983), *The Tory Case*, Longman.

Pym, Francis (1985), *The Politics of Consent*, Sphere, 2nd edition.

Rentoul, John (1989), *Me and Mine: The Triumph of the New Individualism?*, Unwin Hyman.

Riddell, Peter (1983), *The Thatcher Government*, Martin Robertson.

Riddell, Peter (1991), *The Thatcher Era and its Legacy*, Blackwell.

Scruton, Roger (1980), *The Meaning of Conservatism*, Penguin.

Smith, David (1987), *The Rise and Fall of Monetarism: The Theory and Politics of an Economic Experiment*, Penguin.

Taylor-Gooby, Peter (1991), 'Attachment to the Welfare State', in Roger Jowell, Lindsay Brook and Bridget Taylor (eds) *British Social Attitudes: The 8th Report*, Dartmouth.

Tebbit, Norman (1985), Disraeli Lecture, 13 November, Conservative Party News Service.

Tebbit, Norman (1989) *Upwardly Mobile*, Futura.

Thatcher, Margaret (1988), 'A Family of Nations' (speech at Bruges), in Brent Nelson and Alexander Stubb (eds) (1994) *The European Union: Readings on the Theory and Practice of European Integration*, Macmillan.

Thatcher, Margaret (1990), Statement on Rome European Council, 30 October 1990, *Parliamentary Debates*, volume 178, 869-88.

Thatcher, Margaret (1992), 'Don't Undo What I Have Done', *Guardian*, 22 April.

Thatcher, Margaret (1993), *The Downing Street Years*, HarperCollins.

Whitehead, Philip (1985), *The Writing on the Wall: Britain in the Seventies*, Michael Joseph.

Willetts, David (1992), *Modern Conservatism*, Penguin.

Wyatt, Woodrow (1985), *Confessions of an Optimist*, Collins.

Wybrow, Robert (1989), *Britain Speaks Out, 1937-87: A Social History as Seen through the Gallup Data*, Macmillan.

Young, Hugo (1990), *One of Us: A Biography of Margaret Thatcher*, Pan, 2nd edition.

Selected further reading

The impact of Thatcherism on British politics is reflected in a torrent of commentary and analysis from a variety of perspectives. There are several edited volumes, which include essays on almost every aspect of policy during the 1980s. See, in particular, Andrew Adonis and Tim Hames (eds) *A Conservative Revolution? The Thatcher-Reagan Decade in Perspective* (Manchester University Press, 1994); Cosmo Graham and Tony Prosser (eds), *Waiving the Rules: The Constitution under Thatcher* (Open University Press, 1988); Stuart Hall and Martin Jacques (eds.), *The Politics of Thatcherism*, Lawrence and Wishart (1983); Ruth Levitas (ed.), *The Ideology of the New Right* (Polity, 1986); Kenneth Minogue and Michael Biddis (eds), *Thatcherism: Personality and Politics* (Macmillan, 1987); and Robert Skidelsky (ed.), *Thatcherism* (Chatto and Windus, 1988).

Notable books by single authors include Jock Bruce- Gardyne, *Mrs Thatcher's First Administration: The Prophets Confounded* (Macmillan, 1984); John Hoskyns, *Just in Time: Inside the Thatcher Revolution* (Aurum Press, 2000); Dennis Kavanagh, *Thatcherism and British Politics: The End of Consensus?* (Oxford University Press, 1987); and Alfred Sherman, *Paradoxes of Power: Reflections on the Thatcher Interlude* (Imprint Academic, 2005). John Campbell's two-volume biography of Thatcher (*The Grocer's Daughter*, Jonathan Cape, 2000, and *The Iron Lady*, Jonathan Cape, 2003) is a remarkable achievement, written with elegance and impartiality.

For contrasting verdicts on the economy under Thatcher, see Ian Gilmour, *Britain Can Work* (Martin Robertson, 1983); Christopher Johnson, *The Economy under Mrs Thatcher 1979-1990* (Penguin, 1991); William Keegan, *Mrs Thatcher's Economic Experiment* (Allen Lane, 1984); and Alan Walters, *Britain's Economic Renaissance: Mrs Thatcher's Reforms 1979-1984* (Oxford University Press, 1986). Kenneth Hoover and Raymond Plant investigated Thatcherism from an international perspective in *Conservative Capitalism in Britain and the United States* (Routledge, 1988).

CHAPTER 5

Socialism or Social Democracy? The Labour Party, 1979–94

Settling scores, 1979–83

The responsibilities of office normally act as a powerful force for unity within British political parties. After Margaret Thatcher's general election victory of 1979 dissenting voices could still be heard within her party, but they would have been much louder if the Conservatives had lost. After the election Labour did not enjoy this protection. It had the additional handicap of a generally hostile press, ready to publicise any signs of internal bickering. If there had been no rows to exaggerate, they would have been invented. As it turned out, the Conservatives' friends in Fleet Street had no need to be creative, at least until Neil Kinnock began to assert his authority over the Labour Party between 1983 and 1987.

Labour's position after the 1979 election could hardly have been worse. The record of the 1974-79 governments acted as a stimulant to existing ideological difficulties. A major reason for Labour's successes in 1974 had been the perception that the party would ensure good relations with the unions. Yet in 1979 trade union members split their votes almost equally between Labour and the Conservatives. According to moderates within the party, the unions were blamed even by their own members for the disruptions of the Winter of Discontent; on this reading, the buck was passed to Labour in the election because of its close links with the unions (Healey, 1990, 467-8). By contrast, socialists were convinced that Labour had lost because it had let its supporters down. In office it had betrayed the socialist programme of 1974, and the 1979 manifesto had dumped the radical pledges demanded by successive Labour Party conferences. These diagnoses of defeat pointed to rival remedies which could not be reconciled, even by the most skillful party managers.

Labour's performance in government did nothing to reverse the additional problem of declining party membership. Against a published figure of 675,000, it has been estimated that the real number of individual members in 1978 was about 250,000 (Whiteley, 1983, 55). Even Labour was prepared to admit that it was losing members at the rate of 11,000 per year. Ominously for the future, the swing from Labour to Conservative in 1979 was greater among first-time voters than for the electorate as a whole. A diminishing membership would affect finance and morale; it was also likely that those who persevered with the party would be unrepresentative of the average voter. As Labour's factions prepared for a conclusive struggle, the prize for victory was becoming increasingly unattractive.

Since the socialists within the Labour Party had effectively been in opposition since the time of the IMF deal, they were well organised for battle by 1979. At the conference held at Brighton in the wake of defeat the Campaign for Labour Party Democracy gained the first of its constitutional goals, the mandatory reselection of MPs. Constituency parties already had the right to deselect sitting MPs, but the procedure was now greatly simplified. Outwardly this move could be justified as a measure to promote democracy within the party, but it still meant that even popular MPs could lose their seats if they displeased the most active members of their constituency parties. At a time of low morale and dwindling membership, a relatively small number of determined people throughout the country might now be able to control the votes of the entire Parliamentary Labour Party (PLP). The decision on reselection was referred to a Commission of Enquiry which met in June 1980. In the mean time, Tony Benn's ally Chris Mullin published a pamphlet entitled 'How to Select or Re-select your MP' to help the hesitant.

The Commission of Enquiry agreed to reselection, but it had other constitutional matters to consider. The 1979 conference had decided that in future the manifesto should be under the control of the party's National Executive Committee (NEC); and although a proposal to change the method of electing the party leader had been defeated at the conference, the question was revived by the Commission. It suggested that an electoral college should be set up, which would also have the final say over the content of the manifesto. Half of the votes in this college would go to the PLP, 25 per cent to the trade unions, 20 per cent to the constituency parties and 5 per cent to affiliated groups such as the Fabian Society. The 1980 party conference agreed with the idea of an electoral college in principle, although it left the details undecided; the proposal to give the college control over the manifesto was defeated.

By this time the various organisations pressing for change had entered into an alliance, known as the Rank and File Mobilising Committee (RFMC). This embraced ten groups including the CLPD, the LCC, the Socialist Campaign for Labour Victory (SCLV) and the 'Tendency' associated with the Trotskyite newspaper, *Militant*. These groups had a wide variety of aims, and some hated each other more than the Conservatives. The Militant Tendency, for example, thought of most fellow-Trotskyites as 'human rubbish' (Crick, 1986, 91). Despite these unfraternal sentiments, the groups established a temporary tactical unity. They were strong in many constituencies, and enjoyed prominent support within the PLP from Tony Benn, Eric Heffer and others. In his book *Arguments for Socialism* (1980), Benn added another element to the constitutional debate by suggesting that the PLP should decide the membership of Cabinet when Labour was in power, thus further reducing the patronage of a future Labour Prime Minister (Benn, 1980, 172).

Despite Benn's opposition to the personalisation of politics, his prominence in the debate ensured that the media would focus on individuals. On the first day of the 1980 conference he advocated the immediate abolition of the House of Lords, a significant extension of public owner-ship and withdrawal from the EC without a referendum (Jefferys, 1993, 109). It seemed inevitable that when James Callaghan decided to give up the party leadership Benn would be his successor. This prospect caused great alarm among social democrats and even some Tribunites. Benn's personal commitment to democracy (and the traditions of Parliament in particular) cannot be questioned; if anything, over the years these beliefs had strengthened. However, in his dispute with what he regarded as an authoritarian party leadership he had aligned himself with less fervent demo-crats. The Militant Tendency, in particular, was an unusual recruit to the cause; according to one very hostile observer, this revolutionary body threatened 'parliamentary democ-racy and society' (Baker, 1981, 31). Even a more scholarly study claimed that Militant was 'completely intolerant of those who dare to disagree' with its aims (Callaghan, 1987, 199). This was not the only issue that divided Benn from Militant. In the 1970s Benn had advocated the nationalisa-tion of twenty-five major companies, but Militant had a shopping-list of two hundred (with token compensation for previous owners).

A special conference was arranged to finalise the details of a new electoral college. Callaghan promptly resigned in order to ensure that the next leader would be elected under the old rules, which gave the choice to the PLP alone. Benn consulted his advisers, who thought that he should not stand under a system which had no moral authority in their eyes (Adams, 1993, 407–8). The former Chancellor, Denis Healey, was Callaghan's own choice for the succession; but his abrasive manner alienated some of the party's social democrats, who believed that he was taking their support for granted. In the end, Michael Foot emerged as the candi-date who could best unite the party, and Healey was narrowly defeated on the second ballot. This result brought closer the defection of the social democratic 'Gang of Three'(David Owen, William Rodgers and Shirley Williams); although Foot was regarded with personal affection by almost all of the party, the Gang believed that his socialist sympathies would make him unlikely to oppose the mood of radical change. In fact, the circumstances of 1980 meant that Foot's ideas were closer to the social democrats than to Benn; he was wholly committed to the ideals of socialism, but warned against any 'new rigidities of doctrine' which might prove even more destructive than capitalism (Foot, 1983, 14). This position, often labelled as 'soft left', represented the closest thing to a viable compromise within the party; unhappily for Foot, Labour was so polarised that even he was forced to take sides against Benn and his supporters. This did not mean that he was prepared to strike a bargain with those who were preparing to leave the party.

The special conference, held at Wembley in January 1981, confirmed the Gang members in their decision to leave the party. Those who were already uneasy at the direction Labour was taking must have despaired after this meeting. Four main proposals were offered to solve the problem of electing the party leader. The social democrats attempted to outflank their opponents by arguing that every party member ought to have a vote, but this alternative was heavily defeated. The Commission of Enquiry's 50:25:20:5 proposal was also rejected, because it still gave too much say to the PLP. The CLPD preferred that the votes should be divided equally between the PLP, the unions and the constituencies, but this idea also failed.

Ultimately, in bizarre circumstances, the conference plumped for a 40:30:30 division between unions, PLP and constituencies. This plan would also have been defeated, but the Engineers' Union, which had been mandated to cast its block vote only in support of motions which gave the bulk of the electoral college to the PLP, took its instructions too literally and abstained, thus ensuring the success of a system it opposed. This farce was a marvellous christening-present to the Gang of Three (newly-reinforced by Roy Jenkins), who could now argue that the conference block vote produced strange decisions even when the delegates were mandated to support sensible ones. It was a very unhappy beginning for Michael Foot, whose status as a radical hero was already waning. After the crucial votes, a leading member of the RFMC included Foot in a list of 'establishment figures' who had been defeated — a rather odd way of describing a veteran Bevanite rebel who had once been deprived of the party whip (Kogan and Kogan, 1983, 105).

This internal wrangling took place against a background of rising unemployment and economic crisis. Even before the 1979 election the communist academic Eric Hobsbawm had voiced concern that Labour's 'Forward March' had stalled, and urged greater unity among those who upheld working-class interests. But the party's feuding factions made Margaret Thatcher and Edward Heath seem like a married couple (Hobsbawm, 1989, 9–41). Advocates of reform argued that Labour's self-absorption was quite justified, because in its old corrupt state the party could not be trusted to put up effective opposition to Conservative policies. Much still remained to be done. A necessary first step would be Tony Benn's election as deputy leader, particularly since Denis Healey was contesting the position. As Chancellor, Healey's deflationary policies had made him a particular target for socialist hatred, and his uncompromising style represented a danger to their hopes. More seriously, 150 MPs had issued a statement opposing the Wembley decision on the electoral college; significantly, they included Frank Field, who was a member of CLPD and a contributor to the Institute for Workers' Control volume *What Went Wrong?*. This sign of defiance signalled the formation of a Labour Solidarity Campaign (LSC), which attempted to mobilise opposition to the RFMC in the constituencies and the trade unions (Kogan and Kogan, 1983, 107).

The campaign went badly for Benn from an early stage; he was suffering from a debilitating illness, and John Silkin announced his decision to stand, thus splitting the anti-Healey vote. Silkin's candidature gave soft left opponents of Benn (such as Neil Kinnock) someone to vote for on the first ballot without seeming to betray their radical views. At the

Brighton conference of October 1981 the ritual of the new electoral college was played out in full publicity. The impression conveyed to the electorate, however, was not one of a healthy democratic process, but rather of private deals and intimidation. The result was a victory for Healey on the second ballot, but only by less than 1 per cent. Had some MPs not delayed their decision to defect to the SDP until after the vote, Benn would have won. Benn rightly saw that in a close election his interests were best served by defeat: whoever won a narrow victory would seem to lack true authority (Benn, 1994, 155). The arithmetic of the outcome was not a promising basis for a re-union of the party's numerous factions.

While the Labour Party's wounds were being exposed to the public, far-reaching policy decisions were also being taken. Having agreed with Tony Benn that the UK should withdraw unconditionally from the EC, the party gradually established unilateral abandonment of nuclear weapons by the UK as official policy. The relevant votes coincided with the resurgence of the Campaign for Nuclear Disarmament (CND), inspired by the proposed siting of US cruise missiles in British bases. On this issue Foot agreed with the RFMC rather than the moderates who had joined him in opposing Benn. On domestic policy the trend continued with *Labour's Programme 1982*, which one critic dubbed 'a guide book to Bennite Britain' (Mitchell, 1983, 61). It included a reassertion of the Alternative Economic Strategy (AES), featuring a promise to extend common ownership (in various forms), with the disarming proviso that this would not 'reach down into every aspect of economic activity' (Labour Party, 1982, 9). Less publicity was granted to the emphasis laid on the protection of individual rights and open government; Benn's claim that the real threat to liberty came from his opponents was not widely believed, although subsequent events showed that the Labour Party had little to learn from the Militant Tendency on the subject of internal discipline.

By 1982, in fact, the possibility of a thorough socialist takeover of the Labour Party was receding. Michael Foot was now supported by a majority on the NEC, in particular by moderate socialists such as Neil Kinnock. In December

1981 this body set up an enquiry into the activities of the Militant Tendency. The *Militant* newspaper had been established in 1964, although the movement evolved from older groupings. During the 1960s such factions operating within the Labour Party aroused little concern; one study which appeared in 1966 merely poured scorn on Trotskyite groups which remained outside the party, such as the Socialist Workers' Party (SWP) (Gardner, 1966, 115–40). When the movement associated with *Militant* grew in the 1970s the party leadership began to take notice. In 1975 the NEC commissioned a report into Militant's activities; when Reg Underhill, the national agent, presented his findings it was decided not to publish them. After Underhill's retirement in 1979, however, he leaked his report to an eager press, just as the inquest into Labour's defeat was beginning.

Foot's decision to start a new enquiry went against his instincts; as a former victim of 'witch-hunts', he had opposed the publication of the Underhill report on principle. The new powers of constituency parties, however, forced him to act. Inner-city areas (where the nation-wide problem of Labour Party recruitment was accentuated by apathy and unemployment) were particularly vulnerable to 'entryism', the process whereby moribund constituency parties were taken over by revolutionary activists. When the report was finished, Foot agreed that only groups which accepted Labour's full constitution would be eligible for inclusion on a new register. In September 1982 Militant held a conference at Wembley to protest against the decision; the meeting attracted 2,600 members from around the country (Crick, 1986, 199). Inevitably the process dragged on, but in February 1983 the five members of the *Militant* editorial board were expelled from the Labour Party (Jones, M, 1994, 491–7). At the same time, Foot faced a problem over the endorsement of Peter Tatchell as parliamentary candidate for Bermondsey. Tatchell was not associated with Militant, but he had attacked Labour's 'obsessive legalism and parliamentarianism' in the journal *London Labour Briefing* (Jones, M, 1994, 480). Eventually Tatchell stood in a by-election called in February 1983, and his heavy defeat inspired rumours that Foot would be replaced as Labour leader before the next general election. This gossip only subsided when Labour held on to Darlington in a subsequent by-election.

The result of the ferocious infighting during the 1979–83 Parliament was unsatisfactory for all of the warring factions. Even within the Labour Party, the 1983 manifesto (*The New Hope for Britain*) became known as 'the longest suicide note ever written'; more predictably, Margaret Thatcher claimed that it was 'the most extreme ever'. In fact, the distance between key manifesto policies and the views of the electorate has been exaggerated; for example, there was a high level of public support for import controls, the central proposition of the AES (Young, 1985, 20–1). However, the manifesto was based on *Labour's Programme 1982*, and thus reflected decisions taken before the mood of the party turned against Benn and his supporters. Since Bennism had been in decline within the party since the time of the deputy leadership election, members of the RFMC were able to claim subsequently that the leadership had endorsed the manifesto without real conviction. Once again, real socialism had not been given a fair electoral test. Remaining social democrats inevitably saw things differently. By ensuring that the party was both divided and tied to an unpalatable programme, Benn had ruined any chance Labour might have had.

At the level of ideas, at least, this dispute was as far from a settlement as ever. Caught in the middle of the feud, Foot had contributed a passionate rallying-call against Thatcherism in his foreword to the manifesto, but his order of priorities was clearly different from that of many Labour activists. Foot's allies realised that if the 'Bennite' factions were to be defeated it could be done only by means of resolute decisions at the centre. Yet the leader himself did not relish the task. When the election was held the Conservatives won an overall majority of 161 seats; Labour's vote had slumped to 28.3 per cent, its worst performance since 1918. The party's lead over the SDP-Liberal Alliance was only 2 per cent. Within days of this crushing defeat, Foot submitted his resignation as Labour leader.

Confrontation, 1983–87

Despite all his efforts, Michael Foot's record only proves the accuracy of Denis Healey's remark that there is 'no more difficult job in British politics' than leading Labour in opposition (Healey, 1990, 466). According to an early biographer, Neil Kinnock, who was convincingly elected as Foot's successor, was 'born lucky'. Ten years later, Kinnock himself was probably only half joking when he claimed that the balance of his mind had been affected when he made the decision to stand for the leadership (Harris, 1984, 223; Kinnock, 1994, 535). At least Kinnock was spared a potentially bruising contest with Tony Benn, who was ineligible to stand having honourably refused to move from his vulnerable Bristol constituency and suffered the inevitable consequences in the election. The prospects for at least partial unity seemed to be further improved by the election of Roy Hattersley, from the social democratic wing of the party, as Kinnock's deputy. Hattersley's unsuccessful opponent was Michael Meacher, who had worked closely with Tony Benn in the early 1980s.

Neil Kinnock had been elected as MP for Bedwellty in 1970. His parliamentary career had thus begun with a general election defeat for Labour, which inspired the party to adopt a more radical stance in opposition to the Heath Government. Kinnock was still relatively unknown when Harold Wilson returned to office in 1974. Having spent his first Westminster years in opposition, it was natural for Kinnock to anticipate a new Labour government with hopes that were quickly disappointed. His stirring oratory won him a reputation among Labour supporters who were impatient at the government's deviation from the promises of 1974; when circumstances changed, some of these allies were able to turn the accusation of treachery against him. Kinnock was a determined opponent of nuclear weapons, and rejected entry into the EEC on Edward Heath's terms. These views also made life difficult for him later.

As a Welshman, a member of the Tribune group and a friend of Michael Foot, it was natural that Kinnock should write a foreword for a new edition of Aneurin Bevan's *In Place of Fear* in 1978. Here Kinnock explicitly denounced the competitive view of human nature propagated by capitalists, and asserted that the idea of social co-operation went 'with the grain of history'. Like the advocates of the AES, Kinnock called for 'the collective organisation of economic resources under the collective control of democracy'. He summed up his political creed as demanding 'hot ideas with … a cool head' (Kinnock, 1978). This was written when the Labour leadership was preoccupied with survival, rather than idealism. By contrast, as Tudor Jones has written, Kinnock matched a 'reformist' commitment to parliamentary methods with a 'fundamentalist' mission to tranform society (Jones, T, 1994, 570).

As Labour embarked on its civil war after the 1979 defeat, Kinnock began to worry that some who agreed with his fundamentalism were willing to ally themselves to factions within the party who despised his reformism. In the *Political Quarterly* he announced that he would always choose a gradual approach to his goals if the only alternative was revolution (Kinnock, 1980, 411–12). In the context of a polarised Labour Party, this meant that Kinnock had taken sides with the leadership against Tony Benn, who was tainted in Kinnock's eyes by his alliance with the opponents of democratic socialism. At the same time, Kinnock's views were clearly distinct from those of the defecting Gang of Three, who rejected even a long-term commitment to nationalisation and were determined to keep the UK within the EC. In combination with his passionate oratory, these views made Kinnock an ideal successor to Foot, and he gained 71 per cent of the electoral college in the 1983 leadership election.

Unfortunately for Kinnock, he inherited Foot's problems as well as his position. Foot had made only preliminary moves against the Militant Tendency, and the Conservative press was glad to publicise the deeds of so-called 'loony left' councils such as Militant-controlled Liverpool. After wooing former allies of Tony Benn like Tom Sawyer and Michael Meacher, Kinnock was able to use the machinery set up by Foot to continue the expulsions. His campaign was capped by a tough speech at the 1985 party conference, which Labour's image-makers used in a political broadcast for the 1987 election. This was almost certainly a mistake, because it drew unnecessary attention to the party's divisions. After all the scare-stories, hardly any MPs had been deselected, and the leader already controlled policy- making. With local authorities also under attack from the government, it could be argued that Kinnock and Thatcher were working together against democratically-elected representatives who happened to be inconvenient for both of them.

Kinnock's other major headache during these years was the prolonged miners' strike of 1984–85, which ended in a rout for the union movement. Normally the strike would have aroused his wholehearted support; the government's pit closure programme threatened to destroy traditional communities, particularly in Kinnock's Wales. Yet the role of Arthur Scargill prevented the Labour leadership from providing overt support to the strike. Kinnock's rejection of revolutionary activity meant that he was opposed in principle to any attempt to replace a government by extra-parliamentary means, yet this was precisely Scargill's intention. Understandably, Conservative newspapers were not sympathetic to Kinnock's plight. Given his radical past, they could either jeer at him for deserting his old principles or imply that he secretly agreed with Scargill. Often, they did both.

With the economy now recovering and unemployment figures falling, the majority of voters had no reason to scrutinise the Conservative case against Kinnock very closely. Under the circumstances, Labour's slight recovery in the 1987 general election was a reasonable achievement. A new publicity chief, Peter Mandelson, made presentational changes in an attempt to jettison the party's extremist image. The red flag was replaced by a red rose, and broadcasts concentrated on Kinnock's personality rather than the detail of policy. The manifesto, *Britain Can Win*, represented a change of emphasis from previous ideas rather than a fundamental rethink. There was a promise to reduce unemployment by a million in two years, with a detailed breakdown of how this would be achieved. In a clear echo of the Wilsonian approach, Labour proposed to set up a National Economic Summit, which would bring together government, unions and employers. The ambitious AES programme of nationalisation was watered down, and the emphasis shifted to introducing more flexible forms of social ownership (heralded in a 1986 policy document). The manifesto gave more prominence to the idea of a British Industrial Investment bank, to provide the investment funds which capitalists continued to withhold despite the Thatcherite stress on the virtues of free enterprise. Increasingly the Labour leadership was looking to European practices to provide ideas for industrial strategy, in line with Kinnock's agreement that 'Britain's future, like our past and present, lies with Europe' (Kinnock, 1984, 231; Held and Keane, 1984, 170–81; Hattersley, 1987a, 159–74).

Some of these proposals were open to detailed criticism, but Labour's main vote-loser in this election was clearly its defence policy. Despite encouraging world developments after the rise of Mikhail Gorbachev, Kinnock's unilateralism was bitterly attacked. The potency of the issue was increased by the problems experienced by the Alliance during the campaign (see Chapter 3), and it was emphasized by Conservative-supporting newspapers. A humiliating meeting with President Reagan (where the US President managed to confuse Denis Healey with the British Ambassador) served only to underline Kinnock's inexperience as a world leader. Meanwhile, Mrs Thatcher embarked on a triumphal visit to Moscow. Few voters appreciated the irony of this trip to a country which was widely portrayed as a deadly threat to the nation's survival. Conservative posters suggested that Labour would simply surrender to nuclear blackmail from the Soviet Union; a manifesto pledge to increase spending on conventional forces could not protect the party from its critics.

Consolidation, 1987–92

The 1987 election result was double-edged for Labour. The party could be satisfied with its clear defeat of the Alliance for second place — there was now an 8 per cent gap between them. However, the economic boom in the south of England meant that Labour representation was still largely confined to its old 'heartlands' of the north and midlands of England, and Wales and Scotland. The impression that Labour was finished as a national force was not dispelled by an election which suggested that their message was still outdated, despite the new professionalism of the campaign. Kinnock seemed to have exchanged insecurity at the head of restless factions only for a more comfortable life of permanent impotence.

Some consolation could be drawn from a more detached analysis. In 1987, Mrs Thatcher had benefited from an inevitable economic recovery which seemed more exciting by contrast with the previous deep recession. If this trend proved temporary, Labour was now well placed to win in future, particularly if the next recession also hit the Conservative heartlands in the South-east of England. The issue of defence looked likely to fade as Gorbachev negotiated for deep cuts in nuclear weapons, and at least Labour had now abandoned the idea of leaving the EC without a referendum. Finally, the Conservative proposal of a Community Charge to replace the rating system could prove to be a gift to the opposition, although they made little use of it during the election campaign. These factors meant that Labour's frustration after a third consecutive defeat need not be lasting.

The 1987 election was also a serious setback for Tony Benn and his supporters. The traditional explanation that Labour had not been socialist enough could still be rehearsed, but it had become somewhat repetitive by now and Kinnock's tactics had deprived Benn of many allies. Benn himself was back in the House of Commons as MP for Chesterfield; although he failed to win election to the Shadow Cabinet in 1987 he still received sixty-nine votes. Within the PLP his support was centred on the Campaign Group, which had been set up in 1981 with the support of around twenty MPs; Benn also established an informal think-tank in 1985 to keep up socialist momentum. In March 1988 the Campaign Group agreed that Benn should stand against Kinnock for the leadership; Benn's insistence on democracy in all things exposed divisions even within the group, and Margaret Beckett, Clare Short and two other women members resigned as a result of the vote (Adams, 1993, 454). After six months of exhaustive campaigning, Benn was able to secure only 11.3 per cent of an electoral college which exaggerated his support within the Labour movement. His running-mate for the deputy leadership, Eric Heffer, attracted even less support. Benn would always enjoy the allegiance of socialist MPs such as Dennis Skinner, but standing against Kinnock at this time only gave the leader (and the public) a more precise indication of his impregnable status.

This was particularly welcome to Kinnock, who had decided to set up a wide-ranging policy review exercise after the 1987 election. It was already clear which direction this would take. In the year of the election Roy Hattersley published *Choose Freedom*, which attacked the Thatcherite definition of liberty as simply the absence of external restraint. For Hattersley, 'the extension of freedom is an essential element within the philosophy of socialism'; on this view, for example, the concept of liberty is meaningless in the presence of wide economic inequalities. Governments should therefore act towards the goal of equality, even if this should prove impossible in practice (Hattersley, 1987b, 92). Hattersley cited approvingly the American liberal philosopher John Rawls, who had also inspired some of David Owen's work in the early 1980s. He described his position as 'democratic socialist' rather than social democratic, but there was little to separate Hattersley's thinking from that of former allies such as Shirley Williams. Now that the identity of the SDP had become blurred through Owen's ideological migrations, Hattersley's writings could bring Labour back to the legacy of Anthony Crosland.

The first product of Labour's Policy Review, *A Statement of Democratic Socialist Aims and Values* (1988), was mostly written by Hattersley. Like *Choose Freedom*, this document showed a willingness to accept a central role for private enterprise. At the 1988 party conference Kinnock acknowledged that the new position was an adjustment of socialist principles in the light of Thatcherism's electoral success. This sense of a tactical shift was enhanced when the findings of the completed Policy Review were published under the title *Meet the Challenge, Make the Change* (1989). For many voters, the actual content of the new programme was overshadowed by the impression that it did not represent Kinnock's real thinking. The fact that Kinnock was now prepared to give up his life-long commitment to unilateral nuclear disarmament was particularly difficult for Labour's new image-makers to present, either to the party conference or to the electorate.

Meet the Challenge, Make the Change argued (like Anthony Crosland three decades earlier) that the question of industrial ownership was barely relevant to the achievement of socialist goals. From this viewpoint, even the renationalisation of industries returned to the private sector by the Conservatives became less of a priority, and would depend upon circumstances after Labour's re-election. The proposals envisaged greater regulation of private enterprise, rather than other forms of ownership; as the Major Government later found, this compromise solution left everyone dissatisfied. There would be some changes to existing trade union law, but the status quo of 1979 would not be restored. This issue had led to friction between Kinnock and Michael Meacher; the latter had served his purpose by supporting Kinnock on the NEC, and could now be discarded. Meacher's replacement as Employment spokesman by Tony Blair in 1989 removed this difficulty. While the 1987 manifesto had promised to reverse the government's tax cuts, the Policy Review concluded that the rate on higher earners would rise to a maximum of 50 per cent—lower than it had been after Geoffrey Howe's first Budget in 1979. To tackle poverty, a national minimum wage would be introduced, but Labour was now echoing Thatcherites in its opposition to any 'dependency culture';

the state would act as an 'enabler' rather than a nanny (Garner, 1990, 31–6).

The reaction of many commentators was that the social-democratic 'Gang of Four' had won the battle for the Labour Party in their absence (Marquand, 1992, 201; Gamble, 1994, 36). Some felt that the Policy Review lacked any imaginative ideas, and failed to bring Labour's principles up-to-date (Hughes and Wintour, 1990, 205). *Meet the Challenge, Make the Change* had been publicised through a song of the same name; Tony Benn wrote his own version of the lyrics, which now ended 'Pink and harmless we must be/If we want a victory' (Adams, 1993, 458). More seriously, Benn recorded that the Policy Review represented 'the Thatcherisation of the Labour Party. We have moved now into the penumbra of her policy area, and our main argument is that we will administer it better than she will' (Benn, 1994, 546). Whatever the Policy Review had done to Labour's principles, the voters seemed to be impressed. In 1987 67 per cent had considered that the party was too extreme; by September 1989 this figure was down to 29 per cent (Sanders, 1993, 219). In the latter year the party took the constituencies of the Vale of Glamorgan and Mid-Staffordshire from the government in by-elections, and in June it inflicted Mrs Thatcher's first nationwide election defeat in the vote for a new European Parliament. Perhaps Britain was now ready to 'Make the Change' at last.

Events had not been kind to the Labour Party since October 1974. Now the gods decided to do Kinnock a temporary favour in order to be more sadistic later on. The government was well behind in national opinion polls, as inflation and interest rates climbed together. The housing boom which had done so much to help Mrs Thatcher win the 1987 election now turned sour, with mortgage-holders under pressure from the high cost of borrowing. Just as the boom had been greatest in the south of England, now the pain was felt there most. The merged Alliance parties were struggling to find a name, let alone an identity; for a while it looked as though the Green Party would replace them as a remote challenger to the main parties. At the same time, the revolt against the Community Charge was beginning; this brought Labour some problems, as several MPs joined a campaign to break the law, but the effect on Conservative popularity was far worse. Mrs Thatcher now began to look like an electoral asset for Labour, and after the resignation of Nigel Lawson the divisions inside her party could no longer be disguised or contained.

Despite the obvious temptations, Kinnock did not wait for the government to present him with victory. With party membership still only around 250,000, the leader called for a recruitment drive in January 1989. The party was in debt by over £2 million (Butler and Kavanagh, 1992, 59). Initial results were disappointing, but Kinnock's campaign drew attention to a problem which the party had not taken seriously enough. There was always likely to be a transitional phase before the revolutionary reputation of Labour's constituency parties changed sufficiently to attract new members with a different outlook. In contrast to Foot's problems with Peter Tatchell, the Kinnock-controlled NEC began to impose its preferred candidates in certain areas, and two Militant sympathisers in the PLP were expelled in 1991. Meanwhile, after a false start in 1984, Kinnock began to move towards the principle of 'One Member One Vote' (OMOV) to reduce the power of constituency cliques over the selection of parliamentary candidates. Just as Benn's drive to devolve power to the constituencies helped his campaign to radicalize the party, so OMOV was calculated to strengthen the leadership. In the face of opposition from some unions who felt that OMOV was ultimately designed as an attack on their influence, Kinnock was forced to compromise, although individuals members were still given much more influence over the selection process. By 1991 a ballot of all constituency members had also become mandatory for NEC elections (Shaw, 1994, 117–18). In 1992 and 1993 this reform resulted in defeat for Dennis Skinner and Tony Benn. Kinnock's allies claimed that these measures would 'modernise' the party as an institution, to complement the changes in its policies.

If Mrs Thatcher had remained as Prime Minister, Kinnock's reforms might have produced the elusive victory in 1992. Instead, the Conservative Party acted to 'shoot Labour's fox'. After Thatcher's fall in November 1990 John Major was able to replace the Community Charge with a tax that was slightly less regressive. Perhaps more importantly in the light of subsequent events, the Gulf War offered Major the opportunity to look as though he combined a more caring approach to domestic policy with Mrs Thatcher's toughness on the world stage. Ironically, the new economic recession also hit Labour's chances. The party's spending promises were more restrained, but there was still a difficulty about finding the money to pay for them without the threat of tax-increases which might alienate key voters.

Labour's 1992 manifesto, *It's Time to Get Britain Working Again*, began by reaffirming the party's new 'core' principle of individual liberty based on effective community provision. The NHS and education were seen as special priorities. At the same time, a Labour government would 'make families better off' by reforming the tax and national insurance systems. A new top rate of income tax of 50 per cent would apply only to 'individuals with an income of at least £40,000 a year'. The Shadow Chancellor, John Smith, produced an alternative budget to explain the impact of these measures. Revenue would be raised in other ways; instead of Labour's original opposition to council house sales, the party now demanded that councils should be allowed to spend the proceeds as they wished. In contrast to these detailed proposals, promises to cut unemployment were left vague. In place of nationalisation, Labour was now fully committed to partnership between government and private industry, complete with generous investment grants, 'Technology Trusts' and a Minister for Science to promote innovation. Rather than directly intervening in the economy, Labour would cajole industrialists into stepping up investment. This shift from Labour's traditional reliance on the state was also reflected in plans for the decentralisation of power; an elected Scottish Parliament was promised, together with a Welsh Assembly and devolution to the English regions. A charter of rights would entrench civil liberties for all. In a tantalising hint to supporters of the Liberal Democrats, Labour also promised that the findings of a working party on electoral reform (under Professor Raymond Plant) would be taken very seriously.

During the 1987–92 Parliament, Labour was consistently ahead in national opinion polls, and was widely expected to win the April 1992 general election. In the event, the Conservatives scrambled home with a majority of twenty-one. Labour's share of the vote had risen to 35 per cent, but its appeal in the south was still too limited. In part, this could be accounted for by tactical errors, such as the party rally at Sheffield in the last week of the campaign (which the press portrayed as a premature celebration of victory), and the 'War of Jennifer's Ear', which was fought over an emotive election broadcast on the state of the NHS. This was already a strong Labour issue, on which the party had little to gain by taking risks. Similarly, Kinnock's indecision over the question of proportional representation gave the impression that Labour would be prepared to cut an opportunistic deal with the Liberal Democrats if it failed to win an overall majority. Finally, the Conservatives were able to attack the details of Smith's shadow budget, frightening middle-income householders who were already under pressure from high interest rates.

Apologists for Labour governments between 1964 and 1979 commonly argued that the party has been prevented from governing as it wished because of the mess left behind by the Conservatives. After 1992, this theory could be elaborated further. On this occasion the Conservatives had mismanaged the economy so badly that Labour never stood a chance of winning. On this view, a disillusioned electorate refused to believe in the brighter future offered by Labour. In fact, despite the efforts of Kinnock and Smith, voters still did not trust Labour to run the economy better than the Conservatives (Sanders, 1993, 171–213). Instead of the existing government, trends in the world economy and Margaret Thatcher were blamed for this recession. Labour's message had failed to get through – or, perhaps, the opposing message of the Conservative press had got through too well.

The 1992 election result was a personal disaster for Kinnock, who resigned shortly afterwards. Party leaders rarely survive two election defeats in a row, and some attributed the defeat to Kinnock's personality. While the long years of opposition had denied him an opportunity to demonstrate administrative skills, the need to fight his internal opponents (and a well-publicised hot temper) created a divisive image. Not even the skills of Peter Mandelson could make the public regard Kinnock as a Prime Minister in waiting. Perhaps this demonstrated the remarkable impact of Conservative propaganda rather than any serious weaknesses in the Labour leader, but by March 1992 only 39 per cent of the public thought that he was doing a good job. The corresponding figure for John Major was 51 per cent; almost three-quarters of the electorate approved of Paddy Ashdown's leadership (Sanders, 1993, 193). After the 1992 defeat, Kinnock's popularity increased; even the editor of the *Sunday Times* was prepared to acknowledge that he had been 'Labour's Gorbachev'. These token compliments were safe after the event. For whatever reason, Kinnock was not sufficiently respected by the electorate when it mattered, and this must have contributed to Labour's defeat.

Conclusion: the betrayal of socialism?

After more than a decade of additional Labour 'modernisation', the parallel between Kinnock and Gorbachev becomes even more interesting. It is possible to portray Kinnock as a politician who fought to drag his party into the modern world, at the cost of his own future prospects. By personalising the battle for Labour Party reform he acted as a shield for his reforming ideas; when he was gone critics were prepared to tolerate from his successors further changes which they would never have accepted from him. Like Gorbachev, Kinnock was the creation of the system which he attacked. This made him an effective assailant, but it also ensured that he would be destroyed along with the system (Fielding, 1994, 599).

There was, though, at least one major difference between Kinnock and Gorbachev. As soon as the latter emerged as a significant force in Soviet politics, it was clear that he had limited respect for orthodox thinking within the Communist Party. Like most people who are categorised as 'pragmatists', he had strong beliefs of his own; but he recognised the need for compromises in the situation he inherited. His practical approach to politics was appreciated by Mrs Thatcher, who saw him as a straight-dealing opponent even before he took over in Moscow.

By contrast, while the campaign against Militant brought Neil Kinnock's fighting qualities to the fore, he was not a convincing 'moderniser'. His success as an orator depended on the impression of sincerity as he expounded his beliefs. After the policy review he continued to speak with passion about the need for a Labour government; but it was possible for critics to claim that this was the only principle he had retained from the days before he rose to the leadership. In particular, he had been a fiery advocate of unilateral nuclear disarmament, and his stance on this subject had provoked vicious attacks from the Conservatives. When he watered down this commitment after the 1987 general election, allies could applaud his ability to make personal sacrifices for the greater good of his party. But it was not difficult for the Conservative-supporting press to denounce Kinnock as a cynical opportunist.

In short, Kinnock differed from Gorbachev in that he was not temperamentally suited to compromise. He was not impressed by the proposals which emerged from the policy review, feeling that they lacked 'a central philosophical theme' (Kinnock, 1994, 545). In fact, the proposals were reasonably coherent; it was just that Kinnock did not agree with them, and as a result it was not surprising that his speeches between 1987 and 1992 failed to carry conviction.

Contrary to Kinnock's view, it can be argued that Labour's policy platform at the 1992 general election was the closest the party has ever come to embracing social democracy. There was much greater acceptance of private enterprise as a source of economic prosperity; but this was matched by an obvious desire for greater social justice. The programme reflected the influence of Kinnock's deputy, Roy Hattersley, and of John Smith, the Shadow Chancellor. Smith and Hattersley had remained loyal to Labour, although many of their friends had defected to the SDP at the beginning of the 1980s.

The ideological character of the 1992 Labour manifesto was somewhat ironic, since social democracy had been blamed for the failures of British government in the 1970s and the SDP had turned out to be a damp squib. However, the failure of the SDP could be explained without reference to its underlying principles; and even if social democracy had proved unequal to the unique challenges of the 1970s, in the very different context of 1992 it could be presented as a way of restoring a sense of community after the excessive individualism of the Thatcher years.

However, the 1992 general election should not be seen as yet another adverse judgement on social democracy. Whether or not Labour had the right policies at that time, the party had the wrong leader to present them; and this disparity was highlighted by a media which concentrated on party leaders more than ever before. After the election, Labour's post-mortem concentrated on the alternative budget. Kinnock had been unhappy with Smith's approach, on the grounds that the prospect of higher taxation might alienate key voters. Kinnock's annoyance was reported at the time, and caused some controversy. In hindsight, though, this episode takes on even greater significance. The most plausible lesson of the 1992 general election was that Labour might have won if it had been led by someone who could advocate social democratic ideas with genuine conviction. However, some elements within the party took the analysis further. For them, Kinnock had only failed because he had not pushed policy changes far enough. Labour would never return to office unless it truly came to terms with Thatcherism; and no-one would believe that it had changed unless it chose a leader who accepted that Mrs Thatcher had been more than half right.

List of works cited

Adams, Jad (1993), *Tony Benn: A Biography*, Pan.

Baker, Blake (1981), *The Far Left: An Expose of the Extreme Left in Britain*, Weidenfeld and Nicolson.

Benn, Tony (1980), *Arguments for Socialism*, Penguin.

Benn, Tony (1994), *The End of an Era: Diaries 1980-90*, Arrow.

Butler, David, and Kavanagh, Dennis (1992), *The British General Election of 1992*, Macmillan.

Callaghan, John (1987), *The Far Left in British Politics*, Blackwell.

Crick, Michael (1986), *The March of Militant*, Faber and Faber.

Fielding, Steven (1994), 'Neil Kinnock: An Overview of the Labour Party', *Contemporary Record*, volume 8, number 3.

Foot, Michael (1983), 'Labour's Britain in the 1980s', in Gerald Kaufman (ed.) *Renewal: Labour's Britain in the 1980s*, Penguin.

Gamble, Andrew (1994), 'Love's Labours Lost', in Mark Perryman (ed.) *Altered States: Postmodernism, Politics, Culture*, Lawrence & Wishart.

Gardner, Llew (1966), 'The Fringe Left', in Gerald Kaufman (ed.) *The Left*, Anthony Blond.

Garner, Robert (1990), 'Labour and the Policy Review: A Party Fit to Govern?', *Talking Politics*, volume 3, number 1.

Harris, Robert (1984), *The Making of Neil Kinnock*, Faber and Faber.

Hattersley, Roy (1987a), *Economic Priorities for a Labour Government*, Macmillan.

Hattersley, Roy (1987b), *Choose Freedom: The Future for Democratic Socialism*, Penguin.

Healey, Denis (1990), *The Time of My Life*, Penguin.

Held, David, and Keane, John (1984), 'Socialism and the Limits of State Action', in James Curran (ed.) *The Future of the Left*, Polity.

Hobsbawm, Eric (1989), *Politics for a Rational Left: Political Writing 1977-1988*, Verso.

Hughes, Colin, and Wintour, Patrick (1990), *Labour Rebuilt: The New Model Party*, Fourth Estate.

Jefferys, Kevin (1993), *The Labour Party since 1945*, Macmillan.

Jones, Mervyn (1994), *Michael Foot*, Victor Gollancz.

Jones, Tudor (1994), 'Neil Kinnock's Socialist Journey: From Clause Four to the Policy Review', *Contemporary Record*, volume 8, no. 3.

Kinnock, Neil (1978), 'Foreword', in Aneurin Bevan, *In Place of Fear*, Quartet edition.

Kinnock, Neil (1980), 'Which Way Should Labour Go?', *Political Quarterly*, volume 61.

Kinnock, Neil (1984), 'Mobilizing in Defence of Freedom', in James Curran (ed.) *The Future of the Left*, Polity.

Kinnock, Neil (1994), 'Reforming the Labour Party', *Contemporary Record*, volume 8, number 3.

Kogan, David, and Kogan, Maurice (1983), *The Battle for the Labour Party*, Kogan Page.

Labour Party (1982), *Labour's Programme 1982*, Labour Party.

Marquand, David (1992), *The Progressive Dilemma: From Lloyd George to Kinnock*, Heinemann.

Mitchell, Austin (1983), *Four Years in the Death of the Labour Party*, Methuen.

Sanders, David (1993), 'Why the Conservative Party Won – Again', in Anthony King (ed.) *Britain at the Polls 1992*, Chatham House.

Shaw, Eric (1994), *The Labour Party since 1979: Crisis and Transformation*, Routledge.

Whiteley, Paul (1983), *The Labour Party in Crisis*, Methuen.

Young, Ken (1985), 'Shades of Opinion', in Roger Jowell and Sharon Witherspoon (eds) *British Social Attitudes: The 1985 Report*, Gower.

Selected further reading (see also Chapters 1 and 3)

Notable contributions to debate within the Labour Party at this time (some of which seem highly ironic in hindsight) include Tony Benn, *Arguments for Democracy* (Penguin, 1981); David Blunkett and Bernard Crick, *The Labour Party's Aims and Values: An Unofficial Statement* (Spokesman, 1988); Gordon Brown, *Where There is Greed: Margaret Thatcher and the Betrayal of Britain's Future* (Mainstream, 1989); Francis Cripps, John Griffiths, Frances Morrell et al., *Manifesto: A Radical Strategy for Britain's Future* (Pan, 1988); Michael Foot, *Another Heart and Other Pulses* (Collins, 1984); Bryan Gould, *A Future for Socialism* (Jonathan Cape, 1989); Neil Kinnock, *Making Our Way* (Blackwell, 1986); Jon Lansman and Alan Meale (eds), *Beyond Thatcher: The Real Alternative* (Junction, 1983); and Raymond Plant's Fabian pamphlets, *Equality, Markets and the State* (1984) and *Citizenship, Rights and Socialism*, (1988).

Excellent accounts of developments within the party during the Kinnock years include Richard Heffernan and Mike Marquese, *Defeat from the Jaws of Victory: Inside Kinnock's Labour Party* (Verso, 1992); Donald Sasson, 'Reflection on the Labour Party's Programme for the 1990s', *Political Quarterly*, Vol. 62, no. 3 (1991); Patrick Seyd and Paul Whiteley, *Labour's Grass Roots: The Politics of Party Membership* (Clarendon Press, 1992); Martin Smith and Jo Spear (eds), *The Changing Labour Party* (Routledge, 1992); and Gerald Taylor, *Labour's Renewal? The Policy Review and Beyond* (Macmillan, 1996).

From the ideological perspective, this crucial period is well covered in Raymond Plant, Matt Beech and Kevin Hickson (eds), *The Struggle for Labour's Soul: Understanding Labour's political thought since 1945* (Routledge, 2004).

CHAPTER 6

Nationalism in UK Politics

While the fall of communist regimes in 1989–90 brought widespread rejoicing in Eastern Europe, many western observers expressed concern about the likely consequences. World politics were hardly stable during the period of the Cold War, and many populations suffered under regimes which existed only to serve superpower interests. The supposed 'balance of terror' established between NATO and the Warsaw Pact might have had a pleasing symmetry for statesmen and military strategists, but this feeling was mostly confined to those who could hide from the consequences of their mistakes in nuclear bunkers. Yet despite the proxy wars, puppet governments and general insecurities, the presuppositions of the Cold War had brought a few undeniable comforts. Most importantly, as new realities became clearer it seemed that the old system had kept nationalism in check. With this restraint removed, the scope for conflict within and between states suddenly looked greater than ever.

The effects of the end of communism were quickly registered on the map. New republics replaced the former Soviet Union, Czechoslovakia split into two states and Germany was reunited. The processes were relatively smooth compared with the hideous violence that accompanied the break up of Yugoslavia – ironically, a state which had avoided Soviet domination under Marshal Tito. The effects were not confined to Eastern Europe, as refugees keen to exercise new freedoms of movement added to existing migrations into the more prosperous western countries. The result was increased support for nationalist parties in these states, which were already experiencing economic difficulties. Apart from well-publicised incidents in Germany, the Italian Northern League joined a coalition government with the new party Forza Italia (which itself benefited from nationalistic feelings), and the French National Front under Jean Marie le Pen continued to poll well. While rationalistic observers pontificated about the inevitable decline of nation-states under the impact of technological change, activists throughout the world were busy trying to establish or reassert their collective sense of identity. Francis Fukuyama, the prophet of 'The End of History' dismissed nationalism as a transient phenomenon. But it seemed likely to outlast the celebrity of his eccentric thesis (Fukuyama, 1992, 266–75).

Nationalism is certainly an unsettling political force. It is also a highly complex phenomenon, eluding neat definitions. Its effects depend on the context in which it is manifested (Smith, 1995, 13–19). As events in South Africa have shown, it can truly be creative if leaders are skillful and sincere. In other cases it is exploited as a vehicle for personal ambition, and provides a token cause to legitimise the operations of thugs and fanatics. Perhaps because of an imperial history in which liberation movements were inevitably portrayed as public enemies, the British (or rather the English) have tended to overlook the creative side of nationalism. As a result, it is often regarded as an unfortunate malady which only ever afflicts other peoples. Despite the existence of popular nationalist parties in Scotland, Wales and Northern Ireland (and the important role that nationalism plays within English-based parties), books on UK politics usually downplay this awkward sentiment.

The intention of this chapter is to explore the diversity of views associated with each party, and to offer explanations for these variations. It also looks at the response of the major parties to the challenge posed by nationalist movements. Finally, the status of nationalism will be considered – that is, whether it shares the most important characteristics of political ideologies, or should fall into a different category of beliefs.

Scottish nationalism

Scotland lost its independence through the Treaty of Union in 1707. Most Scots originally regarded this as a beneficial measure, especially for economic reasons which soon proved misleading. Despite the bloody aftermath of the 1745 rebellion which tried to restore the Stuart monarchy, nationalist feelings were still mainly directed towards the preservation of Scottish culture rather than an independence movement. During the eighteenth century Scotland produced figures of European renown such as David Hume and Adam Smith. The distribution of power meant that ambitious Scottish politicians had to travel to London in search of glory, but separate legal, religious and educational systems offered opportunities within other professions. The feeling that a distinctive Scottish culture could thrive under the Union is illustrated by the novels of Sir Walter Scott, whose nostalgia for his country's history did not prevent him from being a staunch Tory, opposed to constitutional changes of any kind.[1]

While Irish nationalists struggled for either Home Rule or independence in the early twentieth century, London-based parties became more sensitive to separatist sentiment in Scotland. Just before the First World War, the Liberal Asquith government promised to allow Scotland a degree of autonomy. But the necessary legislation was not passed before the European conflict broke out. After the war parliamentary support for home rule subsided, and a Scottish National Convention was called in 1926. The Scottish Nationalist Party itself was founded in 1934, during the economic slump which hit the country's industries particularly hard. The party itself arose out of a merger between the

---

[1]   Apparently Sir Walter's *Ivanhoe* was Tony Blair's favourite book, which says a great deal about Blair's taste for constitutional innovation since it is probably the most reactionary of Scott's numerous productions.

National Party of Scotland (founded in 1928) and the Scottish Party (1932).

Although the Scottish Nationalist Party (SNP) won a by-election at Motherwell in 1945, the seat was quickly lost. It was not until the 1960s that the SNP became a well-organised mass political party (Webb, 1978, 108). As a strictly constitutionalist party, the SNP was embarrassed by some well-publicised protests performed by other nationalists during the 1950s, such as the theft of the Stone of Destiny from Westminister Abbey. By 1960 it had only 1,000 members, but in that year the siting of a Polaris nuclear submarine base on the River Clyde, after minimal consultation, helped to inspire a rise in interest. The SNP has a long record of opposition to nuclear weapons; in addition to the arguments advanced by CND, the Scots were also aware of the danger of being obliterated in the course of an English quarrel.

In 1962 the SNP performed well in the West Lothian by-election won for Labour by Tam Dalyell, and in 1967 Winifred Ewing pulled off a sensational victory in Hamilton. The discovery of oil off the Scottish coast in the early 1970s added weight to the SNP argument that the country's economy could thrive without interference from London. By October 1974 the SNP had eleven MPs, having secured over 30 per cent of the Scottish vote in the second general election of that year. This achievement has yet to be repeated in a general election, and after the 1992 contest the party was left with only three seats. However, its share of the vote (at 22 per cent) was close to that of the Conservatives in Scotland, and it remained a force to be reckoned with; in 1994 it nearly snatched the late John Smith's Monklands seat, and in the following year it took Perthshire and Kinross from the Conservatives in addition to breaking the 30 per cent barrier once again in the European parliamentary elections.

The SNP benefited in 1974 from general disillusionment with the larger parties, but it is much more than a depository for protest votes. Its main problem has been whether openly to espouse total independence, or to concentrate on more limited demands for devolution as a tactical manoeuvre. The sensitivity of this issue was indicated by the referendum held in March 1979 on the subject of devolved powers to a Scottish Assembly. The proposed powers for this Assembly were severely limited, excluding the authority to raise taxes, for example. One commentator has described the suggested relationship between London and Edinburgh as resembling 'that between central and local government more than that between Washington and the States in the USA' (Kellas, 1989, 154). The SNP campaigned in favour of a 'Yes' vote; after all, the necessary legislation had been promised by the Labour government in return for parliamentary support. Yet this moderate measure was at best a stepping-stone for the party, which would have negotiated for full independence had it won over half the Scottish seats in October 1974 (Miller, 1981, 243). The result of the referendum was inconclusive, with 'Yes' failing to win support from the required proportion of the electorate.

A possible answer to the SNP's dilemma arose through the UK's membership of the European Union (EU). The EU's commitment to reducing economic inequalities between and within member states, exemplified by the development of regional policies during the 1980s, offered the party an opportunity to advocate 'independence within Europe'. Just before the 1992 general election, the Maastricht Treaty set up a Committee of the Regions, which gave Scotland the chance of direct representation in the European policy process (Harvie, 1994). In particular, as nation-states looked less suitable as promoters of economic development, regional bodies were seen as their logical replacement (Marquand, 1991, 36-7). While the oil was running out and nationalists searched for another source of future economic security, this European route to independence looked increasingly attractive — despite the fact that the SNP had originally opposed European integration (Mullin, 1979, 127). This coincided with a promising shift in popular attitudes. In January 1992 one opinion poll revealed that full independence was now favoured by half of the Scottish electorate, instead of the previous desire to stop short at devolution (Butler and Kavanagh, 1992, 73). This change of mood meant that the SNP had not suffered from its boycott of a new Convention, called in 1988 by the Campaign for a Scottish Assembly (CSA) formed from representatives of other opposition parties (McCreadie, 1991). Although the Convention produced many constructive ideas, the SNP's withdrawal showed how the nationalist cause could be hampered by rivalries between Scotland's parties; in this case, the SNP feared that Labour would hijack the meeting.

The outcome of the 1992 general election was a disappointment for the SNP, but the return of the Conservatives was not a disaster. Only a quarter of the Scottish electorate had supported the government (even this was better than many had expected). The Conservative's dismal record north of the border had not prevented it from using Scotland as a guinea-pig for the Poll Tax legislation; the inevitable outcry against the new tax directly benefited the SNP, which campaigned in favour of non-payment. In November 1988 Jim Sillars, formerly a Labour MP, overturned his old party's majority of nearly 20,000 in the Glasgow Govan by-election at the height of the anti-Poll Tax agitation (Butler et al., 1994, 131). The ill-considered tax also called the Union into question. The rump Scottish Conservative Party was in no state to fight back, with the supporters of the Thatcherite Michael Forsythe engaged in guerrilla warfare with the former devolutionists Malcolm Rifkind and Ian Lang. The Scottish electorate had decisively rejected the government in four successive elections; why should it continue to suffer just because other parts of the UK had a different opinion? Those who thought that the London-based government enjoyed democratic legitimacy in Scotland required notable inventive powers to sustain their argument, and it was a short step from denying the Conservative right to rule to accepting the case for full independence.

In the 1997 general election, the Conservatives were confronted with the true extent of ill-feeling in Scotland. They failed to win a single seat in the country. In accordance with its manifesto promise, Labour pressed ahead with a referendum on a devolved Scottish parliament, presenting the electorate with the additional option of limited tax-raising powers. Only a quarter of voters supported the Conservatives in their lonely opposition to the parliament. The outcome on the question of tax-raising powers was closer, but there was still a clear majority (63.5 per cent) in favour.

The achievement of devolution was a mixed blessing to Scottish Nationalists. If the new institutions proved to be successful, they might show that the country could cut remaining ties with the Westminster parliament, and govern itself. However, there was also a chance that Labour's constitutional settlement would be regarded as adequate in itself, and reduce the demand for complete independence. In the first election to the new parliament, held under the Additional Member voting system, the SNP won 35 seats. Labour, with 56 seats, governed in coalition with the Liberal Democrats (17). Scottish Conservatives, meanwhile, were forced to contest elections to an institution which their national leadership had opposed. At least they had the satisfaction of beating the Liberal Democrats, winning 18 seats in 1999.

While the SNP could be satisfied with its showing in 1999, the subsequent parliamentary election (May 2003) was far less promising. It lost 8 seats—two more than Labour, which was prosecuting its unpopular war on Iraq at the time. The main beneficiaries were the Greens and the Scottish Socialists, who could be expected to press for specific policy reforms within the Scottish parliament rather than concentrating on the campaign for full independence. In the 2005 general election the SNP vote fell, leaving the party in third place behind Labour and the Liberal Democrats.

Welsh nationalism

The development of the Welsh nationalist party, Plaid Cymru, shows some striking similarities with the history of the SNP. Although Welsh nationalism was hardly absent before 1914 (Lloyd George, for example, regarded himself as a supporter), the party was not founded until after the First World War. It emerged in 1925 from several Welsh-speaking groups, with particular support from the University of Wales. For many years it seemed to be destined to continue as an agreeable outlet for cultural nationalists, and contested only a handful of Welsh seats in elections. For Plaid Cymru, as for the SNP, the breakthrough did not occur until the 1960s. In 1966 its candidate Gwynfor Evans took Carmarthen from Labour in a by-election. Evans was a well-known and popular candidate; even so, he failed to retain the seat in 1970, when twenty-six Plaid Cymru candidates lost their deposits. Despite this setback, the party, and the attitudes that it represented, could no longer be ignored at Westminster.

The similarities between the SNP and Plaid Cymru are overshadowed by one major difference. From the outset Plaid Cymru's 'principal concerns were the Welsh language, the Welsh identity, and Christianity in Wales' (Butt Philp, 1975, 15). By contrast, although the future of the Gaelic language concerns many SNP activists, it is not their main priority. While a Scottish Parliament was the minimum SNP demand, many members of Plaid Cymru have had mixed feelings about devolution because Welsh speakers are only a minority of the population. The refusal of Welsh nationalists to become 'obsessed' by the question of self-government can be seen as far-sighted at a time when the future of the western nation-state is in question; according to Dafydd Elis Thomas, for example, 'Constitutions are … probably the least important ways of constituting a national or international community' (Thomas, 1991, 67). On this view, cultural factors are more important than institutions.

Despite these sceptical voices, self-government of some kind has always been an official aim of Plaid Cymru. In pursuit of its goals, the party 'is constitutional, decentralist, co-operative, Social Democratic and non-violent' (Balsom, 1979, 141). Like the SNP, it has been handicapped by association with direct action which it rejects, such as the burning of Welsh cottages owned by absentee English people. Since

Wales has suffered more than most other parts of the UK from relative economic decline, Plaid Cymru also has a record of close attention to economic subjects. It shared the SNP's attraction to small-scale enterprises as a replacement for traditional heavy industries, which enhanced a sense of community but also brought pollution and left regions economically vulnerable in a period of technological change. Plaid Cymru is also a long-standing opponent of nuclear weapons.

The years between 1974 and 1979 were as fraught for Plaid Cymru as for the SNP. The February 1974 election focused on issues such as the role of the unions, and therefore did not favour the chances of the nationalist parties, but Plaid Cymru still managed to win two seats at Caernarfon and Merioneth. The October contest was even more satisfactory, as Gwynfor Evans regained his Carmarthen seat to join his two colleagues at Westminster. Elsewhere the outlook was less favourable, and once again only ten Plaid Cymru candidates saved their deposits. Yet this was an exciting time to have even a small representation in Parliament, with Labour holding a tiny majority. For Plaid Cymru as for the SNP, the government's plight would ensure at least a referendum on the issue of devolution.

In Scotland, the 1979 referendum produced a dubious result; but in Wales it was clear-cut. Only 11.9 per cent of the total electorate voted for devolution. Plaid Cymru had campaigned hard for a `Yes', although there was initial hesitation. Afterwards the party continued to join Labour in parliamentary votes, but could not stave off the government's defeat on 29 March. In the ensuing general election the party secured only 8.1 per cent of the Welsh poll, and Evans was defeated once again (Balsom, 1979, 139).

Lacking an emotive issue such as oil to spur supporters, Plaid Cymru has never matched the electoral performance of the SNP in percentage terms. However, while the SNP consistently attracts a respectable vote throughout Scotland, Plaid Cymru concentrates its greatest effort on the five main Welsh-speaking constituencies. The identity of the SNP can be confused by its need to say different things in a wide range of Scottish constituencies, but Plaid Cymru's narrower targets allow for greater clarity, despite the fact that it has suffered splits (notably between socialists and the anti-socialist 'Hydro' group in the early 1980s). In the 1992 general election its percentage support in Wales was less than half that of the SNP in Scotland, but it won more seats (four compared to three).

The nature and level of nationalist sentiment in Wales is very different from that in Scotland, and it is not surprising that this has produced different responses from the main parties. In 1992 both Labour and Conservatives promised concessions to Welsh speakers, but while Labour advocated an Assembly of very limited powers, the government emphasised its practical achievements. The Conservatives could argue that they were already working to meet the demands of most nationalists, by promoting the Welsh language through the National Curriculum and other measures including the establishment of a Welsh Language Board. The Welsh Office (first set up in 1964) enjoyed a surprising degree of autonomy under Mrs Thatcher; this was even more unusual given that her ideological opponent Peter Walker was Secretary of State after 1987. Levels of industrial assistance were therefore somewhat higher than might have been expected, and inward investment was particularly buoyant (Gamble, 1993, 83). This conciliatory approach to Welsh nationalism proved no more successful at winning friends than the confrontational tactics adopted in Scotland; the Tories held only six Welsh seats in 1992, on 29 per cent of the vote. But Conservative measures proved counter-productive in the medium term. As internal discrimination against the Welsh language was reduced, Plaid Cymru became much more relaxed about the prospect of a devolved assembly. Even in 1968 one perceptive commentator noted that grievances about language were 'becoming merely a part of a general resentment at the remoteness and apparent lack of concern of Whitehall' — a feeling which could not be assuaged by the Conservative habit of picking secretaries of state who had little previous connection with Wales (Mackintosh, 1968, 149).

As in Scotland, the Welsh electorate ensured that the Conservatives paid the price in 1997 for 18 years of unpopular rule. The party lost all of its remaining MPs in Wales. However, Plaid Cymru did not benefit from this collapse in Tory support, winning less than 7 per cent of the Welsh vote. Although the new Labour government fulfilled its promise to hold a referendum on devolution to Wales, there was no question of an assembly having tax-raising powers. The Welsh electorate gave a very lukewarm response; the turnout was only just over 50 per cent, and the 'Yes' campaign prevailed by less than 7,000 votes.

In the first elections to the National Assembly of Wales Plaid Cymru performed strongly, winning 17 of the 60 seats. However, Labour chose to govern in coalition with the Liberal Democrats, who had won only 6 seats. In the second contest (2003), Plaid Cymru was reduced to just 12 seats. Like the SNP, the party was still running in second place, but its progress had stalled. In the 2005 Westminster elections it argued for greater social justice and environmental protection, whereas the SNP had concentrated on the need for a more dynamic Scottish economy. It also insisted that the Welsh Assembly should be upgraded to the constitutional status of the Scottish Parliament, rather than arguing the case for full independence. It lost one of its four seats, and its share of the Welsh vote fell by almost 2 per cent, to 12.6 per cent. Arguably Plaid Cymru had done well to remain as a significant presence in Welsh politics, in view of a referendum result which suggested that a limited degree of devolution would satisfy the demands of all but a small minority of voters.

Nationalism in Northern Ireland

The political implications of nationalist feelings in Scotland and Wales are very different, but the SNP and Plaid Cymru share a commitment to constitutional activism. With the exception of the anti-Poll Tax campaign, these parties have discountenanced illegality, and deplored the use of political violence. For various reasons Northern Ireland has been a different case. Whatever the success of current moves towards a constitutional settlement, differences are likely to remain for some time, both in the manifestations of nationalism throughout the province and in the reactions of mainland parties.

The Anglo-Irish Treaty of 1921, which officially divided Ireland into the self-governing Free State and the partially autonomous six counties of Ulster, was difficult to defend on rational grounds. It could always be attacked for creating an 'artificial' Protestant majority in the north of the island. For the British government, however, it was a tolerable means of escaping the unrest which had made rational administration an impossibility. Ireland as a whole had suffered during the nineteenth century, from famine, the violent suppression of any protest, and unscrupulous exploitation by absentee landlords. The grievances of the majority Catholic population stretched back much further, to the atrocities committed by Cromwell's soldiers and beyond. As the United Kingdom became a more democratic state the situation in Ireland was increasingly anomalous, but proposals for peaceful reform, like Gladstone's Home Rule Bills came to nothing. The resulting anger among nationalists was matched by the insecurity of their opponents, and violent outbreaks such as the 1916 Easter Rising were inevitable. About 450 people were killed in the 1916 insurrection against British rule; and many rebel leaders were executed afterwards, creating a potent legacy of martyrdom.

Although sporadic paramilitary activities continued, Ulster itself remained relatively peaceful under the compromise of 1921 until the late 1960s. In 1968 a Northern Ireland Civil Rights Association (NICRA) was formed, in an attempt to emulate the success of similar movements abroad. NICRA's main aims were the reform of an electoral system which had been skewed to favour Unionist candidates, and the end of discrimination in policies such as housing. The Unionist response was predictably hostile, but Northern Ireland's Prime Minister, Terence O'Neill, attempted to satisfy the main demands. This was the signal for the 'Troubles' to begin, and the disorder quickly over-stretched the local security forces. In August 1969 military support was requested from the British government. As the situation continued to deteriorate, soldiers who had originally been sent to protect the Catholic minority in Ulster were increasingly regarded as their enemy; the events of 'Bloody Sunday', when troops opened fire on demonstrators in Derry on 30 January 1972, could only add to this impression. Direct rule from London was established later in the same year. Since then, successive Westminster governments have struggled to find a form of devolution which will satisfy the contending parties.

During most of the 'Troubles', the main constitutional parties in Ulster have been the Ulster Unionist Party (UUP); the Democratic Unionist Party (DUP); the predominantly Catholic Social Democratic and Labour Party (SDLP); and the Alliance Party, which attempts to draw support from moderates on both sides of the dispute. From the early 1980s Provisional Sinn Fein contested elections, but also supported the Irish Republican Army (IRA) in line with the slogan 'the ballot paper in one hand and the Armalite rifle in the other'. In 1974 Sinn Fein was legalized in an attempt to wean its supporters away from their close alliance with the IRA.

In practice, though, it has been difficult to draw a precise line between constitutional and paramilitary activities in Northern Ireland, at least since the early twentieth century, when senior Conservative politicians encouraged Unionists to arm themselves in preparation for a violent struggle. Just as Sinn Fein speaks for those who will accept nothing short of total British withdrawal from Ireland, people who are ready to fight to maintain the Union will rarely disagree with the opinions of the Reverend Ian Paisley's DUP. British governments have long recognised that these incompatible attitudes exist and must at least be listened to. As a result, the main UK parties have tried to isolate Ulster's problems from the usual party conflicts; the formula that the province will remain part of the United Kingdom until a majority decides otherwise has satisfied most mainland politicians.

Although the Unionist parties have historic ties with the Conservatives at Westminster and the SDLP normally sides with Labour, the kind of tactical considerations which affect the main parties' dealings with Scottish and Welsh nationalism at election time have been subdued in the case of Ireland.

The usual terminology applied to the Irish scene equates the Catholic and nationalist populations, and makes similar assumptions about Protestants and Unionism. This approach is understandable given the historic divisions, but it can be misleading. In a sense, all the main parties of Northern Ireland are nationalistic; Sinn Fein and the SDLP both aspire to Irish unity (either immediately or in the long term), but the UUP and the DUP have tried to preserve a culture which is very different from that found in other parts of the United Kingdom. In 1990 a survey found that 27 per cent of the Protestant population identified themselves as 'Ulster' or 'Northern Irish' rather than as British (Jowell et al., 1990). When pressed, the Unionist parties have been prepared to defy the UK government. In 1974, for example, a general strike supported by many Unionists destroyed the devolved 'power-sharing' initiative introduced by William Whitelaw, and relations have been particularly strained since Mrs Thatcher signed the misnamed 'Anglo-Irish' Agreement in 1985. In 1979 the Unionist New Ulster Political Research Group (NUPRG) proposed independence for the province in its paper *Beyond the Religious Divide* (cited in Arthur and Jeffery, 1988, 49).

The ideological situation in Northern Ireland is complicated by divisions within the parties. For example, under Gerry Fitt (1970–79) the SDLP was an avowedly socialist party. Under John Hume, however (1979–2001), a more social democratic outlook prevailed (Rolston, 1987, 60). At one time Sinn Fein was strongly influenced by Marxist ideas, and argued for unity among all working-class residents of Northern Ireland against a common capitalist oppressor. However, this stance did not prevent the murder of many working-class Protestants, and has now been superseded by a social policy which scarcely differs from that of the SDLP. Under the leadership of Ian Paisley the DUP has been united from its base in the Free Presbyterian Church. By contrast, the UUP has suffered from tensions between those (such as Enoch Powell) who advocated full integration within the United Kingdom, and others who prefer a return to the status quo before 1972.

Politics in Northern Ireland since the 1970s have always been strongly influenced by attempts to reach a peace settlement. On the Republican side, progress under John Major and Tony Blair has encouraged a shift towards peaceful methods of effecting change. An IRA ceasefire was announced in 1994, although this proved short-lived because the Major Government needed parliamentary support from the Ulster Unionists. Since the Good Friday Agreement of 1998, however, Sinn Fein has renounced violence in favour of the peaceful, political road to Irish unity. The SDLP is still a relevant factor, not least because Sinn Fein representatives refuse to attend the Westminster parliament. However, in the 2003 elections to the (suspended) Northern Ireland, Sinn Fein overtook the SDLP in terms of seats and vote share.

The change of fortunes has been even more dramatic within the Unionist community. After the 2005 general election the UUP, which once dominated politics in the north of Ireland, was reduced to just one seat. Paisley's DUP, by contrast, had 9 MPs. Thus the trend in Northern Ireland's politics favoured more aggressive nationalists on each side, at a time when terrorist activity had greatly reduced. On the most optimistic rationale, this development meant that the divided citizens of Northern Ireland were now looking towards their toughest politicians for protection, rather than the gunmen who had supposedly fought for their causes in the past. However, even if this meant that Northern Ireland was becoming a wholehearted member of the democratic community, the chances of cooperation between Sinn Fein and the DUP were remote, at least in the short-term. The Blair Government had re-introduced devolved institutions in 1998, but after only four years they were suspended after dubious allegations concerning Republican activity.

English nationalism

Unlike the Scots, the Welsh and inhabitants of Northern Ireland, the English did not feel constrained to debate the question of national self-determination for most of the modern period. This has helped to produce a supercilious attitude towards nationalism. When English people exhibit enthusiasm for their country in the yearly 'promenade' concerts at the Royal Albert Hall, or in more unusual circumstances such as the Falklands War, they generally admit to patriotic, rather than nationalistic, feelings. Patriotism, on this view, is a steadfast love of one's country, which involves aggression only when the homeland is attacked by others. Nationalists, by contrast, are believed to harbour negative feelings about others rather than pride in themselves. On this reading, nationalism is a sure sign of frustrated ambitions or a country in spiritual decline.

A version of this theory was expounded by George Orwell, who wanted to teach socialists that it was not wrong to love one's country (Crick, 1991, 96). As used by Orwell the distinction is important; like Edmund Burke, Orwell thought that one can love one's country only if it is intrinsically lovable. Unfortunately for the English, it has been more common for them to exhibit the unthinking outlook which Orwell abhorred — 'My Country, Right or Wrong'. As the English deplored the evils that can arise from nationalism in other parts of the world, they often failed to appreciate how strongly it affects their own politics.

However, in recent years the question of English nationalism has been revived. On the one hand, English people felt threatened by the development of the European Union (EU). On the other, Scotland now has a devolved parliament with independent tax-raising powers, and Wales has an assembly. There is no corresponding English institution. This realization has come as a shock to many English people, who previously assumed that the Westminster parliament exclusively catered for their interests. At least the ensuing debate over 'Englishness' has attracted some constructive contributions (Scruton, 2000). But recent developments have also given rise to emotions which even the English would have to define as 'nationalistic'.

The immigration question

The United Kingdom has traditionally benefited from immigration, particularly that which accompanied religious persecution in Europe during the sixteenth and seventeenth centuries. During the nineteenth century the confidence of British governments allowed them to give refuge to political dissidents from abroad such as Mazzini and Marx. Whatever the conditions in industrial areas and workhouses, or the treatment of native populations by the British overseas, the symbolism of empire was used to evoke the idea of a nation at ease with itself. Even the criticism of Disraeli's 'Jingoism' during the Russo-Turkish War of 1878 indirectly implied that Britain was strong and righteous enough to base its foreign policy on moral concerns rather than self-aggrandisement. The nation's mission was to spread good government and unimpeachable values to less fortunate countries; when war broke out in 1914 colonies were expected to show their gratitude by fighting on behalf of their generous benefactor, and the response was impressive.

After the Second World War some colonial governments encouraged migration to the UK in response to unemployment at home. Despite labour shortages in certain industries and concerns about a possible fall in the resident population, this trend was discouraged by the British government. The British were beginning their retreat from empire, and did not want the empire to come home with them. In particular both of the main parties were worried about the impact of 'coloured' immigration. Sometimes this attitude arose because policy-makers genuinely feared that racists would react violently to the newcomers; this was borne out when riots occurred in Liverpool and parts of

London between 1948 and 1954 (Layton-Henry, 1992, 37). More often it simply reflected the prejudices of governments and their officials. In fact, inward immigration proceeded steadily during the 1950s and 1960s (though not as rapidly as populist legend implied). Economic growth stimulated demand for unskilled labour in industries such as textiles, and cheap workers were needed in the developing National Health Service. While the economy was healthy the issue did not feature in party conflict, although riots at Notting Hill, West London, in 1958 increased public alarm.

The 1960s was the key decade for the treatment of immigration. Both parties established a dual-track approach which has remained in force ever since. Immigration was limited by law, but legislation was also introduced to curb racial discrimination. Although the Labour Party created the Race Relations Board in 1966, both of the governing parties acted to restrict immigration during the decade. The strategy caused deep misgivings for the opponents of racism within each party, but they had little choice but to accept what was seen as the dictation of electoral necessity. The compromise meant that the Conservative Party could include both the enlightened Iain Macleod and rabid members of the Monday Club, which had been formed to oppose Britain's retreat from empire and now advocated the compulsory repatriation of immigrants in addition to its conspiratorial work with elements of the secret services (Dorril and Ramsay, 1992, 224–8).

In April 1968, however, this fragile unity was threatened when the Conservative Enoch Powell delivered his 'Rivers of Blood' speech. Whatever Powell's motives, his language could only inflame existing prejudices, and he was instantly sacked from the Shadow Cabinet. His defence was that he had only repeated party policy, but his assertion that most immigrants had no desire to be integrated with the rest of the population was a direct assault on the established approach. An opinion poll conducted in the following month found that 27 per cent of the electorate considered immigration to be the most urgent problem facing the country (Wybrow, 1989, 88). It was subsequently claimed that the Conservative victory in the 1970 general election owed much to Powell's personal following in the midlands. In 1971 the Heath government passed an Immigration Act, parts of which have been described as 'blatantly racist' (Layton-Henry, 1992, 89). Certainly the Act had the effect of seriously curtailing rights of entry for non-white Commonwealth citizens. The Home Secretary responsible for the Act, Reginald Maudling, betrayed this attitude when he claimed in his memoirs that 'immigrants had been pouring in to this country from the Commonwealth in large numbers ... they came in numbers that were too large to be assimilated' (Maudling, 1978, 157–8). Yet when Idi Amin expelled 50,000 Asians from Uganda in August 1972 more than half were allowed to settle in the United Kingdom, despite an hysterical campaign in the Conservative press. Heath's refusal to capitulate to racist propaganda disgusted many of Powell's supporters, who began to leave the party even before their hero defected in 1974.

By 1977 Enoch Powell was an Ulster Unionist MP, but his preoccupation with the immigration issue continued. On 21 January he delivered a speech that was consciously intended to test the scope of the third and most powerful Race Relations Act, which Labour had passed in the previous year (Berkeley, 1977, 87). Now that Heath had been replaced, the Conservative Party had a leader who was sympathetic to Powell's economic views. In January 1978 Margaret Thatcher also hinted that she was receptive to his thoughts on race. In a television interview she declared that 'People are really rather afraid that this country might be rather swamped by people with a different culture'. Thatcher 'was taken aback by the reaction to these extremely mild remarks'. However, her comments are difficult to reconcile with her later statement that 'individuals are worthy of respect as *individuals*, not as members of classes or races'. In fact, colour was probably irrelevant to Mrs Thatcher, who instinctively disliked people of any hue if they had absorbed a culture which rejected free enterprise and the minimal state. She might have thought that this applied very strongly to West Indians, but she was equally convinced that it was true of the French. Whatever the reasons for her stance, race joined the extensive list of issues on which she sensed the support of most British people; as she noted in her memoirs, opinion polls after the interview showed that the Conservatives had suddenly established an eleven-point lead over Labour (Thatcher, 1995, 406, 408).

One probable effect of Thatcher's remarks was a sudden reversal of fortune for the racist National Front (NF) party. This had been formed in 1967 from three existing groups which agitated for the repatriation of immigrants. By 1973 the NF was popular enough to take 16 per cent of the vote in a midlands by-election, and was attracting defectors from the Monday Club. These recruits fitted rather uneasily with Margaret Thatcher's assertion that groups like the NF 'were just as much socialist as they were nationalist' (Thatcher, 1995, 406). In fact, the NF was no more 'socialist' than Adolf Hitler, who had used the word to attract a following which was purged as soon as it had served his purposes. In the 1979 general election NF candidates received 189,000 votes. This was a relative disappointment, after some encouraging performances in local elections (Walker, 1979, 199). By contrast, in 1992 the National Front and a splinter group, the British National Party (BNP), fielded only twenty-seven candidates, who scraped 12,000 votes between them.

This did not mean that racists had experienced a mass conversion to more conventional politics since 1979. Some shadowy groups, such as Combat 18, were more interested in direct action against the immigrant community than in the democratic process. Yet it is safe to assume that, after their disillusionment with Heath, a good proportion of NF support returned to the Conservatives once Mrs Thatcher became leader. The Conservatives did not introduce repatriation, but they certainly took every opportunity to discourage further immigration. In Peter Riddell's words, the British Nationality Act 1981 virtually removed automatic rights of entry and settlement from everyone except 'whites with close ties to the UK' (Riddell, 1991, 156). Just in case anyone else could sneak in, the government passed yet another Immigration Act in 1988; in the House of Commons the Bill was introduced by Edward Heath's old ally Douglas Hurd, who had once praised his mentor's 'disgust at colour prejudice' (Hurd, 1979, 50). This was the price that enlightened ministers had to pay for serving in Thatcher Cabinets.

Unlike his predecessor, John Major was an outspoken anti-racist. But this did not prevent his Home Secretary, Michael Howard, from urging more restrictions on immigration, particularly affecting those seeking political asylum. As internal EU borders disappeared, other states 'set out to make it impossible for immigrants and asylum-seekers to enter Europe', but clearly this was a policy from which the Prime Minister was disinclined to 'opt out' (Wheeler, 1993). Conservatives confidence about securing the anti-immigrant vote was indicated by the fact that the party's 1992 *Campaign Guide* devoted only one out of four hundred pages to the issue.

However, by 1997 the Conservatives were in disarray, and open to challenge from more extreme organizations. In 1997 the BNP fielded 56 candidates, who received more than 35,000 votes between them. These were still derisory figures, and all but four of the BNP candidates lost their deposits. But the party began to attract more publicity as anti-immigrant organizations began to make significant gains in other European countries. In 1999 the BNP chose a more media-friendly leader, Nick Griffin, who attempted to tone down the party's official policies and to target constituencies which suffered from a combination of poor living conditions and racial tension. Although the BNP vote increased only slightly in 2001, the party won three council seats in Burnley. Later in the year it won another seat in the Blackburn constituency of the Foreign Secretary, Jack Straw. These victories were achieved in areas which had been scarred by racial violence in 2001. Although the BNP did not come close to winning a parliamentary seat at the 2005 general election, it did secure a record vote of almost 200,000.

The BNP's enemies frequently referred to its members as 'Nazis'. This kind of language has often been used in postwar Britain, but it rarely has any substance. European fascism has taken a variety of forms, but its central idea is that the state, as the embodiment of the nation, should transcend the interests of individual citizens. The appeal of this creed in the contemporary UK is limited, to say the least. The BNP's only chance of achieving an electoral breakthrough, in fact, would be to link its opposition to immigration and the EU to a platform of extreme *individualism*. The BNP's 2005 general election manifesto contained forthright opinions about the impact of immigration; but Adolf Hitler is unlikely to have been very enthusiastic about the title of the document — *Rebuilding British Democracy*. In addition to its stance on immigration, the BNP did advocate the familiar 'right-wing' idea of re- introducing national service; but most of its policies (which included the abolition of income tax) were difficult to place in any ideological pigeonhole. Its party political broadcast in 2005 featured the plight of an impoverished ex-soldier, whose unfortunate history was turned into a plaintive, Dylanesque ballad by Nick Griffin himself.

While the upward trend of BNP support is disquieting, there is little chance that it could ever win parliamentary seats outside its current heartlands. Most evidence suggests that, although opposition to further immigration remains high, attitudes towards the ethnic minorities already settled in the UK have improved. After its election victory in 1997 Labour continued Conservative attempts to crack down on illegal immigrants and 'bogus' asylum-seekers. But ministers were prepared to argue in favour of immigration in general, on the grounds that the economy needed an influx of workers and that the country benefited from diversity. Racial unrest continued, but at least members of ethnic minorities could feel more confident in reporting attacks, after an official inquiry into the 1993 murder of Stephen Lawrence. The resulting concern about 'institutional racism' within the Metropolitan police force led to a recruitment drive among the ethnic minorities. Although the Westminster parliament continued to be dominated by white males, the main parties were keen to address this imbalance.

In the wake of terrorist attacks on New York in 2001, and the London underground in July 2005, anti-Islamic feeling increased in the UK. Attacks on members of the Sikh community, who were assumed to be Muslims because of their dress, showed that race and religion was still a source of confusion as well as hatred. However, the reaction was relatively muted, compared to the kind of upheaval which would have been likely if the incidents had occurred in the 1970s or 1980s. One of the most telling features of the attacks on New York and London, indeed, was the diverse origins of the victims. Far from exposing the injustice and hypocrisy of Western civilization, the nature of the outrages actually drew attention to one respect in which it had registered remarkable improvements.

The European controversy

Although the British electorate confirmed the country's membership of the EEC in 1975, the level of public hostility remained too high to ignore. The solution was similar to the government's attitude towards immigration. In that instance, existing immigrants were appeased by legislation on race relations; but in return it was made increasingly difficult for people to gain the right to enter the country. As regards the EEC, if pro-Europeans were pleased because the UK had joined, Euro-sceptics had to be placated by means of an obstructive attitude—in Stephen George's phrase, the UK had to be at best an 'Awkward Partner' (George, 1994). Hence, Harold Wilson renegotiated the terms of entry after his return to office in 1974, and then held a referendum on the subject at the prompting of Tony Benn, Labour's most prominent anti-marketeer. Margaret Thatcher's vigorous demands for a fairer budget contribution continued the trend. After the Maastricht negotiations of 1991, however, the Conservatives could no longer sustain their European balancing-act.

Nationalism clearly lay at the root of Conservative problems. Had the UK signed the Treaty of Rome in 1957 it would have become a powerful founding-member of the

EC, and controversial measures such as the Common Agricultural Policy (CAP) would have been designed differently. The decision not to join was at least partly the result of a calculation that the UK could thrive outside the Community. This made the unsuccessful applications of the 1960s particularly humiliating, and continuing membership still acted as an affront to those who thought that the UK could survive on its own. A negative attitude towards the Community has trapped the UK in a vicious circle; the annoyance of other European states made it feel like an impotent outsider, and in turn this increased British reservations. In a typical manoeuvre, Euro-sceptics have propagated the myth that the most crucial European decisions are taken by the unelected Commission instead of the Council of Ministers; even ministers who are well disposed to the EU have found the Commission a welcome scapegoat for their own decisions. Thus a nationalistic hatred of power-sharing with foreigners has often been disguised under a more respectable appeal to democratic principles. The fact that the public overwhelmingly approved membership in 1975 (even on unsatisfactory terms) has not deterred those who see the fight against closer European union as a battle 'to save our democracy' (Gorman, 1993, xvii).

Obviously not all 'Euro-phobia' is dictated by prejudice. Some opponents of EU membership base their views on an assessment of UK interests which has little (or even nothing) to do with the fact that foreigners now have some influence over government decisions. However, the Chancellor of the Exchequer, Kenneth Clarke, could not explain the depth of Conservative feeling in mid-1995 without using the word `xenophobia'; during the Maastricht debates, John Major had privately described his opponents in even harsher terms. In fact, Major had done all he could to please these critics short of actually leaving the EU — to the extent, for example, of seriously exaggerating the likely impact of the Social Chapter of the Maastricht Treaty in order to justify the UK's decision to opt out of its provisions. Just as Mrs Thatcher's reference to being `swamped' unconsciously revealed her fears for a culture in decline, the Euro-phobes unwittingly betrayed a concern that the UK economy was too weak to ensure that its interests prevailed in Europe. Whatever the state of the economy, however, obstructive tactics ensured that the UK could not hope to exercise an influence in proportion to its budgetary contribution. Of course, this did not worry the Euro-phobes: evidence that ministers were ignored in European battles helped their argument that the UK should withdraw altogether.

John Major's difficulties over Europe lasted until the final days of his premiership, when he appealed to party members who wanted to constrain his negotiating position. Increasingly, though, he had bowed to pressure from belli-cose backbenchers, over issues like the banning of British beef after the outbreak of the cattle disease BSE. In the 1997 general election the Conservatives lost several seats because of the intervention of the Referendum Party, which was financed by the former pro-European Sir James Gold-smith. The Referendum Party wanted the UK to withdraw from the EU (but only after the public had been consulted on the issue). Goldsmith died before the next election, and his party was replaced as the chief receptacle for anti-EU votes by the longer-established United Kingdom Independ-ence Party (UKIP). In the European Parliamentary election of 2004 UKIP won 12 seats and more than 16 per cent of the vote. Although this reflected a significant trend of opinion within the country, turnout in the election had been dismal. The UKIP bandwagon was soon halted by internal divi-sions. Ironically, while the European parliamentary elec-tions provided UKIP with its most obvious chance of a breakthrough, success was a mixed blessing because it meant that its representatives were now elected members of an institution which they despised.

Before 1997 it was expected that Labour would also suffer serious divisions over Europe. However, while Tony Blair was prepared to argue the case for British membership of the single currency, the opposition of his Chancellor Gordon Brown ensured that he never had the chance to exercise his powers of persuasion. Like most of his prede-cessors, Blair talked of acting as a 'bridge' between the EU and the United States, but even before the 'war on terror' it was obvious that he preferred the English-speaking side of the bridge. In May 2004 the EU expanded to 25 member states. This represented the fulfillment of a long-standing British goal, but it was overshadowed by controversy over a draft EU constitution. Under pressure, Blair agreed that this would not be accepted without a referendum, but the process was put on hold because other EU countries rejected the draft. Meanwhile, several EU states were increasingly attracted to the Anglo-American model of capitalism, in the belief that over-regulation was destroying jobs in their own economies. This represented yet another success for 'Thatcherism', but even Blair was not dexterous enough to use this argument to cajole the UK population into a more positive view of Europe. Indeed, the main effect was to stimulate continental opposition to the EU, particularly from workers who did not relish the prospect of greater job-insecurity. Thus, in ideological terms the UK debate over Europe had scarcely moved since 1975. The only difference was that Thatcherites were now more strongly 'sceptical', out of loyalty to their former leader.

Conclusion: varieties of nationalism

Even a brief survey of nationalism in the United Kingdom reveals the complexity of the subject. Although it would be a mistake to concentrate on single factors in each case, Welsh nationalism is mainly cultural and linguistic, Scottish nationalism focuses on politics and economics, while religion is the most telling feature in Northern Ireland. Wales and Scotland have significant internal differences, but nothing to compare with the rift between the communities of Northern Ireland. Nationalism of various kinds dominates politics in Northern Ireland, whereas it is one of many important influences in Scotland and Wales. Only in Northern Ireland have constitutional parties developed an ambivalent attitude to political violence, although civil disobedience has sometimes been encouraged in the other countries. As Tom Nairn has pointed out, all these varieties of nationalism differ from the experience of the 'Third World', where national consciousness has arisen in tandem with economic development (Nairn, 1981). In fact, nationalism within the UK became a dynamic political force in the 1960s, at a time of growing disillusionment with the economic outlook. Crude deterministic explanations are usually unpersuasive, but in this instance there does seem to be a link between the perception of decline and a more aggressive approach to the outside world.

In England, many would point to the unsuccessful history of the NF and BNP (following the dismal failure of Oswald Mosley's fascists) to back their claim that nationalism is of no account. This view is based on a misconception of nationalism which has arisen from previous English experiences. Nationalism is not simply a struggle to achieve self-government; it can also arise when a nation falls on hard times, and needs to sustain the feeling that it runs its own affairs. The result is a search for the reason why things went wrong in the past, and for present enemies to struggle against; myths are as necessary to governments under pressure as they are to movements for national liberation. After so many years during which economic power and political influence could be taken for granted, it is not surprising that this form of nationalism has emerged in England since the Second World War. The 1979 election gave the UK its first unashamedly nationalistic Prime Minister. However, Margaret Thatcher's nationalism was difficult to reconcile with her classical liberalism, an ideology which dictates that no nation should be protected from the consequences of its failure to compete. For a nation in economic decline this is a hard doctrine — but, in this sense at least, capitalism is 'colour blind', in Mrs Thatcher's phrase (Thatcher, 1995, 406).

The question which remains is whether or not nationalism ought to be considered as an ideology in itself. The answer provided by most books on the subject is affirmative. Ian Adams, for example, claims that it 'is the simplest, the clearest and the least theoretically sophisticated' of ideologies (Adams, 1993, 82). However, Andrew Vincent acknowledges that 'it is difficult to provide any clear and

overarching sense to the diverse claims of nationalism'
(Vincent, 1995, 238). Moving from general works to particular studies of nationalism, Keith Webb has written that it
differs from other ideologies because 'it implies nothing
specific about the internal organisation of the state or the
nation' (Webb, 1978, 19). When cohesive ideological groups
win power they might disagree over the details of subsequent policies, but they can at least understand the reasoning behind different positions. There is no reason why
successful nationalists should be so fortunate, unless their
common desire for liberation is matched by agreement
about the best kind of social organization.

Of course, there may be cases of activists whose political
desires have been fully satisfied once national liberation has
been achieved. Yet nationalism is more often a means to an
end. The enemy is regarded not just as a force which pre-
vents self-government, but as an obstacle to the fulfilment
of human potential in a specific form of social organisation.
On these grounds, since nationalism itself does not pre-
scribe any social form, it cannot be regarded as an ideology
in the full sense of the definition used here. Instead, it
should be understood as a motivating principle which can
be held by members of any ideological grouping. Once
national feeling has been satisfied, ideology takes over. In
short, there are liberal nationalists, conservative nationalists, and so on.

The major exception to this argument is fascism. In the
form espoused by Adolf Hitler this is certainly a distinctive
ideology, because it upholds a specific view of human
nature. For fascists, life is a quasi-biological struggle, in
which those who truly belong to the nation assert themselves against alien forces either at home or abroad. In practice, this leads to unquestioning obedience to the state, as
the guardian of the national principle; by extension, the
leader becomes the focus of hero-worship, as the embodiment of the state. It can be argued that such views were a
product of specific historical circumstances. However,
Hitler's Germany is not the only example. Although it is
widely regarded as one of the last examples of a communist

regime, North Korea is more accurately portrayed as a fascist state. The Soviet Union under Stalin falls into the same category, as does Saddam Hussein's Iraq.

There are times when the UK appears to be in the grip of a totalitarian mentality — the aftermath of the death of Diana, Princess of Wales, was such an occasion when an individualistic population was engulfed by a desire to enforce conformity. More generally, the influence of the media ensures an unhealthy prominence for 'charismatic' political leaders. It is possible that fascism could creep up by stealth, after a series of petty humiliations rather than a national catastrophe like defeat in a major war. However, although there are numerous nationalists of various kinds in the UK, to date fascism has played an insignificant role. It seems unduly alarmist to expect that this will change in the foreseeable future.

List of works cited

Adams, Ian (1993), *Political Ideology Today*, Manchester University Press.

Arthur, Paul, and Jeffery, Keith (1988), *Northern Ireland since 1968*, Blackwell.

Balsom, Denis (1979), 'Plaid Cymru: The Welsh National Party', in Henry Drucker (ed.), *Multi-Party Britain*, Macmillan.

Berkeley, Humphrey (1977), *The Odyssey of Enoch: A Political Memoir*, Hamish Hamilton.

Butler, David, and Kavanagh, Denis (1992), *The British General Election of 1992*, Macmillan.

Butler, David, Adonis, Andrew and Travers, Tony (1994), *Failure in British Government: The Politics of the Poll Tax*, Oxford University Press.

Butt Philp, Alan (1975), *The Welsh Question: Nationalism in Welsh Politics 1945-1970*, Cardiff University Press.

Conservative Research Department (1992), *The Campaign Guide 1992*, Conservative Central Office.

Crick, Bernard (1991), 'The English and the British', in Bernard Crick (ed.), *National Identities: The Constitution of the United Kingdom*, Blackwell.

Dorril, Stephen, and Ramsay, Robin (1992), *Smear! Wilson and the Secret State*, Grafton.

Drucker, Henry (1978), *Breakaway: The Scottish Labour Party*, EUSPB.

Fukuyama, Francis (1992), *The End of History and the Last Man*, Penguin.

Gamble, Andrew (1993), 'Territorial Politics', in Patrick Dunleavy, Andrew Gamble, Ian Holliday and Gillian Peele (eds) *Developments in British Politics 4*, Macmillan.

George, Stephen (1994), *An Awkward Partner: Britain in the European Community*, Macmillan.

Gorman, Teresa (1993), *The Bastards: Dirty Tricks and the Challenge to Europe*, Pan.

Harvie, Christopher (1994), *The Rise of Regional Europe*, Routledge .

Hurd, Douglas (1979), *An End to Promises: Sketch of a Government 1970-74*, Collins.

Jowell, Roger, Brook, Lindsay, and Taylor, Bridget (eds) (1990), *British Social Attitudes: The 7th Report*, Dartmouth.

Kellas, James (1989), *The Scottish Political System*, Cambridge University Press, 4th edition.

Layton-Henry, Zig (1992), *The Politics of Immigration*, Blackwell.

McCreadie, Robert (1991), 'Scottish Identity and the Constitution', in Bernard Crick (ed.), *National Identities: The Constitution of the United Kingdom*, Blackwell.

Mackintosh, John (1968), *The Devolution of Power: Local Democracy, Regionalism and Nationalism*, Penguin.

Marquand, David (1991), 'Nations, Regions, and Europe', in Bernard Crick (ed.), *National Identities: The Constitution of the United Kingdom*, Blackwell.

Maudling, Reginald (1978), *Memoirs*, Sidgwick and Jackson.

Miller, William (1981), *The End of British Politics? Scots and English Political Behaviour in the Seventies*, Oxford University Press.

Mullin, W. A. Roger (1979), 'The Scottish National Party', in Henry Drucker (ed.), *Multi-Party Britain*, Macmillan.

Nairn, Tom (1981), *The Break-up of Britain: Crisis and Neo-Nationalism*, Verso, 2nd edition.

Riddell, Peter (1991), *The Thatcher Era and its Legacy*, Blackwell.

Rolston, Bill (1987), 'Alienation or Political Awareness? The Battle for Hearts and Minds of Northern Nationalists', in Paul Teague (ed.) *Beyond the Rhetoric: Politics, the Economy and Social Policy in Northern Ireland*, Lawrence and Wishart.

Smith, Anthony (1995), 'The Dark Side of Nationalism: the Revival of Nationalism in Late Twentieth-Century Europe', in Luciano Cheles, Ronnie Ferguson and Michalina Vaughan (eds) *The Far Right in Western and Eastern Europe*, Longman, 2nd edition.

Thatcher, Margaret (1993), *The Downing Street Years*, HarperCollins.

Thatcher, Margaret (1995), *The Path to Power*, HarperCollins.

Thomas, Dafydd Elis (1991), 'The Constitution of Wales', in Bernard Crick (ed.) *National Identities: The Constitution of the United Kingdom*, Blackwell.

Vincent, Andrew (1995), *Modern Political Ideologies*, Blackwell, 2nd edition.

Walker, Martin (1979), 'The National Front', in Henry Drucker (ed.) *Multi-Party Britain*, Macmillan.

Webb, Keith (1978), *The Growth of Nationalism in Scotland*, Penguin.
Wheeler, Francis (1993), 'The New Europe: Immigration and Asylum', in Tony Bunyan (ed.) *Statewatching the New Europe: A Handbook on the European State*, Statewatch.
Wybrow, Robert (1989), *Britain Speaks Out, 1937-87: A Social History as Seen through the Gallup Data*, Macmillan.

Selected further reading

For nationalism in general, see Eric Hobsbawm, *Nations and Nationalism since 1780* (Cambridge University Press, 1990), and Ernest Gellner, *Nations and Nationalism* (Oxford University Press, 1983).

On specific aspects of nationalism in the UK, see Steve Bruce, *The Edge of the Union: The Ulster Loyalist Political Vision* (Oxford University Press, 1994); Simon Heffer, *Nor Shall My Sword: The Reinvention of England* (Phoenix, 1999); Andrew Marr, *The Day Britain Died* (Profile, 2000); John Osmond (ed.), *The National Question Again: Welsh Political Identity in the 1980s* (Gower, 1985); Roger Scruton, *England: An Elegy* (Pimlico, 2001); and Alan Trench (ed), *Has Devolution made a difference? The State of the Nations 2004* (Imprint Academic, 2004). The impact of nationalism on the Conservative Party is thoroughly explored in Philip Lynch, *The Politics of Nationhood: Sovereignty, Britishness and Conservative Politics* (Macmillan, 1999).

On immigration and race relations, see Colin Holmes, *A Tolerant Country? Immigrants, Refugees and Minorities in Britain* (Faber and Faber, 1991), and John Solomos, *Race and Racism in Britain*, (Palgrave, 3rd edition, 2003). An excellent account of fascist ideology is Noel O'Sullivan, *Fascism* (Dent, 1983). On Britain and 'Europe', see Andrew Gamble, *Between Europe and America: The future of British politics* (Palgrave, 2003), and Hugo Young, *This Blessed Plot: Britain and Europe from Churchill to Blair* (Macmillan, 1998).

CHAPTER 7

The Conservatives since Thatcher, 1990–2006

Background: Thatcher to Major

Margaret Thatcher's sudden departure from office in November 1990 has been variously attributed to her style of government, her championship of the Poll Tax, the economic recession, the insecurity of Tory MPs, and the petty vindictiveness of former ministers such as Michael Heseltine, Nigel Lawson and Sir Geoffrey Howe. The question which her fall left unanswered was whether or not Thatcherism would survive Thatcher. The signs here were mixed. At the time of the 1990 leadership contest John Major was regarded as Mrs Thatcher's favourite political son, but almost all the reasons that were advanced for her unpopularity were linked in some way to her political beliefs. Heseltine, whose opposition to Mrs Thatcher went beyond questions of style, had failed to win a majority of Conservative votes, but his supporters were numerous enough to suggest that some changes, at least, would be necessary to restore the party's fortunes under its new leader.

A crucial factor in the future direction of the party was the thinking of the new Prime Minister. His emergence as the person most likely to promote unity was significantly helped by the obscurity of his views. After entering the House of Commons in 1979 he had worked his way steadily through the government hierarchy, joining the Cabinet as

Chief Secretary to the Treasury in 1987. In July 1989 his promotion to Foreign Secretary in place of Sir Geoffrey Howe caused general surprise, but Thatcher's decision to make him Chancellor of the Exchequer when Nigel Lawson resigned in October of the same year was an even bolder move. With a background in finance, Major was better qualified to work in the Treasury than in the Foreign Office, but he could now be regarded as the favoured candidate to succeed the Prime Minister on her eventual retirement. When that time came, the fact that he had avoided being identified with any ideological section of the party would help rather than hinder his prospects.

Major had not been Foreign Secretary for long enough to create much impression, but soon after becoming Chancellor he showed that he was more than just Mrs Thatcher's yes-man by joining with Douglas Hurd to persuade the Prime Minister that the UK should join the ERM. This ran counter to Thatcher's instincts in two crucial respects; it represented a move towards deeper European integration, and it also contradicted her belief that currency exchange rates should be decided by the free market. Major's only Budget provided some relief for Poll Tax payers, and introduced a new tax-free account for savers. It was not a spectacular Budget after the fireworks of the Lawson years, but it made no additional enemies for the party at a difficult time.

Major officially supported Margaret Thatcher on the inconclusive first leadership ballot, but he was recovering from a timely surgical operation when the rest of the Cabinet were asked for their views about her prospects in a second contest. Probably he would have echoed the majority, arguing that although she deserved to win she would be better advised to stand down. After running a skillful campaign Major defeated Heseltine on the second ballot by 185 votes to 131; Douglas Hurd, whose love for his new job at the Foreign Office made him a surprising challenger, received 56 votes. A notable feature of the campaign was its inverted snobbery, with the Old Etonian Hurd offering lame excuses for his privileged background. Major had gained few academic qualifications, and a great deal was made of his relatively humble origins in Brixton, South London. Labour leadership elections have never concentrated so narrowly on class issues.

In keeping with his image, Major declared that he wanted Britain to become a 'classless society' (Junor, 1993, 253–4). This theme had featured in Labour and Liberal propaganda, although each party meant different things by it. Major, a known opponent of discrimination, was indicating his preference for the kind of equal opportunity which had benefited him. It was another question whether his personal experience – in the days when governments made full employment a high priority – was relevant in 1990. Old definitions of class were becoming blurred in a consumer age, but social inequalities were rising. Yet at least Major's rhetoric hinted at a change of emphasis from the Thatcher years. The former Prime Minister had argued that 'Class is a communist concept' (Thatcher, 1992).

Major's selections for his first Cabinet continued to give the impression that he was above any party infighting. Michael Heseltine was brought back into the Cabinet as Environment Secretary, charged with a thorough reform of the Poll Tax. The only important casualty was Cecil Parkinson, who had been Mrs Thatcher's personal favourite, but there was no general purge. Other ministers closely associated with the old regime kept their places; even Kenneth Baker, who had been party chairman while Tory fortunes declined, was moved to the Home Office. Baker had once been an ally of Edward Heath, but had prospered under Thatcher. The new Chancellor, Norman Lamont, was well placed as both a convinced Thatcherite and a friend of the new Prime Minister. Lamont was a member of the so-called 'Cambridge Mafia', whose members had all been prominent in Conservative circles at Cambridge University in the early 1960s. Other past and present Cabinet ministers from this group included John Selwyn Gummer, Michael Howard, Kenneth Clarke, Leon Brittan and Norman Fowler. At Cambridge, Howard had been such an outspoken opponent of racism that some doubted whether he would remain within the Conservative Party, but by 1990 he was seen as a standard-bearer of Thatcherism (Crick, 2005, 194–220). The others were suspected of secret 'wet' leanings, although their ministerial records showed that they had disguised their secret very effectively. Such ministers, along with the Health Secretary William Waldegrave, could be described as 'Career Thatcherites', who would probably have implemented very different policies if they had enjoyed a free hand. Christopher Patten, the new chairman of the party, had made his dissent from Thatcherism very public in the early 1980s, but like the members of the 'Cambridge Mafia' he had finally succumbed to the call, agreeing to oversee the Poll Tax as Environment Secretary in 1989. The subsequent behaviour of these flexible ministers would be a useful barometer of Major's intentions.

If John Major had wished to move away from Thatcherism, there was little to stop him. One authoritative study in 1989 found that only about 20 per cent of the Parliamentary Conservative Party were convinced believers in the 1980s revolution; and if Major felt that his colleagues were unrepresentative, in 1988 half of the electorate rejected the Thatcherite nostrum that inflation was a greater curse than unemployment (Norton, 1993, 33–5). The Poll Tax was regarded as the flagship of Thatcherism; now that this was sinking to loud popular applause, why not torpedo the whole fleet? With a secure parliamentary majority, Major had more than a year before a new election to signal the beginning of an ideological counter-revolution.

After the Conservative victory in the 1992 general election, some commentators claimed that changes had taken place, although the shift had not been dramatic. Philip Norton, a seasoned observer of the Conservative Party, wrote that Major had no distinctive ideological leanings'; he differed from Thatcher in 'being a pragmatist'. Admittedly, he had declared his loathing of inflation in a forthright manner which his predecessor must have applauded, but according to Norton the undoubted change of style under Major did reflect substantive policy differences (Norton, 1993, 60). If the country had sought a change of government in 1990, John Major seemed to have given it what it wanted without the trouble of going through a general election.

This verdict can be accepted only on the view that ideological politics are invariably linked with crusading zeal and radical change. Between 1990 and 1992 the Thatcherite revolution did not accelerate, but when the circumstances of economic recession are taken into account this was always unlikely. In most areas, change simply proceeded at a steadier pace. The education reforms introduced under Mrs Thatcher were maintained by the energetic Kenneth Clarke. Clarke introduced a new source of controversy with the first suggestion of league tables to evaluate school performance. At the Department of Health the bruising Clarke was replaced by Virginia Bottomley, but the change of style did not bring an end to reform, despite public concerns that the Conservatives were planning to privatise the health service. The much-publicised 'Citizen's Charter' meant that state employees could now be identified by name-badges, but their numbers continued to diminish. The 'Next Steps' programme initiated under Thatcher continued to transform government departments into independent agencies, which could be regarded as a temporary halt on the road to privatisation (Giddings, 1995). The Major government seemed even more anxious to replace local government with unelected and secretive quangos, even though such bodies had once been a target for Thatcherite criticism (Holland, 1981). By 1994 a joint study by Essex University and Charter 88 found that there were 5,521 of these appointed bodies in the UK; working on a more forgiving definition, the government only admitted to 1,345 (Marr, 1995, 78). The idea of private prisons, which had once provoked either laughter or nightmares among non-Thatcherites, brought only muffled protests when it became a reality. Returning railways and the coal mines to private hands remained high priorities, as did tax cuts. In short, the government acted on Thatcherite principles in all of these areas, sometimes proceeding boldly when Mrs Thatcher would have hesitated. Even the misleading difference in personal style between Major and Thatcher had its limits; Major was touted as a 'listening' Prime Minister, but he could not hear the arguments of trade unions while they continued to be barred from Downing Street.

Actions which superficially suggest a retreat from Thatcherism should also be examined in context. In some cases, when the new government was asked to clear up debris left by the previous regime, it was convenient for ministers to hint that Mrs Thatcher had been personally responsible. The Pergau Dam affair, which involved the misapplication of £56 million from the overseas aid budget to facilitate an arms deal with Malaysia, could easily be blamed on the previous regime (Marr, 1995, 248-9). But the short-term success of this strategy concealed dangers. Since it demanded that ministers should disown policies which they had once helped to implement, its usefulness depended upon the short attention span of the electorate. Sometimes, as in the case of the Scott inquiry into the sale of arms to Iraq, the issues were too spectacular for the government to rely on public amnesia. Hence, rumours quickly spread that ministers were keen to delay the publication of Scott's findings for as long as possible. Sometimes the government seemed to be spending more time on damage-limitation than on constructive work; as a result, ministers were more likely to make additional mistakes of their own. Even the previous Labour government, living with the constant threat of parliamentary defeat, had never been as accident-prone as the Major administration.

The best evidence that Major represented a new start was his prompt abandonment of the Poll Tax. Its eventual replacement, the Council Tax, took some account of house values and reflected a greater concern for 'the ability to pay' (Butler et al., 1994, 176-83). When the new tax is compared to the old rating system, however, its effects are still regressive. It can be argued that Michael Heseltine simply substituted a superficially-plausible Thatcherite policy for an idea which had been poorly planned and hastily implemented. If the abolition of the Poll Tax really was a defeat for Thatcherism, it implied no more than a minor tactical withdrawal. These had been fairly common during the 1980s, but Mrs Thatcher's occasional fits of pragmatism were now fading in the memory of commentators. Instead of comparing Major with other post-war Prime Ministers, the media wanted to measure him against an exaggerated image of his immediate predecessor. As a result it was not surprising that public opinion polls consistently showed that Major was regarded as pitifully weak (King, 1994).

The government's macro-economic strategy showed no serious deviation from the Thatcherite approach. Inflation remained the chief enemy, and interest-rate policy was still the weapon used to control it. Unemployment climbed back to around 13 per cent before the 1992 election, but the government took the same 'hands-off' approach as Mrs Thatcher had done. The Chancellor, Norman Lamont, caused uproar in May 1991 when he declared that unemployment was 'a price worth paying' for economic recovery. In its handling of recession, the Major Government was scarcely more flexible than Thatcher's had been; it courted electoral defeat through its inactivity when economic problems were affecting its natural supporters in the South of England. The small business people who formed the backbone of the party suffered as much as anyone; 44,000 small concerns went bankrupt in 1991 (Norton, 1993, 64). If the budget deficit rose, this was inevitable at a time when unemployment was climbing and fewer people were paying stamp duty as the housing market collapsed.

This evidence shows that if Thatcherism was slain by Tory back-benchers in November 1990, its ghost made a very effective understudy. It is normally a mistake to draw a clear distinction between perceived style and the content of policy, but in Major's case the difference between the two was unusually vivid. Major's style brought the Conservative Party some credit for a rethink that never took place. His predecessor played an important part in creating this impression; with Mrs Thatcher herself now free from ministerial responsibility it was natural that she should criticise Major whenever his resolution seemed to be weak. In particular, she failed to appreciate that Major's tactic of remaining as an obstructive force within the EC was essentially the same as her own. Short of total withdrawal from the Community (which she never advocated while in office) it is difficult to see how she would have achieved different results.

In the run up to the 1992 general election, almost all of the public opinion polls pointed to a narrow Labour victory, or at least a hung Parliament which would end thirteen years of Conservative rule (Sanders, 1993). A fourth successive victory in spite of a severe economic recession was an impressive achievement, even if the majority was now down to twenty-one seats. If Major could win in such unpromising circumstances, how could the Conservatives ever be beaten? The Labour Party had already redesigned its image, and dropped most of the policies which its leaders rated as electoral liabilities. Although the Liberal Democrats had recovered from Owenite distractions, they still seemed unable to win the necessary support for a breakthrough. Yet the news was not all good for the Conservatives. For the first time since 1979 parliamentary unity would be essential to maintain a relatively slender majority. The party had not been wholly united at any time since 1970, and now the issue of Europe loomed as a possible threat to Major's authority, despite the opt-outs negotiated at Maastricht in December 1991.

More worrying still, the party was experiencing a serious membership crisis. A study conducted in the election year showed that estimates of well over 2 million members in the 1960s were now well out of date; the figure in 1992 was not far above 750,000. Of these, less than 5 per cent were younger than 35 (Whiteley et al., 1994, 25, 42). Under similar circumstances in the 1980s Labour's weakness in the constituencies had encouraged revolutionaries to practise `entryism'; for the Conservatives, apart from a little-publicised row which led to the disbandment of the Federation of Conservative Students in the 1980s, there was little sign of even unwanted enthusiasts joining the ranks. But while party members were becoming both fewer and older, they were also increasingly difficult to manage. The party conference, once unfairly derided as a synchronised orgy of deference, has certainly become more consistently unruly since the fall of Margaret Thatcher (Kelly, 1994, 221-60). In the Charter Movement the Conservatives now had their own version of Labour's RFMC, demanding greater democracy within the party.

In Thatcher's shadow, 1992–97

Having led his party to an election victory against the odds, John Major was well placed to signal a retreat from Thatcherism. Instead, the government lost no time in demonstrating its commitment to the ideas of the 1980s. In October 1992 Michael Heseltine announced that more than 30,000 miners would lose their jobs, as 'uneconomic' pits were closed prior to the privatisation of the industry. Even some Tory MPs were shocked by these proposals. The move followed the publication, in July, of a White Paper on the privatisation of the railways. Even Mrs Thatcher had been concerned about this sale, although her governments had starved the industry of necessary investment. One Conservative MP, Robert Adley, described rail privatisation as 'the Poll Tax on wheels'. Ministers had taken advice from the Adam Smith Institute, rather than from experts who warned against splitting British Rail into separate companies, responsible for maintaining the track and for running the trains. Adley died in May 1993, just a few months before the legislation was passed. His predictions were verified, although the full effects of rail privatisation did not register until after the fall of the Major Government.

This evidence that Thatcherism was still in control of government thinking made no impression on the former prime minister herself. After the 1992 election, Mrs Thatcher launched an explicit attack on her successor, in which she denounced any suggestion of a compromise between 'Heathite' (or 'One Nation') Conservatism and her own position. Between 1990 and 1992 Christopher Patten had tried to show that this was possible by drawing on the arguments of European Christian Democracy (Patten, 1991). Patten lost his seat in the 1992 election and departed to govern Hong Kong. In his absence David Willetts, the former head of the CPS and newly elected as MP for Havant, prepared a different version of this unlikely synthesis (Willetts, 1992, 1994). In particular, Willetts attempted to show that Thatcherism was compatible with a tangible sense of community. Willetts had been taught at Oxford by John Gray, a disciple of the conservative philosopher Michael Oakeshott; his skillful argument was undermined when Gray repudiated Thatcherism as a departure from the conservative tradition (a view which Oakeshott privately shared) (Gray, 1993). Gray subsequently wrote a powerful series of articles in the *Guardian*, in which he showed that communitarian rhetoric would mean nothing unless it tackled the economic roots of social breakdown (Gray, 1995). Despite this setback, the views publicised by Patten and Willetts filtered through into John Major's speeches (Major, 1994). But nothing was done to reverse the Thatcherite reforms which had provoked the new concern with community in the first place.

Skillful advocates like Willetts could make the rebuilding of community seem plausible in books, but the experience of the 1980s suggested that it could not be done in practice. The mobile workforce demanded by the free market (at least in its British guise) was unfriendly to social cohesion. As the police found during the riots of 1981 and the miners' strike of 1984-85, expressions of communal solidarity were generally hostile to the operation of 'market forces'; under the Major premiership even prosperous communities began to obstruct road-building projects and the free market in live calves (see Chapter 8). The beneficiaries of the Thatcher revolution seemed to be rootless individuals — notably the so-called 'Yuppies', whose main concern was their own pleasure. For the policy-makers of both main parties, the choice lay between more individualistic policies, which might divide the country further, or the end of the Thatcherite project, permitting a new emphasis on social priorities which would go beyond rhetorical gestures.

Claims that Thatcherism was solely responsible for the social problems of the 1980s were seriously exaggerated; indeed, if community spirit had been strong in 1979 it is unlikely that Mrs Thatcher would ever have been elected. However, classical liberalism had certainly accentuated the problem. If politicians genuinely believed that a country 'at ease with itself' would be easier to govern, it was in their interest at least to explore the possibility of alternatives to Thatcherism. Since Thatcherism had never impressed a majority of the electorate, this approach should have been even more attractive for both parties. However, repeated opinion polls suggested that the public was confused; people wanted both lower taxes and more public spending. In the US, it had proved possible to square this circle, and Ronald Reagan had satisfied conflicting demands for tax cuts and higher defence spending by running a massive budget deficit. This option was not practicable for Britain in the 1990s. For politicians of both leading parties, it was much more convenient to interpret the poll findings as evidence that the public was desperate for lower direct taxes – after all, a saloon-bar philosopher in a tight corner will always count on greed rather than altruism (Marquand, 1988, 93-5). When another opinion poll (conducted in the same month that Tony Blair rid himself of Clause IV) found that 60 per cent of voters agreed that the basic rate of income tax should be raised from 25p to 30p in the pound to finance public services, politicians refused to take the hint (Linton and Wintour, 1995).

One of the key assumptions which underpinned Mrs Thatcher's classical liberalism was that British people would behave responsibly if left to themselves. This meant that any social problems must have been caused by the unwise meddling of benighted legislators in previous years. The reforming Labour governments of the 1960s were frequently identified as the worst culprits here. Given her remarkable faith in the moral instincts of most Britons, Thatcher felt that the occasional homily on the themes of 'Victorian Values' (added to the effect of her economic policies) would do more good than direct government action.

This approach had clearly failed, and the impression that Britain had become an uglier place in recent years worried John Major. At the party conference in 1993 the theme of his speech was that the country should go 'Back to Basics'. The immediate result of this rallying call was an argument about Major's intentions: was he referring to individual moral standards, or to the rectitude of the government's programme? Whatever the Prime Minister meant, his slogan released nostalgic visions among Conservative supporters of a world in which it was safe to walk down unlit streets and back doors were always open to the neighbours.

The public reaction to 'Back to Basics' was awkward enough, as the government had few solutions to offer beyond the negative ones of tougher sentencing and greater resources for the police. What made matters worse was that the individual moral standards of senior party figures could not withstand the extra scrutiny which the speech unintentionally invited. For the press this was particularly welcome at a time when the government was contemplating a crackdown on intrusive journalism. Spectacular ministerial resignations followed, including that of the Heritage Secretary (or 'Minister of Fun') David Mellor, who had recently warned the press that they were 'drinking in the Last Chance saloon'. One MP, Stephen Milligan, died at his home in bizarre circumstances, thus triggering off the Eastleigh by-election which gave voters a chance to register their disapproval of a 'sleazy' government. The campaign gradually broadened to include allegations of financial impropriety concerning donations to the Conservative Party, favours to ministers and cash payments in return for parliamentary questions. In January 1994 the *Sun*, which had boasted of ensuring Major's re-election in 1992, was warning the Prime Minister to 'wake up and get a grip'. The long-term damage of 'Back to Basics' was revealed in October, when the *Sunday Telegraph* published an opinion poll showing Tory support down to below 23 per cent, while Tony Blair was rated more highly than John Major in every leadership category.

While 'Back to Basics' was widely regarded as an own goal by the Major Government, it merely unmasked the real moral ambiguities of Thatcherism. For the ex-Prime Minister worldly success and spiritual health presupposed each other. A celebrated example of this was her argument that the Good Samaritan's laudable moral sentiments would have been unavailing if he had lacked material resources (Riddell, 1991, 2). Throughout her premiership Thatcher was advised by moralists (such as Brian Griffiths of the Downing Street Policy Unit) who believed that markets make good citizens. Unfortunately the severity of her views on 'socialism' undermined this optimism. If post-war governments up to 1979 had really sapped the ethical strength of the country through policies designed to promote dependency and permissiveness, could the people be trusted to act responsibly now that their economic chains had been struck off? Some of her ministers had actually been young adults during the 1960s; perhaps they, too, had been tainted by the ethos of those years? In other words, if the Conservatives were right in their analysis of post-war society, some sort of direct moral reforms would be needed. If they were wrong, then their moral case against 'socialism' was wrong too. Thanks to her dauntless faith Mrs Thatcher seems not to have examined this problem very closely. As with other matters, it was left to John Major to wrestle with the consequences.

Divisions over Europe

While the association of the Conservative Party with 'sleaze' caused long-term damage, its MPs were more obsessed than ever with 'Europe'. After postponing a decision, Thatcher was stampeded into joining the ERM when sterling was over-valued. The new economic recession was prolonged as a result. Before leaving office Mrs Thatcher had made her hostility to European developments very clear, and this created uncertainties about Britain's future in the developing Community. Most Euro-sceptics were pleased with Major's handling of the European Council Meeting at Maastricht, but other European governments were not so impressed. If the pound came under speculative pressure on the exchange markets, the necessary co-operation from Germany and France might not be forthcoming.

In September 1993 the markets turned against sterling, and despite firm statements from the Prime Minister and Chancellor Norman Lamont the pound's position within the ERM could not be sustained. Ironically this gave the government more flexibility, particularly in interest rate policy, and 'Black Wednesday' actually assisted the slow process of economic recovery. Yet once again Major had been made to look weak in comparison with his predecessor. This was particularly unfair, as Thatcher had brought the UK into the ERM; she had been most reluctant to do so, but that proved only that she, too, had suffered moments of weakness. Such subtleties were ignored by the media, who sensed that Major was in serious trouble. This mood was not altered by the removal of Norman Lamont, who had privately rejoiced after the ERM debacle.

Despite this sacrificial sacking, Major's European problems only worsened, technically costing him his overall parliamentary majority in late 1994 when eight Conservative MPs lost the party whip for voting against the government on a motion of confidence (a further MP resigned the whip in protest). The normal practice in such cases is for a party to let its rebels rejoin after a token period of ostracism; this time it seemed that the 'whipless ones' were themselves dictating terms, and would oppose the government again on European questions.

By this time the Conservative Party had been continuously in office for sixteen years. The popular feeling that it was 'time for a change' prevented the signs of economic recovery from registering with the voters. Bad news proved more interesting to the media. After the 1992 election the government had extended the scope of VAT to include domestic fuels, even though there had been no indication of this during the campaign. Before these charges were imposed, the new Chancellor Kenneth Clarke hastened to protect welfare claimants from their full impact, but the damage was done. Ministerial talk of a healthy economic revival only reminded the public that this had already been forecast, when Norman Lamont claimed to have seen 'the green shoots of recovery' prior to the 1992 general election.

At that time, John Major had said 'vote for me on Thursday and the recovery will start on Friday' (Junor, 1993, 253). The Conservatives were faced with a Catch-22 situation; they needed to generate a 'feel-good factor' in order to win re-election, but it seemed that the voters would not feel good until there was a change of government. If the economy really was improving, this meant that for once Labour would win a promising inheritance, and the Conservatives might be out of power for decades.

Only one escape route looked feasible. As in 1990, the party could create the impression that there was a new government by replacing its leader. After the ERM debacle and 'Back to Basics' a challenge to John Major before the next election looked a certainty. The only problem concerned the identity of the challenger. Major had defeated Heseltine in 1990 because he looked more likely to unite the party, and his successor would have to share this advantage. Unfortunately all the obvious candidates had strong views about Europe. A victory for either Heseltine, Kenneth Clarke or Michael Portillo would look like the triumph of one party faction, whereas Major had skilfully allowed MPs on both sides to think that he privately agreed with them. Conservative feelings over Europe had grown so bitter that this delicate balancing act could not be maintained for much longer; in particular, Euro-sceptics wanted Major to rule out in advance any prospect that the UK would join a single currency. It seemed that even the prospect of electoral disaster could not restrain the more determined sceptics from forcing a contest in 1995.

The feverish atmosphere of rumour left Major with only one card if his authority was to survive. In June 1995 he announced that he was resigning as party leader in order to precipitate a vote on his future. His opponents were preparing themselves for a challenge later in the year, and were caught unawares. The shock of Major's announcement looked like a master-stroke, and it immediately caused a rise in his poll rating. He had consulted the Cabinet, but one member in particular thought that this process had not gone far enough. John Redwood, the Secretary of State for Wales, duly announced that he would challenge Major for the vacant leadership.

Redwood was a determined Euro-sceptic, but his intervention meant that the election would not focus entirely on one issue. The Thatcherite legacy as a whole was at stake. As a committed supporter of the ex-Prime Minister, Redwood acknowledged that Major had persevered with the policies of the 1980s. Rather, his campaign was motivated by personal ambition, and a sense that Major's lack of fervour might cost the Conservatives the next election. While Major's emphasis was on consolidation, Redwood wanted the crusade to start again. Further tax cuts were needed, and waste in government departments should be attacked more vigorously.

In basing his campaign on substantive issues, Redwood was leaving himself open to the charge that he had stayed within a Cabinet which lacked direction until he saw an opportunity to strike. Yet the same accusation had not prevented Mrs Thatcher herself from beating Heath in 1975. The majority of the Conservative press supported Redwood, and in the election itself he secured eighty-nine votes. One-third of the parliamentary party refused to vote for Major, even though the Prime Minister had started with a significant tactical advantage. Redwood's impressive performance was due to his recognition that in contemporary British politics a lukewarm attachment to principles is not enough; the public needs to be convinced that these ideas are held with genuine enthusiasm. Major was not prepared to rise to this challenge. Whatever his real views; his performance in government showed him to be no more than a 'Career Thatcherite'; he carried out the policies of classical liberalism, while creating the impression that his heart was not really in it. His main weapon, after all, was the perception that he was the candidate of party unity, and any evidence of ideological zeal might upset that delicate position. As a result, his defeat of Redwood simply left the Conservative Party where it had been before the election was announced. The campaign offered an opportunity for senior figures to abuse the Labour Party on television without being challenged, but the inevitable boost in opinion polls proved temporary.

Major delayed the general election for as long as possible, clearly hoping for some positive news to rally his divided and demoralised troops. But the message of the opinion polls suggested that the only question at issue was the scale of the government's defeat. In December 1994 Gallup had placed the Conservatives an astonishing 40 per cent behind Labour; at the time, the government's record was approved by less than 10 per cent of the electorate. There was a minor improvement in the early months of 1997, but the Conservatives were still around 20 per cent behind. In February they lost a by-election in Wirral South, their eighth such defeat in a parliament which had seen relatively few contests. Significantly, the Wirral seat was predominantly middle-class, but it fell to Labour rather than the Liberal-Democrats. The same thing had happened in the previous year, when Labour won Staffordshire South East.

The record of the Major Government was not as bad as the public clearly thought. For example, Kenneth Clarke emerged as the only Chancellor since 1979 to have presided over an era of relative economic stability. Greatly to his credit, he resisted any temptation to bribe voters, in the hope that this would limit the government's defeat and leave Labour (yet again) with a difficult economic inheritance. However, the Conservatives had lost their reputation for economic credibility on 'Black Wednesday'. Elsewhere, Major made significant progress towards peace in Northern Ireland. But his efforts were undermined by his vulnerable parliamentary position, which forced him to strike deals with the Unionist parties.

Up until the end of his premiership, Major was dogged by the problem of Europe. Unrest within the party was fuelled even further by a ban on British beef, imposed in March 1996 because of fears that the cattle disease, BSE, would be transmitted to humans. Under pressure from his back-benchers and the tabloid press, in May Major threatened to disrupt EU business if the ban was not lifted. 'Major goes to war at last', the *Daily Mail* trumpeted. However, British resistance was short-lived and inglorious.

The general election was finally called for 1 May 1997. Major tried to repeat his personal success in the previous contest by touring the country and speaking from a soap-box. This time, though, the image of a plucky, street-fighting underdog failed to move the voters. Indeed, the most striking impression of Major was provided at a campaign press conference, when he appealed to his unruly colleagues to allow him a free hand in negotiations with Britain's European partners. While many backbenchers wanted Major to rule out membership of the single currency, Clarke and Heseltine refused to contemplate this concession. In any case, many Conservative voters preferred the position of James Goldsmith's Referendum Party, which advocated withdrawal from the EU.

At the election itself, the gap between Labour and the Conservatives was less than 13 per cent. This margin compared favourably with all of the opinion polls since late 1992. But Britain's electoral system translated these figures into a humiliation for the party. It was left with only 165 seats. Even in the landslide defeat of 1945, 213 Tories had been returned. Some ministers, including Michael Portillo, suffered spectacular defeats. But the most significant results came in Scotland and Wales, which failed to elect a single Conservative MP between them. During the campaign, Major had attacked Labour's plans for devolution and claimed that only the Conservatives could prevent the break-up of the UK. The decisive rejection of this policy, along with all the other failures of the Major years, brought the survival of the Conservative Party into question at the end of a century which it had dominated.

Nationalism and nostalgia, 1997–2006

Bruised by his years in office, Major resigned straight after the election. This decision was understandable, but opened him to further criticism since it gave the party no time to digest the lessons of defeat before choosing a successor. The media focus on the leadership contest fostered an unreal atmosphere within the party; after eighteen years of political dominance, MPs could be forgiven for thinking that their opinions still mattered as they toured the television studios.

The list of contenders for the vacant position did not include two of the men who had been tipped as possible leaders before the general election. Portillo had decided not to stand against Major in 1995. Now he was ruled out because he had lost his seat. Michael Heseltine was excluded on health grounds, having suffered heart problems just two days after the general election.

Even without these leading figures, when MPs voted in the first leadership ballot on 10 June they had a choice of five candidates. From the outset, they were appraised in terms of their attitudes to Europe. For those who wanted the Conservatives to take a positive approach to the developing EU, Kenneth Clarke was the only realistic option. His opponents were all Eurosceptic. John Redwood, Peter Lilley and Michael Howard were all well known for their opposition to further integration. William Hague, the 36-year old former Welsh Secretary, made it clear during the campaign that he opposed membership of the single currency. But compared to the others his feelings on this key issue were relatively temperate. Initially, Hague had agreed to support Michael Howard's campaign. But he and his supporters soon realised that his moderate scepticism, combined with his youth, gave him an excellent chance of winning the election. His decision to abandon Howard was justified when the latter was subjected to a damaging personal attack by Ann Widdecombe, who had served with him at the Home Office.

On 10 June, Howard came bottom of the poll with just 23 votes, one behind Lilley. Both candidates withdrew, pledging their support to Hague. This was highly damaging to John Redwood, who broadly shared their attitude to Europe and had come third in the poll against expectations, with 27 votes. If the supporters of Howard and Lilley had switched to him, he would have been well placed to win on the second ballot. Clarke had topped the first poll, but had only received 49 votes compared to 41 for Hague. On the second ballot held on 17 June Clarke still led, with 64 votes. But Hague was closing the gap, on 62. Under the rules, third-placed Redwood was eliminated from the contest after the second ballot, with only 38 votes.

The third ballot took place only 2 days later, but this left plenty of time for dramatic developments. Redwood suddenly announced that he was asking his supporters to vote for Clarke. No doubt he had calculated that a Clarke victory would give him his best chance of winning a senior post in the shadow cabinet. Clarke, for his part, knew that he had no chance of winning without attracting a significant number of Redwood's supporters. However, this pact of mutual convenience proved counter-productive. Redwood's supporters were under no obligation to follow him into the Clarke camp, and those who were disinclined to do so were emboldened by Lady Thatcher, who took this opportunity to endorse Hague. In the third ballot, Hague won easily, by 92 votes to 70.

Immediately after the election Hague promised to unite his party, while Labour argued that the Conservatives were now hopelessly divided. In fact, the most interesting feature of the contest was the extent of ideological agreement between the candidates. This may seem a surprising judgement, in view of the bitter legacy of the Major years. Yet the European issue cannot be understood under the traditional terms of ideological debate in the UK. As we have seen, the 1975 referendum forged an improbable alliance between socialists and classical liberals. Tony Benn and Enoch Powell feared European integration for very different reasons, and they remained fierce antagonists on almost every domestic question. The same was true in 1997. Socialists still had every reason to dislike the EU, which was unequivocally capitalist despite its fondness for regulation. Classical liberals concentrated on these regulations — invariably exaggerating their impact — and overlooked the fact that the EU tried to enforce free market competition in many areas which had previous been subject to economic intervention by member states.

In terms of domestic policy, there was little to choose between any of the candidates in 1997. They were all Thatcherites, with varying degrees of enthusiasm. Clarke, indeed, was associated with some of the more controversial measures of the Conservative period, notably the enforcement of market-style practices within the NHS. Nevertheless, during the leadership contest he was invariably described in the media as the 'left-wing' candidate. It was often claimed that he belonged to the 'One Nation' tradition within the party, and it was pointed out that he had been a junior minister in the Heath Government. Such details gave a seriously misleading impression of Clarke's beliefs.

In June 1997 Clarke was easily the most popular of the Conservative candidates among the electorate as a whole. For a party which has always been interested in the exercise of power, this should have been a primary consideration. To make the decision easier for his party, Clarke had made sceptical noises about the single currency during the election campaign. Clearly John Redwood believed that the prospect of a Clarke leadership was perfectly palatable. The pact with Clarke was mainly inspired by self-interest, but such calculations also suggested a sequence of events which would benefit the party as a whole. Realistically, the Conservatives were unlikely to win the next election. Clarke could therefore be seen as a caretaker leader who would keep up party morale by landing heavy blows on the new government. He would have to modify his pronouncements on the EU; and in any case he would never have the chance to put his views into practice.

However, even if MPs were pragmatic enough to see the logic of this scenario, a clear majority decided that Clarke would be too divisive. This conclusion says a great deal about the state of the Conservative Party in 1997. Many of its members, and a significant number of its elected representatives, were in the grip of nationalistic fervour. For them it did not matter that Clarke was unlikely to become prime minister; they simply did not want to be led by someone who was sympathetic towards the EU.

As we saw above, in its typical manifestations nationalism cannot be regarded as a distinctive ideology like socialism and liberalism. Nationalism is a product of a specific situation – a positive desire to achieve national self-determination, or a defensive reaction against a perceived threat to an existing nation. The necessity for concerted action allows members of various ideological groupings to overlook their disagreements on fundamental issues about human nature and social arrangements; but if their movement is successful their underlying ideological differences will soon re-emerge. Yet the fact that nationalism is different in character from ideological thought does not mean that it is incapable of inspiring political action; indeed, it is one of the most potent of political forces.

Nationalism within the Conservative Party after 1992 was obviously of the defensive kind. Eurosceptics believed that the EU had already undermined British sovereignty, and was on the verge of subsuming the UK into a federated 'superstate'. This suspicion had always been present within the Conservative Party; few members had rejoiced when Britain joined the EEC, or when the 'Yes' vote prevailed in the 1975 referendum. But it was no accident that misgivings turned into obsessional hatred of 'Europe' after 1992. Feelings were whipped up by Lady Thatcher, and by newspaper proprietors whose hatred for the EU was much deeper than their love of the UK. But the ageing members of the Conservative Party had other reasons for resenting European interference. Many of them had memories of the Second World War. This produced a lasting suspicion of Germany, and contempt for France. But opposition to the EU also reflected a sense of bewilderment about Britain's reduced status in the world. Many Conservatives had taken at face value Mrs Thatcher's claims about making Britain great again, and in their eyes the victory in the Falklands conflict had backed up her rhetoric. Yet by 1992 the limits of the revival were clear to all but the most blinkered observer. The US regarded its ties with Britain as of no more importance than its relationship with Germany; the second recession under Conservative rule showed that the British economy was still weak; and the ERM fiasco was an international humiliation.

Euroscepticism was not confined to the Conservative Party, and many observers expected that Labour's divisions of the 1970s would re-open after it was returned to office. This proved not to be the case, for understandable reasons. Although some of the historic reasons for anti-European sentiment applied to Labour members, the impact of more recent developments was confined to the Conservatives. The potent mix of memories, both near and remote, meant that in 1997 their party was seething with discontent. Some members blamed Major for his weak leadership, while others thought that parliamentary party had made strong leadership impossible. There was also a general feeling that the Conservatives were the natural party of government, and that the electorate would soon tire of its frivolous flirtation with Labour.

Almost certainly, Hague was guilty of the latter misapprehension; otherwise he would not have run for the leadership in 1997. Even if the Conservative Party had been governable, Hague would have struggled to make an impression as a potential prime minister. The electorate was constantly reminded of his appearance as a teenager at a Conservative Party conference. If he had served a longer apprenticeship as a cabinet minister it would have been easier for voters to forgive and even forget the smug speech he had made back in 1977. As it was, when he became leader his precocious interest in politics was the only thing for which he was famous. Attempts to appear more 'normal', including visits to a theme park and the Notting Hill Carnival, rebounded against him. Less fairly, he was criticised for responding to the death of Princess Diana with a sober speech when most of the country was convulsed with hysterical grief.

Initially, Hague and his inexperienced advisers hoped to broaden the party's appeal. However, he was acutely aware of feelings among grass roots activists. During the leadership campaign he had promised to give members a say in the election of future leaders. In keeping with this democratic pose, he also asked the party to endorse his policy of ruling out membership of the single currency for the course of the next parliament. His proposals won overwhelming support from the dwindling membership, which by this time included very few pro-Europeans. For Hague, these endorsements were all the more important because he lacked other sources of authority. He performed well against Tony Blair at Prime Minister's Question Time, but this ritual encounter was not taken seriously by many voters. Hague's vulnerability within the party was emphasised in November 1999, when Michael Portillo re-entered parliament after a by-election. Hague could not deny Portillo a senior post, and made him Shadow Chancellor. But there was no personal rapport between the pair, and the leader's entourage felt that Portillo was plotting to replace him.

Since Labour had accepted most of the key Conservative reforms since 1979, Hague had little scope for distinctive policy initiatives. Some younger members of the party wanted to present a more tolerant image (Vaizey, Boles and Gove (eds), 2001). But Hague was inhibited in this area by the knowledge that he would be opposed by traditionalists. He tried out several themes to encapsulated the Conservative case, notably 'The Common-sense Revolution'. The slogan might have worked in 1979, when there was a real difference between the two main parties. But for most of Tony Blair's first term, voters registered a high level of satisfaction with the government's performance. The idea of a 'revolution' could only appeal to the minority who remained dissatisfied. It was a sign that Hague had given up any hope of winning the next election, and wanted to concentrate his appeal on the 'core' Tory vote. The assumption was that some people who had deserted the party in 1997 would return to the fold if they felt that the Conservatives really meant business this time. There would be a significant recovery in terms of seats, and the party could expect a considerable advance on the 31 per cent vote-share it had received in 1997.

Left to himself, Hague would probably have concentrated on the prospect of tax cuts, financed by efficiency savings. However, Portillo watered down the party's commitments in order to reflect the popular demand for better public services. Denied any opening for 'revolutionary' proposals in this area, Hague took a reckless gamble in the only field where his party could hope to outflank Labour. In March 2001 he claimed that Britain was in danger of becoming a 'foreign land' under the present government. Ostensibly, the speech was about the growing influence of the EU. But Hague's catch-phrase could be extended to cover other developments which were affecting the lives of ordinary Britons. In particular, the tabloid press was increasingly exercised by the growing numbers of people who arrived in Britain to claim political asylum. As a result, Hague's speech was attacked by Labour as an attempt to play the 'race card' in the forthcoming election.

During the election campaign, a chastened Hague concentrated on the EU, under the slogan 'In Europe, not run by Europe'. Attacking alleged Labour plans to scrap sterling at the first opportunity, Hague developed the habit of holding up a pound coin during his speeches. If anything this actually undermined his case, since the coin was itself a recent innovation which had been widely resented when it was introduced in 1984. In any case, Hague could not promise that his party would always oppose UK membership of the single currency, for the very good reason that the euro might prove to be a runaway success. As a result, not even die-hard Conservatives could support Hague's party with much enthusiasm. In the election, held in June 2001, the Conservatives gained only one seat, and their vote share rose by less than 1 per cent. Hague immediately resigned from the leadership.

With hindsight, having chosen a 'core vote' strategy Hague might have been better advised to persevere with his 'foreign land' critique of the Labour government, but with a subtle change of emphasis. In itself, the asylum question was a valid topic for political debate, although it had to be addressed in the context of tight immigration policies, and a declining UK birth-rate. Hague had also been accused of opportunism during 2000, after offering support to the farmer Tony Martin, who had killed an intruder, and criticising the Macpherson Report into the police handling of the murder of Stephen Lawrence. His mistake was to deal with each of these questions as they arose, in a way which was designed to please his core constituency. If Hague had bided his time, he could have produced a general indictment of a government which imposed radical change on abstract liberal principles, rather than implementing gradual reforms which took account of the diverse attitudes of the British public. Instead, by March 2001 Hague's repeated attempts to associate himself with populist causes had earned him the nickname of 'Billy Bandwagon' (Garnett and Lynch, 2002).

Hague's departure meant that the party was once again in the media spotlight after an election which left it politically impotent. This time the leadership contest was held under different rules. MPs voted in the initial rounds, which reduced the field to the two most popular candidates. Party members then exercised the decisive choice. The final part of this process lasted three months, to give the candidates time to take their messages to the grass-roots members. It was not until September 2001 — four months after the general election — that Conservatives knew the identity of their new leader.

The result proved that the party was now more interested in principle than in power. Iain Duncan Smith, who had frequently rebelled against the Major Government even in crucial votes, was elected in a run-off against Kenneth Clarke. It was not very surprising that the Eurosceptic Duncan Smith was able to beat Clarke in a contest which was decided by ordinary members. But most observers were amazed that Duncan Smith was able to progress to the final round. This time, Michael Portillo had been a candidate, and he had led the field during the first two rounds of voting among MPs. But in the next round he had finished third, trailing Duncan Smith by just one vote. For some time, rumours had been circulating about Portillo's sexuality, and he had admitted

to some homosexual experiences. Quite possibly these revelations made the vital difference. Shortly after the election,
Portillo announced that he would be leaving politics.

Duncan Smith held the leadership for just over two years.
During that time, it became clear that his implacable opposition to the single currency was irrelevant as an electoral
issue, because Labour was unlikely to 'scrap the pound'
while Gordon Brown remained as Chancellor. After he
returned to the backbenches, Duncan Smith began to campaign on behalf of the under-privileged. This approach
promised to embarrass the Labour government, which had
allowed economic equality to increase. However, while he
was Conservative leader Duncan Smith's commitment to
social justice remained obscure.

In October 2003, Duncan Smith lost a vote of confidence
among Conservative MPs by 90 votes to 75. It had become
clear that the party could never hope to reclaim power
under his leadership, and the parliamentary party used the
revised leadership rules to remove him. Whether or not the
ordinary members would have liked a contest, MPs
ensured that they would never be allowed to exercise a
choice. In November 2003 Michael Howard was anointed
without a contest. Howard's unanimous elevation was an
ironic commentary on the 1997 leadership election, when he
had finished bottom of the poll in the first ballot. Hague had
made him Shadow Foreign Secretary, but he had not held
the post for long and seemed likely to concentrate on a
career outside parliament. Duncan Smith had brought him
back as Shadow Chancellor, and his skillful Commons performances against Gordon Brown seems to have convinced
MPs that they had been wrong to overlook him in 1997.

Under Howard, the Conservatives made limited electoral
headway, despite the government's unpopularity in the
wake of the war in Iraq. On this subject the Conservatives
were handicapped by the fact that both Duncan Smith and
Howard had been consistent advocates of strong action
against Saddam Hussein; later attempts to attack the government because it had distorted the case for war only made
Howard look opportunist. In the 2005 general election the

party won 198 seats, and its share of the UK vote increased to 32.3 per cent. No-one had expected the Conservatives to win, but these results were very disappointing and Howard followed the example of Major and Hague by announcing his resignation at the first opportunity. This time, though, he remained as a caretaker for several months, while the party selected his successor.

Despite the discouraging statistics, the Conservatives were in much better shape when Howard stood down than they had been when he took over. In particular, the party was much more united. Conservatives had learned important lessons after eight years in opposition. By this time, even they had realised that constant arguing over Europe had damaged their electoral prospects. But the path to enlightenment was smoothed by Howard, whose attitude to Europe was shared by most MPs and activists.

Howard's brief stint as leader was also interesting because at any early stage he made an explicit declaration of principles. In January 2004 he took out a newspaper advertisement, under the heading 'I Believe'. Among the 16 key points, the most striking is Howard's view that 'the people should be big ... the state should be small'. On the same theme, he argues that 'People are most likely to be happy when they are masters of their own lives, when they are not nannied or over-governed'. These statements are highly characteristic of classical liberalism. Indeed, Howard begins his list with the claim that 'It is the duty of every politician to serve the people by removing the obstacles in the way of [their] ambitions'. This was closely comparable to Isaiah Berlin's famous definition of 'negative liberty', and is clearly distinct from the prevalent post-war view that the state should actively *help* citizens to develop their talents (Garnett, 2004).

Howard's statement of faith aroused little interest, and certainly did not trigger a debate within his party. This implied that Thatcherite views now commanded universal assent among Conservatives—a stark contrast to the position in 1975, when Mrs Thatcher had taken over from Edward Heath. There was general agreement that the party had to present a more 'compassionate' image; indeed, 'Compassionate Conservatism' had been one of the slogans which William Hague road-tested after 1997. At the 2005 election, Howard identified £34 billion of public spending which was allegedly 'wasted' on unnecessary bureaucracy. Of this sum, only £4 billion would be used to finance tax cuts. This was an important departure from previous electoral promises. Yet it was difficult to see how the party could construct a persuasive narrative on this theme, given its ingrained suspicion of the state.

Howard wanted the party to change the way in which leaders were elected, giving the final choice back to MPs. However, this initiative was rebuffed by the membership. When the parliamentary party embarked on the laborious process which had given the leadership to Iain Duncan Smith, four candidates had been nominated. Clarke stood once more, and his views on Europe generated far less antagonism on this occasion. But MPs could now reject him on the less controversial pretext of age. He was eliminated in the first round of voting.

The second candidate to go was Dr Liam Fox, who had previously been co-chairman of the party and a spokesperson on Health. Fox attracted strong support with a robust, unapologetic Thatcherite message. Initially seen as the outsider of four, he failed by only 6 votes to make the final run-off. As it was, the membership was confronted with a choice between David Davis and David Cameron. Davis had started as favourite, but support had ebbed away after a disappointing speech at the 2005 party conference. Cameron had only been elected to parliament in 2001, at the age of 34. However, his campaign had run smoothly and on the second ballot of MPs he established a convincing lead, winning 90 votes compared to 57 for Davis. The membership ballot, conducted in November and early December 2005, showed that Cameron had made an even more favourable impression outside Westminster. Nearly 200,000 Conservatives cast votes, and Cameron won by just over 70,000.

Conclusion

Cameron's election was hailed by many Conservatives as the beginning of the road back to power. He also received very favourable coverage from the media, which relished the prospect of a closer political battle. Cameron certainly had an attractive personality, and looked better on television than his three predecessors. However, his principles were obscure. In his first weeks several controversial policies were scrapped, and the party moved even further away from its tax-cutting agenda. Oliver Letwin, who had been put in charge of a policy review, even argued in favour of reducing the gap between rich and poor, which had increased markedly in the Thatcher years. When Cameron launched a statement of principles (entitled 'Built to last') at the end of February 2006, he argued that economic policies should help the underprivileged. He also asserted that government could be 'a force for good'.

Lady Thatcher's old ally, Lord Tebbit, was prominent among Cameron's early critics. In some respects, the policy proposals did mark a departure from the Thatcherite agenda. Even before the 2005 general election Cameron was arguing for a more 'practical' approach to politics. He claimed that the successes of the 1980s arose from pragmatism rather than ideology, but that towards the end of the Thatcher years the party became preoccupied by its victory in the battle of ideas (Cameron, 2005).

Cameron's early decisions certainly showed that he was flexible; he had, after all, drafted the 2005 general election manifesto, yet lost no time in ditching some of its central policies. His approach invited comparisons with Tony Blair — which, for some members of own his party, meant that he was ready to abandon any principle in the quest for office. However, even at his most open-minded Cameron betrayed certain key assumptions. For all his talk of communities and the positive role of the state, his most distinctive policies reflected a strong belief in the rational, self-interested individual. This ideological view underpins the Conservative approach to public service reform, where an extension of the profit motive is regarded as the most likely source of efficient provision. Under Cameron, the Conservatives will promise greater choice to the consumers of public services. Such policies are characteristic of the classical liberalism which has dominated the Conservative Party since the 1980s. In this sense, Cameron only represents a significant departure from his party's recent past because he has a more realistic chance of convincing the public that the Conservatives stand for 'Thatcherism with a human face'.

List of works cited

Butler, David, Adonis, Andrew, and Travis, Tony (1994), *Failure in British Government: The Politics of the Poll Tax*, Oxford University Press.

Crick, Michael (2005), *In Search of Michael Howard*, Simon & Schuster.

Garnett, Mark (2004), 'The Free Economy and the Schizophrenic State: Ideology and the Conservatives', *Political Quarterly*, Vol. 75, no. 4, October–December, 367–72.

Garnett, Mark, and Lynch, Philip (2002), 'Bandwagon Blues: The Tory Fightback Fails', *Political Quarterly*, Vol. 73, no.1, January–March, 29–37.

Giddings, Philip (ed.) (1995), *Parliamentary Accountability: A Study of Parliament and Executive Agencies*, Macmillan.

Gray, John (1993), *Beyond the New Right: Government and the Common Environment*, Routledge.

Gray, John (1995), 'Hollowing Out the Core', *Guardian*, 8 March.

Holland, Philip (1981), *The Governance of Quangos*, Adam Smith Institute.

Junor, Penny (1993), *The Major Enigma*, Michael Joseph.

Kelly, Richard (1994), 'The Party Conferences', in Anthony Seldon and Stuart Ball (eds) *Conservative Century: The Conservative Party since 1900*, Oxford University Press.

King, Anthony (1994), 'Tories Suffer from Sleaze Factor', *Daily Telegraph*, 10 October.

Linton, Martin, and Wintour, Patrick (1995), 'Voters Say Yes to Tax for NHS', *Guardian*, 13 April.

McSmith, Andy (1994), *Kenneth Clarke: A Political Biography*, Verso.

Major, John (1994), 'Major Pledges Continuity and Stability', *Times*, 15 October.

Marquand, David (1988), *The Unprincipled Society: New Demands and Old Politics*, Fontana.

Marr, Andrew (1995), *Ruling Britannia: The Failure and Future of British Democracy*, Michael Joseph.

Norton, Philip (1993), 'The Conservative Party from Thatcher to Major', in Anthony King (ed.) *Britain at the Polls 1992*, Chatham House.

Patten, Christopher (1991), Interviewed by David Marquand, *Marxism Today*, February.

Riddell, Peter (1991), *The Thatcher Era and its Legacy*, Blackwell.

Sanders, David (1993) 'Why the Conservative Party Won — Again', in Anthony King (ed.) *Britain at the Polls 1992*, Chatham House.

Thatcher, Margaret (1992), 'Don't Undo What I Have Done', *Guardian*, 22 April.

Vaizey, Edward, Boles, Nicholas, and Gove, Michael (eds) (2001), *A Blue Tomorrow: New Visions for Modern Conservatism*, Politico's.

Whiteley, Paul, Seyd, Patrick, and Richardson, Jeremy (1994), *True Blues: The Politics of Conservative Party Membership*, Oxford University Press.

Willetts, David (1992), *Modern Conservatism*, Penguin.

Willetts, David (1994), *Civic Conservatism*, Social Market Foundation.

Selected further reading

While the dramatic changes of the Thatcher years attracted enormous scholarly interest, academics shared the general view that the Major premiership was an anti-climax. Dennis Kavanagh and Anthony Seldon produced an illustrious cast of contributors for *The Major Effect* (Macmillan, 1994), but this confirmed the impression that Major had barely deviated from the Thatcherite agenda. Peter Dorey's edited volume, *The Major Premiership: Politics and Policies under John Major, 1990-97* (Macmillan, 1999) is also well worth consulting. Another interesting volume which focuses on this period is Steve Ludlam and Martin J Smith (eds), *Contemporary British Conservatism* (Macmillan, 1996).

Although many key figures (including Major and Lamont) have published their memoirs, the best 'insider' account of these years is Gyles Brandreth, *Breaking the Code: Westminster Diaries* (Phoenix edition, 2000). This provides some fascinating insights into a regime which was decaying from the inside.

The most substantial account of developments since 1997 is Mark Garnett and Philip Lynch (eds), *The Conservatives in Crisis* (Manchester University Press, 2003). Keiron O'Hara's *After Blair: Conservatism Beyond Thatcher* (Icon, 2005) is a lively assessment of the dilemmas facing the contemporary party.

CHAPTER 8

'New' Labour

Party strategists drew two main lessons from Labour's defeat in the 1992 general election. Neil Kinnock complained bitterly about the impact of the press, particularly the *Sun*. On the eve of the election that newspaper had poured vitriol on the Labour leader, suggesting that sensible people would want to leave the country if he became Prime Minister. Despite Kinnock's justified outburst, many of his colleagues decided that it would be advisable to court the Conservative newspapers in future.

The second lesson pointed towards a similar solution. It was decided that the despite Kinnock's reforms, the electorate still thought that Labour was still controlled by the trade unions. The answer was to press on with 'modernisation'. Eventually, it was reasoned, even the *Sun* would be appeased; and this would allow the party's real message to reach the voters.

Of course, there were still people within the party who felt that it had lost because the reforms had already gone too far. But by 1992 their influence had waned, and their alternative analysis was ignored. It was also possible to argue that Kinnock had been the party's greatest liability; after all, since Thatcher's removal from office he had consistently trailed John Major in the popularity polls, encouraging the *Sun*'s campaign of vilification. However, most party members recognised that this second electoral defeat was a personal tragedy for Kinnock. Even those who thought that Kinnock blundered by indulging in premature celebrations of victory at the party's pre-election rally were inclined to forgive him after his resignation.

Kinnock's successor was the Shadow Chancellor, John Smith. Smith had been challenged for the post by Bryan Gould. Gould was unhappy with some developments within the party, notably the new warmer relationship with the business community in general and the City of London in particular. Shortly after his crushing defeat, Gould left to take up an academic post in New Zealand, complaining that Labour no longer stood for 'the goals of greater equality and freedom for ordinary people' (Gould, 1995, 281). The new deputy leader, Margaret Beckett, had benefited from the campaign to deselect the moderate Dick Taverne in Lincoln during the early 1970s. Later she had denounced Neil Kinnock for failing to support Tony Benn in his own campaign for the deputy leadership. She had now repented of these ideological errors, and unlike Taverne (and Gould) she saw no reason to leave the party.

Smith himself had joined Taverne in the 1971 parliamentary rebellion on membership of the EEC. Unlike many of his fellow-dissidents, however, he had resisted the lure of the SDP. A brilliant Scottish lawyer, he had worked on Labour's plans for devolution before entering the Cabinet as Secretary of State for Trade. This governmental experience made him unusual among Labour's current front-bench team, if not in the PLP as a whole. Apart from his obvious debating skills, Smith at least gave the impression of listening to opinion from all sections of the party.

In the eyes of Kinnock's critics this made Smith a change for the better, although listening and acting on unwelcome advice are different things. Smith's 'shadow budget' of 1992 had been identified by some as the main cause of Labour's defeat, but this was not enough to prevent his victory. He had also recently recovered from a serious heart attack. The size of his vote — 91 per cent of the electoral college — showed that these handicaps were dwarfed by his personal popularity.

Smith immediately promised to complete the 'modernising' reforms of the Kinnock years, and to unite the anti-Conservative majority in the country. Even the *Sun* was forced to accept that he would have led Labour to victory in the next general election. But Smith died after a further heart attack in May 1994, after less than two years as leader. The most important development during his brief spell as leader was a vote at the 1993 party conference which adopted a version of OMOV. However, the party retained an electoral college system for electing its leader, with re-adjusted proportions which gave a third of the vote to MPs, constituency parties and trade unions. On policy matters Smith set up a Social Justice Commission under Sir Gordon Borrie. When this reported after Smith's death, it advocated a national minimum wage and spoke of a social security system which offered 'a hand-up rather than a hand-out'.

The Borrie Commission placed a new emphasis on opportunity, rather than dependency. This approach was consistent with the social democratic tradition, to which Smith belonged. But the report was also influenced by Thatcherite assumptions about rational individualism. For example, it urged that young people should be encouraged to plan for their retirement. This advice could not be very impressive after more than a decade of widespread economic insecurity. Significantly, the Borrie report did not suggest that Labour should restore its post-war target of full employment.

The independent status of the Borrie Commission meant that Labour was not bound by its conclusions. By the time it reported, the party had another new leader. After Smith's death, speculation focused on two young MPs who were closely associated with 'modernisation'. Gordon Brown was the senior of the two, having been Shadow Chancellor under Smith's leadership. Tony Blair had earned favourable coverage for his performance in a series of front-bench jobs. Recently he had been Shadow Home Secretary, and had made effective use of a slogan coined by Brown: 'Tough on crime, tough on the causes of crime'.

In the era before television, Labour would certainly have chosen Brown. However, Blair's image was ideally suited to the modernising project. He looked cheerful and gregarious — even a little naïve. By contrast, Brown gave the impression that the world's woes had accumulated on his shoulders. Blair also had a young family, whereas Brown was unmarried.

For party strategists like Peter Mandelson, these considerations helped to sway the decision in favour of Blair. Normally there would have been no problem in allowing the final choice to be taken by party members, especially in the light of recent reforms to the voting system which made it most unlikely that an uncongenial candidate could take advantage of the split in the modernising vote. However, there was a reasonable chance that Brown would win if he contested the post. His roots lay deep in the Labour Party, and he had even written a book about James Maxton, a hero to many socialists from the inter-war period. By contrast, Blair's father had been a Conservative whose views would have made him a reliable Thatcherite MP, had he not been struck down by ill-health. If the spotlight had fallen on Blair's allegiance to the Labour Party, critics could easily have asked why he had ever joined. This question was never satisfactorily answered, despite a series of biographical studies of Blair.

After Smith's death his supporters could only wonder what might have happened if he had lived to become prime minister. But although his death was a shock, the party had been aware of possible health problems when they elected him. Brown's decision not to stand against Blair provides a more interesting thought-experiment for those who like to ask 'what might have been'. If he had stood unsuccessfully, there is no reason to think that his friendship with Blair would have been affected. As it was, he agreed to step aside after a discussion with Blair in a North London restaurant. This has become a legendary meeting, mainly because the friendly rivals were supposed to have struck a deal which guaranteed the succession to Brown. It is equally interesting, though, to speculate about the arguments which were used to persuade Brown that a contest would be damaging to the modernising cause.

Despite the mysterious deal, Blair was not elected unopposed. Margaret Beckett, who had served as a caretaker leader after Smith's death, joined John Prescott in running for the permanent position. The result suggested that Blair would have had a very difficult fight if Brown had decided to stand. He received more than half of the electoral college votes (57 per cent); but unlike Brown neither of his rivals was seriously regarded as a potential prime minister. The fact that Prescott received nearly a quarter of the votes was particularly troubling for the modernisers, since he had very strong trade unions links and was sceptical, to say the least, about the benefits of further radical reform. However, after winning the deputy leadership in a further contest against Mrs Beckett, Prescott proved to be an invaluable ally for Blair, as William Whitelaw had been for Margaret Thatcher.

'New' Labour in Opposition

It is doubtful whether many Labour members voted for Blair in the hope that he would move well beyond Smith's reforming agenda and completely transform the party. But just ten weeks after he became leader, he gave a clear signal of his intentions. At the party conference of October 1994 he announced that Labour should present 'a clear, up-to-date statement' of its objectives. This was another way of saying that its existing objectives were out-of-date. Blair was obviously hoping to succeed where Hugh Gaitskell had failed and where other leaders had feared even to try. His target was Clause IV (section 4) of the party's constitution, with its commitment to nationalisation.

For the modernisers, the existing Clause IV was redundant because the party no longer had aspirations to control 'the commanding heights of the economy'; indeed, it could be argued that only a minority of its members had ever taken the idea seriously. In the past, Labour could win elections despite this piece of ideological baggage. But in Blair's view that time was over. Clause IV merely provided an easy target for the party's enemies — for Conservatives, who cited it as evidence that Labour could never befriend the free market, and for socialists, who had criticised previous leaders for ignoring it. But the campaign to revise the constitution also gave Blair the chance to exert his authority over the party while enjoying the usual honeymoon period for incoming leaders. If this meant defying the trade unions, so much the better; Blair and his advisers were convinced that the connection with the unions was a major contributory factor to Labour's electoral disasters since 1979. Finally, ditching Clause IV maintained the impression that Labour was not complacent about its chances of winning power in the near future. Blair's initiative was the most effective answer to Smith's allies, who believed that 'one last heave' would be enough to bring electoral victory.

Blair's calculated risk paid off, and the historic clause was removed after a special conference held in April 1995. The new version attracted some criticism on the grounds that it was much too vague. In fact, it left significant room for debate. For example, it described Labour as 'a democratic socialist party'. If Blair was serious in using this phrase, he could only mean that Labour was committed to the peaceful pursuit of distinctively socialist goals. Since nationalisation was such a goal, Blair's words could be seen as a re-statement of the old pledge which he found so objectionable. This interpretation was supported by the commitment to 'a community in which power, wealth and opportunity are in the hands of the many not the few'. However, the remainder of the new clause showed that Blair was working with a rather novel (not to say eccentric) definition of 'socialism'. He went on to refer approvingly to 'the enterprise of the market and the rigour of competition'. As we have seen, even a qualified endorsement of free-market practices is incompatible with socialism, on the grounds that economic competition invariably results in unacceptable inequality, and that the struggle for profit produces exploitation and spiritual unease.

At the time, Blair could escape serious censure on these points because he added warm words about the benefits of social co-operation. In any case, he had promised to ensure that 'power, wealth and opportunity' were no longer the monopoly of the few. However, it soon became clear that Blair had no intention of dismantling the broad policy framework erected by the Conservatives since 1979. In these circumstances, how could 'the many' really be expected to take a fair share of 'power, wealth and opportunity'? Blair had also envisaged a society in which 'undertakings essential to the common good are either owned by the public or accountable to them'. Yet the Conservatives had entrusted the provision of crucial amenities, including water, to the private sector. Such natural monopolies were subject to a system of regulation which was not 'accountable' to the public in a meaningful way. The obvious answer was to take such utilities back into public ownership, but Blair gave no sign that this was to be the case.

Fears about Blair's intentions grew in July 1995, when he flew to Australia to give a speech to senior executives of Rupert Murdoch's News Corporation. Perhaps it made tactical sense to establish a personal rapport with the publisher of the *Sun* and the *Times*, who had been Mrs Thatcher's most vehement media supporter. A relationship of mutual respect, based on a recognition of ideological opposition, could have been helpful in toning down the inevitable criticism of Labour before the next election. However, Blair seems to have gone far beyond this objective. Murdoch certainly received the impression that Blair was an ideological *ally*. The Labour leader possibly had not noticed that the *Sun* had been loud in its lamentation when John Smith died. Obviously the newspaper had realised that the Conservatives were certain to lose the next election. Even if Blair did secretly agree with Murdoch's free-market views, he was in a position to deal with the media magnate on equal terms. Instead, he flew half way across the world in an effort to win his support. What Blair's supporters regarded as a stunning *coup* for the new leader was actually an unexpected gift for Murdoch.

Long before Blair took over the leadership, even the most pessimistic of party strategists should have realized that a decisive swing in electoral opinion had really taken place. In the June 1994 European elections, Labour scored a clear victory, winning sixty-two out of the UK's eighty-four seats with 44 per cent of the vote. This was not just a sympathy vote after the death of John Smith; the trend continued after Blair became leader, as the Conservatives lost control of almost all of their urban councils and Labour performed well in parliamentary by-elections. Labour's recovery in the south was particularly chilling to Conservative MPs. Meanwhile, the drive for new members which had begun under Kinnock was now succeeding.

In the months before the 1997 general election Blair seems to have realised that his reference to 'democratic socialism' had been a mistake. This explains why he embarked on a quest for alternative soundbites to characterise his views. Initially he spoke about the importance of community, triggering a sudden interest in the work of an obscure academic, Amatai Etzioni. Being a 'communitarian' at least gave the impression of rejecting Thatcher's ill-judged remark that there was 'no such thing as society'. But evidently the label was found wanting, because Blair soon began to talk of a 'stakeholder society'. This concept, inspired by the British journalist Will Hutton, was equally short-lived.

In his search for an ideological identity, Blair overlooked two well-established traditions which might have been more apposite. As we have seen, social democrats had contributed a great deal to Labour thinking in the post-war period. Although they placed their main emphasis on collectivity, social democrats upheld the importance of individual character-development; and they also envisaged an important economic role for private enterprise.

Social democracy can usefully be regarded as a 'Third Way' between fully-fledged capitalism and socialism. It is highly significant that, after becoming prime minister, Blair frequently talked of the 'Third Way' as a new invention of his own, as if social democracy had never existed. He might have feared being associated with a position which was widely (if inaccurately) blamed for Britain's problems during the 1970s. Within the Labour Party, the phrase 'social democracy' had not been very popular since the split of the early 1980s, and Blair did not want to invite comparisons with his real role-model, David Owen. However, it is also possible that he was anxious to avoid being judged against a relatively clear set of principles. Even before he became prime minister, it was difficult to square his views with those of well-known social democrats (like the former deputy leader Roy Hattersley) who were still active within the Labour Party. After 1997, Hattersley became one of Blair's most eloquent opponents, without shifting from his previous views (which, ironically, had consigned him to the 'right wing' of the Labour Party for most of his career).

The other label which Blair might have adopted would have been even more controversial within the party. By 1997, Labour had become much more sympathetic towards Europe. Social democrats within the party had always been interested in European ideas, taking particular inspiration from Sweden. In many European states, notably Germany, the electoral battle lay between social democratic parties and Christian Democrats. This made it impossible for any Labour leader to claim allegiance to the Christian Democratic tradition, which allowed a constructive role for the state while placing a greater emphasis on the individual. In many respects, Christian Democracy resembled the British tradition of New liberalism. The main difference was that Christian Democracy was heavily influenced by the Roman Catholic church. This element made it strongly moralistic, allowing much greater scope for state intervention in personal conduct than either New liberalism or social democracy. Tony Blair's wife Cherie was a Roman Catholic, and he showed clear signs of being attracted to that church's teachings. Although he could not acknowledge any debt to Christian Democracy, this tradition is the closest approximation to Blair's ideas up to the end of his first term as Prime Minister.

'New' Labour in government

In the 1997 general election campaign, Blair focused on five pledges which were distributed in a (highly appropriate) credit-card format. Although the pledges covered familiar Labour issues like health, education and work-creation, the first was a promise to 'Halve the time from arrest to sentence for persistent young offenders'. The final pledge committed the Labour Party to preserving rates of income tax at the levels which Margaret Thatcher had established.

From a purely tactical perspective, Blair's conduct of the 1997 general election campaign can be regarded as a success. Keeping down public expectations of change deprived the Conservatives of their usual propaganda weapons. However, Blair did not regard the 1997 manifesto as a starting point from which Labour could build once it had displaced the Tories. After his landslide victory, which gave his party an overall majority of 179 seats, he promised to govern according to the 'New' Labour approach which he had established in opposition. Even he was shocked by the scale of the victory, which strongly suggested that the public was ready for a radical departure from Thatcherite policies. Indeed, an overwhelming parliamentary majority was disagreeable to Blair, because it removed any pretext for reaching a meaningful understanding with the Liberal Democrats. The Blair 'Project', which promised to end a century of division between the opponents of the Conservative Party, was thus extinguished before the planning could move from the secretive stage. Blair was also left with so many MPs that only a fraction could be bought off with government posts. In the short-term, a semblance of party unity was maintained by the system of party discipline which had been established in opposition. From their headquarters in the Millbank Tower along the River Thames from the Palace of Westminster, Labour's 'spin-doctors' did their best to ensure that MPs stayed 'on message'.

Yet there had been several flaws in Blair's attempt to contain public expectations. The most obvious of these was the party's campaign song: 'Things can only get better'. Like so many aspects of the Blair strategy, the idea of an upbeat anthem was stolen from Bill Clinton who had won the US Presidency in 1992 and 1996. But whereas Clinton's song ('Don't Stop' by Fleetwood Mac) had been resolutely forward-looking, 'Things can only get Better' invited the electorate to compare 'New' Labour's performance against the record of the past. 'Sleaze' was an obvious respect in which Blair's Government could have restored public faith which had been shaken by Major's Tories, and after his victory the new Prime Minister made an explicit promise to clean up politics. But within months of the 1997 general election it was revealed that Labour had accepted a million-pound donation from Bernie Ecclestone, a leading figure in motor sport. Ecclestone himself made no pretence of supporting traditional Labour aims and objectives. He did, though, have an interest in the new government's policy towards advertising. When Ecclestone's sport of Formula 1 was exempted from a ban on tobacco advertising , voters drew their own conclusions. Blair's plea that he and his colleagues were 'pretty straight guys' was an early indication of his ability to assume an air of injured innocence, whatever the evidence against him (Cohen, 2003). He extended this cloak of moral invulnerability to his closest allies. Peter Mandelson and David Blunkett were both quickly forgiven and re-appointed after enforced departures from the government. In both cases, the ministers subsequently had to leave again in the face of new allegations. Mandelson's achievement was the more remarkable, since he resigned from the Cabinet twice within the same parliament. Undeterred, Blair subsequently made him an EU Commissioner.

The Ecclestone affair, and Blair's personal intervention on behalf of the ill-fated Millennium Dome, underlined the fact that he and his ministers had no governmental experience; indeed, few of them had more than a distant acquaintance with any significant organisation, apart from the Labour Party itself. It was no surprise that ministers merely tried to copy the techniques which had supposedly brought them success in opposition. Blair himself by-passed the cabinet, taking decisions after private conversations with the relevant ministers. It was widely thought that Labour had been well served by its 'spin-doctors', who tried to ensure that the media always gave positive coverage to Labour's initiatives. Blair's chief media spokesman, Alastair Campbell, was able and loyal. However, he made no attempt to disguise his contempt for most of his former media colleagues, and his status within the government was highly ambiguous. Although he was a political appointee, he was given special dispensation to exercise authority over civil servants. In some quarters, he, rather than John Prescott, was regarded as the real deputy prime minister. While Campbell attracted most of the hostile comment, the government's media service was being revolutionised by an influx of Labour supporters, who were now paid to lavish praise on the party at taxpayers' expense. One of them was sacked after sending an email which described the terrorist attack on New York as an opportunity 'to bury bad news'.

Despite these problems, the new government continued to win high approval ratings. In large part, this was a mirror-image of the 1980s, when the popularity of the Conservatives had been exaggerated by the lack of a realistic alternative. However, there were some positive achievements. In one of its first decisions, the government gave authority over interest-rates to a committee of the Bank of England. This move was widely welcomed, since it reduced the temptation for ministers to manipulate the economy for electoral advantage. The government also introduced a minimum wage, although the level fell a long way short of trade union demands. There was a 'New Deal' for the unemployed, as part of the government's drive to lift people out of welfare dependency and into work. Changes to the benefits system were designed to help low paid workers with children. Although there was little chance that Labour could abolish child poverty entirely — as it rather rashly promised to do — the government did make significant progress in this area.

These reforms had one common factor. They were all championed by Gordon Brown, rather than Blair. This reflected the 'deal' struck in 1994 between the government's leading figures. Recent Labour Chancellors had tended to be unpopular, often shielding the prime minister from blame after enforced decisions. Harold Wilson had wanted to reduce the power of the Treasury, believing that it acted as a brake on economic growth. Under Blair and Brown, this situation was transformed. If anything, tension between the Downing Street neighbours was greater than ever before. But this Chancellor enjoyed strong support among backbenchers, while the prime minister was regarded with suspicion. Their respective supporters regularly briefed the media when friction arose. For example, Blair was keen to press ahead with membership of the European single currency. But Brown was far more sceptical, and since this issue clearly fell within his remit as Chancellor his judgement prevailed.

The frequent reports of difficulties at the top gave rise to media talk of a split between 'Blairites' and 'Brownites'. This battle was often presented as an ideological division, with Blair's allies struggling to preserve the 'New Labour' reforms, while Brown was supposedly more sympathetic to 'Old Labour'. The 'New' and 'Old' Labour tags did make some sense, although they were too simplistic. Since the term encompassed everyone within the party who opposed 'modernisation', 'Old' Labour embraced the social democrat Roy Hattersley as well as people who considered themselves to be socialists, like Tony Benn. As we have seen, 'New' Labour was difficult to categorise ideologically; but since it was neither social democratic nor socialist, it could not be included within any distinctive Labour Party tradition prior to 1994.

From this perspective, there would be a case for saying that the split between Blair and Brown had an ideological element. Certain aspects of Brown's policy as Chancellor can be squared with the social democratic tradition. Significantly, before the 2001 general election Blair said that he was content with the widening gap between the rich and the poor. It is unlikely that Brown would have made such a comment. However, on the key subject of public sector reform there has been no suggestion of a disagreement between Blair and Brown. Initially Brown insisted that ministers should not exceed the spending limits established by the Conservatives before 1997. This was carrying Brown's much-vaunted 'prudence' to masochistic levels, since the Conservatives had never seriously intended to stick to their plans. Brown even had to propose cuts in some social benefits in order to honour his spending pledge.

In the year 2000, though, the government was faced with growing public dissatisfaction about the state of public services, and Brown agreed to a relaxation in spending policy.

However, Blair and Brown agreed that increased spending would have to be matched by reforms. Their joint strategy attempted to make public servants behave as if they were operating within a free market, complete with targets, league tables, and 'performance-related' pay. The underlying idea is that public sector workers are just as competitive as their profit-seeking counterparts in the private sphere. To underline this point, Blair and Brown both encouraged private-sector involvement within the public services. The most notorious example of this trend is the Private Finance Initiative (PFI), which Labour inherited from the Conservatives. Under this policy, favoured private-sector firms undertook capital-intensive projects like the building of schools and hospitals. In return, they would enjoy a guaranteed income from the taxpayer, stretching over several decades. In short, the PFI was rather like a welfare state for capitalism; the only difference was that the scope for abuse was much greater, and far less likely to be reported in the tabloid press. The government could also distribute consultancy fees to favoured companies, with rewards far in excess of the work that was done; and it could continue to pour money into private IT companies, even when their products had proved unsatisfactory.

While the 'welfare to work' programme implied that people should truly earn a living rather than accepting meagre state handouts, policies like the PFI distributed enormous sums to incompetent private companies. In both instances, Gordon Brown was the responsible minister. Even on a superficial view, this evidence places Brown amongst the ideological ranks of 'New' Labour; although a social democrat could be happy with his drive to reduce child poverty, his overall strategy was based on a full-hearted acceptance of the profit motive which no social democrat could share. Significantly, Brown was an ardent admirer of life in the United States, where he took his annual holidays. Blair, by contrast, preferred to soak up the sun in countries like Italy and Egypt, whose commitment to democratic ideals was open to serious question.

Iraq

Tony Blair's spin doctors played up his close relationship with the US President Bill Clinton, at least before he was enveloped by scandal. This allowed Blair to argue that the 'Third Way' was sweeping the Western World; after all, Clinton represented the Democrats, who were seen as Labour's ideological allies; and Blair had copied many of his ideas. By contrast, the Republican Ronald Reagan had deliberately humiliated Neil Kinnock before the 1987 general election. It was natural to assume that UK–US relations would cool after the Republican George W Bush won the US Presidential election of 1999. Bush, after all, was a Republican whose approach to foreign affairs was similar to that of the hawkish Reagan.

However, Blair was determined to stay on good terms with the US administration, whoever happened to be in office. This had very serious implications for British foreign policy. New Labour had come to office promising to introduce an 'ethical dimension' to its international role. This phrase was quickly dropped, when critics pointed out that the government had been insufficiently 'ethical' to prohibit the sale of arms to repressive regimes. Nevertheless, Blair was strongly inclined to take a moralistic role in foreign affairs. In 1999 he outlined his view that the international community should, in certain circumstances, intervene in the internal affairs of sovereign states. In accordance with this doctrine, US and UK forces took action to prevent repression of ethnic Albanians in Serbian-controlled Kosovo. Many observers believed that the campaign had been contrary to international law. British troops also saw action in the former UK colony of Sierra Leone, in West Africa.

Since Gordon Brown controlled the key elements of domestic policy, Blair was already pre-disposed towards foreign affairs — a subject in which he had no experience, even from his days in Opposition. After the events of 11 September, 2001, he was the first world leader to visit the United States and offer support for George Bush in the 'war on terror'. His gesture cemented the relationship between the two men, but Blair clearly hoped that he could act as a restraining influence on Bush.

Initially, it seemed that Blair's strategy had been successful, because the US restricted itself to military action against the Taliban regime in Afghanistan, with strong international backing. However, elements within the Bush administration had much more ambitious plans. Some even dreamed of intervention in the Middle East which would trigger off a series of popular revolts against authoritarian governments. On this argument, the region could be transformed with minimal bloodshed; and the resulting governments would be pro-American. This would secure US oil supplies, and also guarantee the security of Israel. The first stage of the plan involved the deposition of Iraq's Saddam Hussein, who was accused of running a nuclear weapons programme in defiance of tough United Nations sanctions.

Blair also had an ambitious agenda for the Middle East. But his main goal was to bring an end to the long-running problem of Palestine. Thanks to his persuasive powers, Bush did at least begin to show some constructive interest in this subject. However, the long-standing US friendship towards Israel meant that he was never likely to push very hard for a settlement which favoured the Palestinian people. The death of the Palestinian leader Yasser Arafat in 2004 removed a key obstacle to closer US involvement, but even then it seemed content with an Israeli plan for limited withdrawal from occupied areas.

In the meantime, Blair had agreed to UK participation in the American action against Iraq. This presented him with major domestic difficulties, because while Saddam's regime had few admirers in Britain, Labour MPs were well aware of the attendant risks and many members of the public shared their reservations. The case for intervention could not rest on alleged links between Iraq and the 2001 terrorist atrocities in New York; whatever the state of opinion in the US, Britons knew that Saddam was detested by Islamic fundamentalists. Instead, Blair focused on the threat posed by Iraq's 'weapons of mass destruction'. Saddam was alleged to have built up significant stockpiles of biological and chemical weapons, even if he had yet to secure a nuclear device.

Unfortunately for Blair, the concrete evidence on this subject was thin. Since the weapons were supposed to be hidden, this was not altogether surprising. Even so, it was clear from the outset that the intelligence reports were largely based on the testimony of Iraqis who were opposed to Saddam's regime; and US spy satellites had failed to detect any incriminating activity. Subsequent inquiries proved that the case for war had been bolstered by imaginative presentation, and that Alastair Campbell had been closely involved in the compilation of dossiers which purported to summarise the existing intelligence. However, the first inquiry, conducted by Lord Hutton, gave the government the benefit of any doubt. Instead, Hutton's findings were sharply critical of the BBC, which had broadcast allegations about the way in which intelligence had been distorted.

Blair's authority at home was seriously weakened; and although he was still regarded as a hero by many Americans, his reputation elsewhere was diminished. He had persuaded Bush to appeal for backing from the United Nations, but the international community was generally opposed to the action and the war had to be launched (in March 2003) without a conclusive endorsement. In Britain, a march through London in the month before the war attracted a million protestors. Robin Cook, the leader of the House of Commons and former foreign secretary, resigned from the Cabinet; he was later followed by Clare Short. These dissenting opinions were registered when most people assumed that UK involvement in combat would be relatively brief, and that Saddam was sure to be toppled. It soon became clear that the removal of the dictatorship was only the beginning of the campaign in Iraq, as various 'insurgents' waged war against the occupying forces. Thousands of ordinary Iraqis were also killed, as terrorists tried to provoke a civil war. Despite remarkable turnouts in a series of elections, it remained unclear whether the intervention would produce a peaceful, democratic Iraq even in the long term. The more likely outcome was the break-up of the nation.

Blair and Thatcherism

As well as reducing its popularity, the Iraq war had a marked effect on the government's domestic policy agenda. It had come into office promising to boost civil liberties. It incorporated the European Convention on Human Rights into UK law, and introduced (limited) legislation on Freedom of Information. However, the 'war on terror' provoked a radical rethink. Even before 9/11, the government had introduced legislation which contravened some aspects of the Human Rights Act. Afterwards, it extended the time-limit for detention of terrorist suspects without trial, and pressed forward with proposals for a system of identity cards.

Blair argued passionately in support of these measures; as well as dominating foreign policy, at times he seemed to be acting as his own Home Secretary. He was sincere in his desire to protect British citizens, and in the wake of the bombings on the London underground in July 2005 it was clear that new measures were needed. However, no-one could seriously doubt that the war on Iraq had made an attack in Britain more likely. Also, when Blair argued that he would never forgive himself if he failed to take the necessary actions to thwart a major atrocity, it seemed that he attached more importance to his own peace of mind than to civil rights which had been safeguarded for centuries.

A year before the bombings of July 2005, Blair had revealed the extent of his 'conversion' on civil liberties. Outlining a new five-year plan to reduce crime, he claimed that the social liberalism of the 1960s had gone too far. Although there had been important reforms, the overall effect had been to undermine respect for authority, and a decline in morality. Too many people had forgotten that rights imply responsibilities. In future, policy on law and order would be dictated by the preferences of the 'law-abiding majority'.

Blair had obviously come a long way since he spoke of being 'tough on crime, tough on the causes of crime'. Many of his new policies, especially those which targeted 'anti-social behaviour', were highly popular. But the nature of his remarks suggested something more than pre-election populism. It was possible to argue that he had at last found a settled ideological identity. Margaret Thatcher had believed in 'the free economy and the strong state'. On this view,governments should leave law-abiding citizens to enrich themselves; but the forces of law and order and of national security should be strong enough to repel foreign threats and to control unruly elements at home. Many commentators had argued that this made 'Thatcherism' a contradictory mixture of economic liberalism and social conservatism. But this interpretation was based on the mistaken assumption that liberals are invariably soft on crime. The classical variant of liberalism, in fact, depends on the rigorous punishment of individuals who threaten the operations of the free market. There is, of course, scope for the rehabilitation of such offenders, in the hope that they could become more 'rational' and join the ranks of the law-abiding majority. But no classical liberal can launch a sustained attack on the *causes* of crime. To do so would involve a massive redistribution of wealth, to reduce social inequalities. Whatever he had felt in the past, by 2004 Blair's ambitions in this sphere were limited to the reduction of *absolute* poverty; hence his admission before the 2001 general election that he was perfectly happy to have presided over a widening gap between the rich and poor. As Mrs Thatcher had found, it was much more simplistic to blame social disorder on well-meaning social reformers of previous decades. The problem, of course, was that the reforms of the 1960s were heavily influenced by rising living standards, which led to demands for greater freedom. Thus the Thatcher/Blair position was actually an unconscious critique of the very affluence that both politicians promoted.

It was therefore a sure instinct which had led Lady Thatcher to hail Tony Blair as a worthy successor. However, if by 2004 Blair himself had become a Thatcherite in the classical liberal tradition, the vast majority of his parliamentary party still had very different ideas. Labour had won the 2001 general election with a majority of 166. But the turnout was below 60% for the first time since Britain became a full democracy, and Labour attracted fewer votes than it had done in the supposedly disastrous 1992 contest. Despite its dominant parliamentary position, towards the end of the 2001–5 parliament the government could no longer feel secure. There were massive rebellions on Iraq and on the introduction of student tuition fees (which was a clear breach of an election promise).

Before the 2005 general election, Blair took the unprecedented step of announcing that he would step down before the end of the next parliament. On one hand, this gave his critics a glimpse of light at the end of the tunnel, giving them less reason to speak out during the campaign itself. The result of the election left Blair looking even more of a 'lame duck', since Labour's majority was cut to just 66. The party's vote-share fell to just 36 per cent, making any talk of a popular 'mandate' for its policy programme even more bogus than usual. However, Blair was now impatient to leave some kind of constructive legacy, setting him on a collision course with emboldened backbenchers. The list of habitual rebels now extended far beyond the usual 'Old Labour' suspects, and included several ex-ministers who had given loyal support in happier times.

Many of Blair's critics continued to hope for a dramatic change of direction once Gordon Brown stepped into his shoes. However, Brown made it clear that he supported Blair's new programme of public sector reform. In Opposition, New Labour had denounced Conservative policies on health and education, which were based on the idea of competition between providers in a pseudo-market environment. In Blair's first term, these measures had been scrapped. It now appeared that Blair regretted this, because his proposals were closely comparable and were based on the same ideas about human nature. If in doubt, the free market was always to be preferred to state direction, because competition forced people to maximise the efficiency of service provision. Consumers of these essential services would not be charged directly. But there were indirect costs, especially in the education system where concerned parents felt constrained to purchase properties in the catchment areas of the best-performing schools. Before 1997, it was well known that the middle classes drew disproportionate benefits from the welfare state, since they had the knowledge and incentive to take full advantage of their entitlements. Blair's reforms were designed to increase consumer 'choice'; as such, their main effect would be to reward the middle class for switching from the Conservatives to New Labour. Of course, the middle class had greatly expanded since 1979. Presumably this was what Blair had meant when he spoke of giving power to the many, not the few.

Blair did have some achievements to his credit. In particular, he worked hard to build on John Major's peacemaking efforts in Northern Ireland, although he spoiled the effect by talking about 'the hand of history' when the deal of April 1998 had been struck. The new devolved institutions subsequently had to be suspended, but this time there was no return to violence.

Sympathetic observers might argue that Blair's real legacy lies in his constitutional reforms. However, his record in this sphere was patchy at best. Scotland and Wales achieved varying degrees of home rule, and London was given a new assembly with a directly-elected mayor. Yet Blair was reluctant to lose his direct influence over these institutions. He tried to impose his own candidate as first minister in Wales, and worked hard to prevent Ken Livingstone from winning the first mayoral election. The worst blot on his constitutional record, though, concerned the House of Lords. Initially Blair had hoped to remove all of the hereditary peers, who allegedly had no place in a 'meritocratic' society. A subsequent compromise allowed 92 hereditaries to remain for a transitional period. But the 'transition' proved to be greatly prolonged, thanks largely to Blair who wanted to retain a wholly-appointed second chamber in spite of increasing cross-party demands for a significant elected component. Attempts to construct a series of assemblies based on English regions encountered public opposition, and the scheme was abandoned.

Blair could not even share Mrs Thatcher's consolation, of having helped to change the policies and outlook of the main opposition party. Mrs Thatcher had been a vehement ideological opponent of socialism, and although her personal definition of that word was eccentric, she did recognise and welcome the fact that Labour had moved towards her position. Blair was equally cavalier in his use of ideological terms. In 1999, for example, he branded everyone who opposed his reforms, for whatever reason, as 'the forces of conservatism'. It was clear that this was the most insulting word in his vocabulary. In contrast to Mrs Thatcher's attitude towards Labour, Blair apparently hated the Conservative Party as an institution, and hoped to destroy it rather than forcing it to adopt 'stakeholding', or 'the third way', or whatever phrase was currently in vogue. This evidence of 'tribal' emotion was difficult to explain. Did it have something to do with the fact that his father had been a Conservative? But it was just as likely to have been yet another tactical ruse. After all, hatred of the Conservatives was one of the few themes that the Prime Minister could exploit to rally the dwindling and disorientated members of his own party.

Conclusion: a new consensus?

As the major parties prepared for the 1997 general election, an unfamiliar word crept back into political analysis. Was it possible that the ideological strife of the previous twenty years, both between and within parties, had subsided into a new form of consensus? The leaders of both main parties agreed that private enterprise was superior to state intervention in the economy; that low inflation should take priority over full employment; and that public services of adequate quality had to be delivered without raising direct taxation. Since Tony Blair's time as shadow Home Secretary, Labour and the Conservatives had competed over law and order. Although there were important differences in their approach to sentencing at that time, both parties wanted a larger and more visible police force. With differing degrees of success, they tried to sprinkle the rhetoric of compassion over the policies of unrelenting competition.

There were, of course, differences of emphasis over issues such as the regulation of privatised utilities, constitutional reform, and the minimum wage. However, by this time scholars had begun to question the original notion of a post-war 'consensus'. According to the late Ben Pimlott, for example, the idea that the parties had once agreed on the broad framework of policy was a myth. According to Pimlott, significant disagreement over fundamentals had remained, despite the appearance of unanimity on the substance of policy (Pimlott, 1988).

The argument of the present book supports Pimlott in so far as it shows that ideological disagreement did not cease in the years before 1979, when Mrs Thatcher came to office with the explicit intention of destroying the 'consensus'. Yet the vast majority of MPs within all three major parties were able to support similar policies, even if they did so for different reasons. It is unrealistic to confuse 'consensus' with complete agreement: after all, as Stalin once said, unanimity can be achieved only in a graveyard. On this reading, Pimlott's analysis is overstated, although it has provoked a valuable debate. If the existence of a consensus means that a new government will not initiate radical changes in the framework of policies and institutions left by its predecessor, the signs are that we have indeed entered a new age of consensus, and that the changes brought about during the Thatcher years will be lasting ones. On current trends, indeed, the new consensus differs from its predecessor because it comes closer to disproving Stalin's quip. Between 1945 and 1979 many politicians accepted institutions like the NHS because it was possible to justify free medical treatment from a variety of ideological standpoints. Since 1997, by contrast, there has been a tendency for party leaders to exaggerate differences over the details of policy because their underlying principles are increasingly similar.

Perhaps the most interesting aspect of this new consensus is the fact that it has yet to achieve the kind of public support once enjoyed by the post-war settlement. Indeed, long before the end of the period of Conservative government it was clear that pre-Thatcherite views commanded greater public loyalty (Taylor-Gooby, 1991). Tony Blair defended the changes in Labour's philosophy by arguing that during the 1980s his party 'lost touch' (Blair, 1995). Actually, the evidence for voters' preferences from those years shows that they regarded the Conservatives and Labour as equally distant from their own thinking (Heath et al., 1991, 217). Yet the changes were supposedly inspired by the Labour leadership's perception of electoral necessity. The reasoning was that even modest promises lost votes in 1992, and the blurring of substantive differences with the Conservatives would guarantee Labour against press attacks. In the mean time, as one commentator observed, Blair's position took the support of non-Conservatives 'pretty much for granted' (Young, 1995). It was calculated that traditional Labour supporters would either hold their noses and vote for the 'modernised' party, or (more likely) abstain. As late as 2005, after 8 years of 'Blairism', this assumption seemed to be verified. Despite taking a stance on the Iraq war which appealed to Labour voters, the Liberal Democrats still found it difficult to make progress in marginal seats held by the government.

Labour's current leadership claims that its policies reflect a mood of 'realism' within the party. This is a word which students of politics should treat with extreme caution. The interpretation of political 'reality' depends upon the values of the observer. Some people will always try to prove that apparent acceptance of the status quo really masks a yearning for radical change; others will demonstrate that acquiescence in reform is merely a sign that the public is desperate for a period of calm. 'Reality', for New Labour, is defined by its experience between 1979 and 1992. During this period ambitious people within the middle-class professions learned to act like Thatcherites in the workplace, even if their dinner-party talk still included token references to social justice. They came to accept that although compassion makes friends, competition makes the world go round. These individuals remain a small minority of the electorate, but their voices are louder than the rest. They are the kind of people who dominate the thinking of New Labour strategists like Philip Gould, because they tend to be 'floating voters' (Gould, 1998). Despite the overwhelming majorities of 1997 and 2001, New Labour continued to be obsessed with the perceived needs of this small fraction of the community. The only reasonable conclusion is that the people in control of the party identified with the floating voters, and shared their acquisitive outlook on life. This suggestion is supported by the steady stream of financial scandals which affected New Labour. Even when ministers were forced to resign, they invariably claimed that they had done nothing wrong; and Blair himself seemed to think that dubious deals were compatible with rectitude in public life.

Despite the similarities between Tony Blair's early thinking and the key tenets of the Christian Democratic tradition, for most of his time as Prime Minister he is best understood as an ideological follower of Margaret Thatcher. That is, for all his talk of 'community', his ideas on domestic policy were inspired by the hope of satisfying the perceived requirements of rational, self-interested individuals. Blair's 2004 attack on the social reforms of the 1960s revealed that his 'conversion' to classical liberalism was sincere. As a direct appeal to Thatcherites, it threatened to alienate any traditional Labour supporters who had remained loyal despite the war on Iraq. When a politician like Blair takes an electoral risk, it is safe to assume that the sentiments are genuine.

Any suggestion that Gordon Brown will discard classical liberalism seem misplaced; his most vocal support for Blair has been reserved for those policies which Lady Thatcher would also have applauded. If anything, Brown's ideological odyssey has been even more dramatic than Blair's; almost every page of his emotive 1989 attack on Thatcherism (*Where there is Greed*) now seems like a far-sighted satire on 'New' Labour . If the key elements of the welfare state survive a Brown premiership, it will only be because the voters indicate that they want to hang on to the empty shell of post-war policy, even if the substance has long departed.

Such is the dominance of leaders like Blair and Brown that dissent within the Labour Party is likely to be contained, regardless of provocation. This prediction can be made with greater confidence since even the Liberal Democrats seem to be embracing classical liberalism. This is yet another irony, since the party has an obvious interest in presenting a distinctive programme. However, Liberal Democrats are very conscious of opinion among floating voters, which lends superficial plausibility to a strategy which brings them closer to their competitors who have targeted the same audience.

Under William Hague, Iain Duncan Smith and Michael Howard, the Conservatives tried to find 'clear blue water' to distinguish them from 'New' Labour. With the election of David Cameron, it seems that these attempts have come to an end. Cameron's argument assumes that the battle for the free market has already been won, and that it is now time for Conservatives to focus on issues which they had previously neglected. This strategy implies an attempt to beat 'New' Labour at its own game, rather than any radical ideological departure. In copying 'New' Labour, the Conservatives under Cameron are merely imitating a more voter-friendly variant of their own Thatcherite inheritance.

List of works cited

Blair, Tony (1995), 'Left with No Option', *Guardian*, 27 July.

Cohen, Nick (2003), *Pretty Straight Guys*, Faber and Faber.

Gould, Bryan (1995), *Goodbye to All That*, Macmillan.

Gould, Philip (1998), *The Unfinished Revolution: How the modernisers saved the Labour Party*, Little, Brown.

Heath, Anthony, Evans, Geoff, Field, Julia, and Witherspoon, Sharon (1991) *Understanding Political Change: The British Voter 1964-1987*, Pergamon.

Minkin, Lewis (1992), *Contentious Alliance: Trade Unions and the Labour Party*, Edinburgh University Press.

Pimlott, Ben (1988), 'The Myth of Consensus', in L. M. Smith (ed.) *The Making of Britain: Echoes of Greatness*, Macmillan.

Taylor-Gooby, Peter (1991), 'Attachment to the Welfare State', in
    Roger Jowell, Lindsay Brook and Bridget Taylor (eds) *British Social
    Attitudes: The 8ᵗʰ Report*, Dartmouth.
White, Michael (1994), 'So Far, So Good', *Guardian*, 27 December.
Young, Hugo (1995) 'Voters want to hear the painful truth', *Guardian*,
    27 July.

Selected further reading (see also Chapter 8)

Although there have been several biographical studies of leading
'New' Labour figures, Andy McSmith's *Faces of Labour: The Inside
Story* (Verso, 1996) includes several balanced pen-portraits. The
same author's biography of John Smith (Verso, 1993) makes poi-
gnant reading in the light of ensuing events. Andrew Rawnsley's
Servants of the People: The Inside Story of New Labour (Hamish Hamilton, 2000) quickly established itself as the standard overview.
Philip Gould's *Unfinished Revolution; How the modernizers saved the
Labour Party* (Little, Brown, 1998), is an unflinching account of the
party's pursuit of power. Peter Mandelson and Roger Liddle's *The
Blair Revolution* (Faber and Faber, 1996) indicated that Blair would
only be a 'revolutionary' in his determination to disappoint the
hopes of Labour activists; *The Blair Revolution Revisited* (Politico's,
2004) updated the story. Mark Perryman (ed), *The Blair Agenda*
(Lawrence and Wishart, 1996) was a more balanced prospectus,
and its chapters provide a good basis for a critique of 'New'
Labour in office.

The record since 1997 has been appraised in several good books,
notably Steven Driver and Luke Martell, *Blair's Britain* (Polity,
2002); Colin Hay, *The Political Economy of New Labour: Labouring
under False Pretences* (Manchester University Press, 1999); and
Richard Heffernan, *New Labour and Thatcherism* (Palgrave, 2001).
From a less critical perspective, Polly Toynbee and David Walker
have assessed the evidence in *Did Things Get Better? An Audit of
New Labour's Successes and Failures* (Penguin, 2001). This survey
can be contrasted with David Beetham, Iain Byrne, Pauline Ngan
and Stuart Weir (eds), *Democracy under Blair: A Democratic Audit of
the United Kingdom* (Politico's, 2002). The assessment delivered by
this book is the more damning since it was completed before
'New' Labour plunged headlong into authoritarianism in the
wake of the Iraq war.

On Blair's ideology, the most notorious contributions are from
Anthony Giddens (*The Third Way: The Renewal of Social Democracy*,
Polity, 1998, and *The Third Way and its Critics*, Polity, 2000). Amitai
Etzioni's *The Spirit of Community* (Crown Publishing, 1993) is still

worth reading by anyone interested in the distance between 'New' Labour's performance and the ideas of its supposed gurus.

On the effect of globalisation on political ideology in Britain and elsewhere, see Will Hutton, *The World We're In* (Little, Brown, 2002). The current hegemony of liberalism is explored in Mark Garnett, *The Snake that Swallowed its Tail: Some Contradictions in Modern liberalism* (Imprint Academic, 2004).

CHAPTER 9

Pressure Groups and the Rise of Apathy

So far the discussion has concentrated on political principles which have been advocated by members of the most
significant UK parties, with particular emphasis on ideas
which underlie manifesto pledges and government policies. In 1951, when Labour and the Conservatives shared
almost 97 per cent of the public vote, it was possible to provide a satisfactory account of political ideas in the UK without mentioning any developments outside the two main
parties. Since February 1974, support for these parties has
only climbed above 80 per cent on one occasion, and a much
broader view of the political scene is now essential.

Over the years since 1970 it has become increasingly
apparent that the UK parliamentary system is failing to
cater for the range of ideas expressed by various groups in
society. Like most political phenomena, the resulting disillusionment resists simplistic quantitative analysis. For
example, it is often claimed that the electorate has become
more 'volatile' thanks to the declining influence of class, but
the evidence for this is inconclusive (Heath *et al.*, 1991,
10-31). One complication is that lying to opinion pollsters
became a popular national pastime after 1987 (Crewe,
1992). If people are prepared to lie about their voting intentions before a general election, they might be equally cynical when reporting their attitudes to political participation.

However, the message of some statistics is unmistakable.
The first edition of this book appeared after the 1992 general
election, in which turnout was a respectable 77.7 per cent.

At that time, the author criticised an argument advanced by the late Henry Drucker, that 'it is difficult to believe that highly disaffected people would bring themselves to vote for any party' (Drucker, 1979, 8). But the habit of voting, once acquired, dies hard. It was suggested in the first edition that Britain was experiencing a trend towards '"apathetic participation" — voting which is motivated by a feeling that one ought to take part in a national ritual, rather than any idealism about party politics. The Grand National or the Derby provide parallel examples; many people feel that they should follow the tradition of "having a flutter" on [the outcome] of these events, but this does not prove that they are very interested in horse-racing' (Garnett, 1996, 162).

This remark was supported by the evidence of the 2005 general election, when turnout subsided to 71.5 per cent. As those who had acquired the voting habit shuffled off to the polling booth in the sky, they were not being replaced. This phenomenon was partly the product of social developments, but also reflected the fact that the leading parties were targeting their appeal on a smaller section of the UK electorate. The most dramatic change lay ahead. In 2001, turnout was 59.4 per cent. This lamentable statistic showed that Britain's politicians were failing; while they imposed league tables of performance on hard-working professionals in the public service, they had achieved a new record for consumer dissatisfaction without incurring any financial penalties. In 2005 turnout improved slightly, but only because the government resorted to a series of gimmicks in order to bolster the figures. Postal voting, which had previously been restricted to people who actually expected to be away from their constituencies, was now made available to everyone. In short, New Labour pulled out all the stops to win the participation of apathetic voters; and in that context the results were deeply unimpressive.

In the first edition of this book, declining turnout was predicted because Labour and the Conservatives had established a new consensus on the basis of principles which can only appeal to a minority of the population. In other words, the *ideological nature* of the new consensus was the problem.

After all, even in 1959, when the old consensus was at its height, almost 80 per cent of voters took the trouble to register a preference. On reflection, the hegemony of classical liberalism can still be identified as the main culprit. Appeals to self-interested individualism might have a genuine attraction for floating voters, but there is good reason to believe that an exclusive focus on their perceived demands leaves the rest of the electorate out in the cold. Between 1974 and 1986, the proportion of British people who thought that they had no chance of influencing government policy jumped by 10 per cent (Topf, 1989). This finding probably reflects developments such as UK membership of the European Community, and Labour's problems with the IMF. But there is also a good chance that much of the alienation arose from thwarted antagonism towards Thatcherism, which owed its electoral success to the fact that the opposition parties were divided.

Since 1979, the membership of the main political parties has dwindled even more dramatically than electoral turnout. Despite concerted efforts to bring in new recruits, by 2006 both Labour and the Conservatives had around 200,000 active members. As recently as 1970, Conservative membership had been estimated at around 1.5 million. Changes in the link between Labour and the trade unions made comparisons more complicated, but although recruitment picked up after Blair became leader the party was soon heading back on a downward trend. These developments suggest that the eras of mass parties have come to an end, leading to the dominance of London-based cliques who try to gain support *via* the electronic media and telephone canvassers who concentrate their attention on individuals who are presumed to be 'key voters' in the few seats that might change hands at a general election. According to Keith Sutherland, 'The political party is an anachronism. It serves no useful purpose and we are better off without it' (Sutherland, 2004, 21).

In view of the decline of political parties and electoral participation, no survey of ideology in the UK would be complete without some reference to pressure groups, which provide an alternative outlet for people who want to change the world in their different ways. Traditionally, pressure groups have been distinguished from political parties because they do not contest elections. In recent years, though, this distinction has become more blurred. Pressure groups thrive on publicity; and standing for election often provides an excellent opportunity for media exposure. In the general election of 2001, for example, Dr Richard Taylor was elected to represent Wyre Forest after running a campaign to save a local hospital. Dr Taylor won again in 2005, providing an auspicious precedent for candidates who based their appeal on a specific issue. The former BBC correspondent Martin Bell was also elected in 2001, on an 'anti-sleaze' platform. Another independent victor in 2005 was George Galloway, who won in Bethnal Green and Bow after being expelled by Labour because of his vocal opposition to the war on Iraq. But the most spectacular result of the 2005 general election was caused by the Labour Party's imposition of an uncongenial candidate. Peter Law won the seat of Blaenau Gwent as an independent, having decided to stand in protest against Labour's use of an all-woman shortlist. Ironically, the protest vote which brought Law to Westminster was itself partly a reaction against feminism, one of the most effective protest movements of the post-war period.

In 2001 Tony Benn brought an end to a career in parliament which had begun more than five decades earlier. However, he announced that he was leaving the Commons in order 'to go into politics', suggesting that the real action now lay elsewhere. The principles and movements briefly examined here are feminism, the Campaign for Nuclear Disarmament and environmental movements (with particular emphasis on the animal rights movement). Obviously those who support these causes have had contrasting fortunes since 1970, and it can be argued that all of them have some keen supporters at Westminster. The broad factor which connects them is that some of their members have resorted to extra-parliamentary action, often provoked by a feeling that the urgency of their views was not sufficiently conveyed by other means.

Feminism

The first national conference of the Women's Liberation Movement (WLM) was held in 1970. The movement was inspired in part by civil rights activism during the 1960s, and coincided with the publication of notable feminist writings such as Germaine Greer's The Female Eunuch (1970). This new feminist impetus seemed to produce results very quickly; 1970 saw the passage of the Equal Pay Act, which promised to end the exploitation of women in the workplace, and the Matrimonial Proceedings and Property Act, which recognised that a woman's work in the home entitled her to a share of the family property if a marriage broke up; provisions also protected women from domestic violence. The Sex Discrimination Act of 1976 was designed to ensure that women were not at a disadvantage when they applied for jobs or training. Fifty years after women had secured full democratic rights, it seemed as if the barriers to economic equality would also be removed.

This picture quickly proved to be over-optimistic. For example, the terms of the Equal Pay Act could easily be evaded by employers who wrote special job-descriptions for women's jobs. The delay in implementing the Act provided a useful opportunity to discover loop-holes. Whatever the intentions of legislators, the figures verified the claim that 'we have an Equal Pay Act but we don't have equal pay' (Coote and Gill, 1974, 21). By 1981 the average gross weekly earnings of women were about half those of men. In part-time occupations women already outnumbered men by almost ten to one — a trend that would continue during the Thatcher years (Wainwright, 1984, 211, 204). Workers in these jobs had never enjoyed much protection from trade unions, and the Thatcherite attack on the unions left women employees even more vulnerable. The Sex Discrimination legislation seems to have been fairly successful, at least to the extent of changing reported attitudes about women at work. In part, however, this evidence has been influenced by the decline in the old manual occupations. By 1984, for example, 89 per cent of respondents to a survey thought that women and men were equally suited to computer programming, and only 39 per cent thought that managing a bank was more suitable for a man. Between 1980 and 1984 the percentage of respondents who thought that 'a wife's job is to look after the home and family' dropped from 46 to 32 per cent (Witherspoon, 1985, 76-8). Yet there remained a suspicion that successful women in business and politics were the exception not the rule, and those who fulfilled their ambitions—like Mrs Thatcher herself—seemed to have done so by taking on the characteristics of men. Meanwhile, women were still grossly underrepresented even in supposedly 'enlightened' professions such as academia.

It is often remarked that Mrs Thatcher did very little for the cause of women. Although her rhetoric about traditional family life was never followed up with concerted action, she also failed to improve child care, which would have made life easier for working mothers. In fact, her determined assault on local government often meant that existing facilities deteriorated. The effect of Thatcherite policies did not end there; between April 1979 and April 1990, the Conservative government cut the real value of child benefit by 21 per cent, having frozen it from 1988 (Gilmour, 1992, 158). Under Mrs Thatcher, ministers also noticed the attractions of making single mothers the scapegoat for social evils, even though at least one of the Prime Minister's closest supporters had contributed to the problem himself.

Overall, the feminist movement stalled during the Thatcher years. In one respect it was a victim of its own partial success; the legislation of the 1970s made many people feel that women had already achieved equality. This contributed to the negative public perception of those feminists who pointed out that more needed to be done. However, this image problem was at least partly attributable to differences within the women's movement. Three broad strands of feminism have been identified. Liberal feminists demand equality of rights; socialist feminists interpret gender issues within the context of class; while radical feminists celebrate the difference between men and women, and attack a 'patriarchal' society in which men are natural aggressors (Vincent, 1995, 172–207). During the 1980s black feminists added a distinctive and urgent voice to the debate, and women's participation in anti-nuclear protests illustrated the growing attraction of 'ecofeminism', which emphasised the intimate relationship between women and the environment. This diversity gives rise to questions about the ideological nature of feminism. Only the radical version seems to be a distinctive ideology in itself, since a fully consistent liberal who believes in complete equality of opportunity would inevitably support the demands of liberal feminism. The same could be said for thorough-going socialists, who logically should demand liberation for women, but would doubt that this could be achieved in a capitalist society. Liberal and socialist feminists, then, are liberals and socialists of either sex who place special emphasis on women's issues. However, radical feminists, who believe that male aggression is inevitable and advocate segregation as a result, have a world-view which cannot be squared with any other ideology.

This interpretation is only a sketch, but it suggests why unity of purpose among all these groups was never likely. In particular, once demands began to be satisfied tension was inevitable between liberal feminists (who are often accused of concentrating on the needs of middle-class women) and others whose priorities had not been met by the legislation of the 1970s. These strains came to a head at the 1978 WLM conference (Lovenduski and Randall, 1993, 360). Unhelpfully, the media gave most prominence to radical feminists, whose ideas could be used to inflame popular prejudices. This group suffered the most open attack from government policies, particularly Section 28 of the Local Government Act 1988, which outlawed the promotion of homosexuality by local authorities.

Some sections of the media had a commercial interest in arousing public hostility towards feminists. In 1986 the Labour MP Clare Short attempted to ban the use of 'Page Three' pin-ups in newspapers. During her speech on a ten-minute rule Bill she was subjected to childish heckling by

Conservative MPs; one, Robert Adey, declared that the Bill 'deserves the booby prize' (Short, 1986). It is difficult to imagine that parliamentarians of the 1970s, when the image of feminism was more positive, would have indulged in this kind of exhibition. Short's campaign highlighted the continuing exploitation of women during the Thatcher decade; indeed, the introduction of the Daily Sport newspaper meant that standards in the press sank even lower, while television, advertising and the film industry gladly exploited the new relaxations. The anti-pornography movement drove a further wedge between feminist groups, as liberal opponents of censorship began to claim that in some cases the sex industry actually enhanced the power of women. While such abuses continued, however, it was difficult to see how men could regard women as equals at home or in the workplace. Perpetrators of domestic violence were also unmoved by the legislative protection of women in 1976, and refuges for battered partners became more common. Cases like that of Sara Thornton, who was convicted of murder after killing her violent husband, illustrated the inherent sexism of the legal system. During one week in 1980, two women who murdered a barbaric father were sent to jail for three years, while the killer of a so-called 'nagging wife' escaped with two years' probation (Sebestyen, 1985, 95).

By the early 1990s the prospects for feminism looked ambivalent. There were some important gains to set against recent reverses; notably, Labour and the Liberal Democrats both promised a ministry for women, and Labour accepted that more women candidates should be chosen in safe seats. This example of positive discrimination was controversial, yet something clearly needed to be done; after the 1992 election women still only accounted for one-tenth of the House of Commons (Lovenduski et al., 1994, 626). After an interesting and occasionally bitter debate, the Anglican church finally accepted that God could speak through both sexes, and allowed the ordination of women. Bizarrely, this helped to provoke one female member of the government into becoming a Catholic. UK society might have become a poor copy of the USA in most respects during the 1980s, but at least MPs refused to succumb to US-style hysteria about abortion, and women's rights over their bodies were secured by the failure of the Alton Bill in 1988. The fight against this measure brought many women's groups together again, but it is telling that their defensive purpose was very different from the radical days of the late 1960s and early 1970s.

Of course, an essentially defensive campaign could bring positive results, and some could draw comfort from similar movements during the 1980s. For instance, the miners' strike of 1984–85 could not have been sustained for so long without the dynamism infused by numerous women's support groups (Lovenduski and Randall, 1993, 122–5). The Greenham protest against the introduction of cruise missiles to the UK was probably the most-publicised campaign of the decade, however. Beginning with a march in August 1981, the women's peace camp at Greenham was a remarkable example of political commitment in the face of discomfort and intimidation. If it also proved easy for sections of the media to distort the nature of the camp (particularly over the decision to exclude men) this was hardly the fault of the protesters, who at least had taken action while others acquiesced in an astonishing policy. The same newspapers which thundered against the infringement of sovereignty represented by membership of the EC were quite happy for nearly one hundred cruise missiles to be deployed at Greenham, even though the weapons would remain under US control (Campbell, 1986, 259–60, 297–338). World developments might have played a greater role in removing the missiles than the civil disobedience of the Greenham women, but this example of principled protest for a moral purpose was a notable reminder that a healthy democracy cannot survive if it depends entirely on the ballot box.

Twenty-five years after the start of the Greenham protest, the public image of feminism was very different. The 2005 general election produced a record 128 women MPs (including 98 for Labour, 17 Conservatives and 10 Liberal Democrats). There were 6 women in the new cabinet.

Women still did not enjoy equal opportunities to rise to the top of their professions, and pay differentials remained. Rape, and violence against women in the home, were still under-reported. But there had undoubtedly been a significant advance in all of these respects since 1970.

The nature of the changes, though, underlined the diversity of feminist thought. While liberal feminists could be generally pleased by recent developments, there were few crumbs of comfort for their socialist counterparts. Women were now accepted as equal competitors with men in the work-place, and as consumers they shared in the expansion of choice in the free market economy. They could also exercise more choice in their relationships, thanks to changes in the divorce laws. However, they continued to be exploited in various ways. But even people who called themselves 'feminists' now tended to defend non-violent pornography, on the grounds that women could use their bodies as economic assets so long as the decision arose from an unconstrained choice. It was commonly argued that women were 'empowered' by such activities as lap-dancing. For socialists, of course, such attitudes remained abhorrent. However, such dissident voices were rarely heard. By 2006, it was reasonable to characterise most attitudes towards the status of women as 'post-feminist'. For liberals, the phrase could mean that all the initial demands of the movement had either been met, or were close to being realised. For others, it meant that liberal feminism had been exposed as a sham.

The Campaign for Nuclear Disarmament

The Greenham protest was just the most publicised episode during the revival of an anti-nuclear movement which had first emerged in the 1950s (Taylor, 1970). The Campaign for Nuclear Disarmament re-emerged from obscurity in 1980 after the coincidence of several worrying developments. The Soviet Union invaded Afghanistan in late 1979, soon after the election of the fiercely anti-communist Margaret Thatcher. At the same time, plans to install cruise missiles in

Europe were announced, supposedly in response to the development of the Soviet SS-20 missile. On 22 June 1980 the veteran campaigner and new Labour leader Michael Foot joined a major CND demonstration through London (Jones, 1994, 443). Labour might be in opposition, but at least CND could be sure of principled support from its leadership for the first time; after all, it had been a Labour administration which secretly decided that the UK should be a nuclear power.

By 1986, CND membership was estimated at around 60,000 (Byrne, 1988, 55). The true figure probably exceeded 100,000, when local groups are included. This was even more impressive given that the Labour Party (along with the nationalists and the Greens) were also committed to unilateral disarmament at the time. The growth of the movement caused alarm within the Conservative government, and a propaganda war intensified after Michael Heseltine became Secretary of State for Defence early in 1983. The government's argument was that nuclear weapons had maintained peace in Europe since 1945; only the retention of the most advanced nuclear technology would continue to deter potential aggressors. The UK was a responsible power, and without nuclear weapons it would be unable to exert much world influence. Against this, CND could claim that there had always been a conflict somewhere during the 'post-war' period, whether or not it had taken place in Europe. Furthermore, the possession of nuclear weapons itself acted as a source of danger. If a dispute between two nuclear powers escalated, each side would be tempted to launch a devastating first strike to ensure that the enemy could not respond in kind. Technological developments had not been matched by a growth in human wisdom; hence, an impulsive decision could lead to a holocaust within minutes. Even worse, missiles could be launched in error.

Since nuclear weapons could not be dis-invented, there were strong arguments on each side of the debate. Given the high stakes involved, the government was not prepared to let the contest be decided by logic, and it resorted to smear

tactics to discredit both the cause of unilateralism and individuals within CND. Its tactics succeeded; in 1981 public
support for the objectives of CND stood at about 33 per cent,
but by the 1983 general election this figure had slumped to
16 per cent (Byrne, 1988, 211). Perhaps the Falklands War
had reassured the public that Britain could rule the waves
without actually detonating any warheads. The war also
caused some disruption within CND. The movement was
opposed to weapons of mass destruction, rather than being
committed to complete pacifism. This position was wholly
logical, but many members went further in their objection to
violence, and there was some dismay when Michael Foot
supported the government's decision to recover the Islands.
At least a hard-core of supporters remained loyal, and even
after the war the 1983 annual demonstration organised by
CND in Hyde Park attracted an estimated 300,000 people
(Byrne, 1988, 152).

Nevertheless, 1983 was a bad year for CND. In the general election the Conservatives succeeded in convincing
voters that Labour was an extremist party; since
unilateralism was included in the party's manifesto, the
policy became identified as an example of the 'loony left' in
action. This perception was enhanced when CND
responded to Labour's national defeat by encouraging local
authorities to declare themselves 'nuclear free zones'. By
1987 Neil Kinnock was forced to compensate for his continued commitment to unilateralism by promising additional
expenditure on conventional weapons. Even this did not
prevent the Conservatives from sensing a vote-winning
issue, and they damaged Labour by claiming that the party
would surrender to the Soviets instead of defending their
country (Shaw, 1994, 78).

The 1987 controversy over nuclear weapons looked even
more unreal in the mid-1990s because by that time world
developments had made a disarmament programme much
more practicable, even on the government's premises. The
rise of Mikhail Gorbachev had ensured a thaw in East-West
relations, and President Reagan's 'Star Wars' initiative
promised to make nuclear weapons (or at least those pos-

sessed by the Soviet Union) obsolete. At the Reykjavik summit in 1986 Reagan startled Thatcher by rivalling CND in his enthusiasm to rid the world of the nuclear threat. Yet the issue caused more mayhem in 1987 than in any other election year; in addition to the Labour-Conservative clash, it brought underlying disagreements within the Liberal-SDP Alliance to a head. While most pressure groups are delighted to win support from political parties, CND discovered that the irrational conflicts of a modern election campaign only distorted the real message they were trying to convey. When the cruise missiles departed after the fall of communism in 1989 and 1990 the Conservatives tried to claim this as a triumph for their deterrence theory.

However, the decline of East-West tension had involved several factors. It was commonly argued that the arms race had exposed the underlying weakness of the Soviet economy. But the inefficiencies of the communist system had extended far beyond its bloated military machine. In any case, while the end of the Cold War made it more difficult to claim that the presence of nuclear weapons was making Britain more vulnerable, it did not affect the moral argument for unilateralism. CND attracted fewer headlines, but there was no possibility that it would dissolve while nuclear weapons remained available for use.

Pacifism is not in itself an ideology; opposition to war on conscientious grounds is open to everyone with a respect for human life, and this principle is shared by all ideologues (except for fascists, and some terror groups who claim to be inspired by Islamic fundamentalism). Originally, CND was not an exclusively pacifist organisation. Many of its members agreed that war might be necessary and even a moral course of action in certain circumstances. However, over time CND has tended to speak out against all world conflicts, whether or not the UK is involved and even when there is no possibility of a nuclear exchange. It is also opposed to the civilian use of nuclear energy, which is connected to the development of weapons-grade radioactive material.

This broader outlook has inspired continuous CND campaigning. At the beginning of the twenty-first century, membership had declined to around 30,000. However, the Iraq war caused a revival; CND helped to organise the massive London demonstration of February 2003. It also demonstrated against the continuing US military presence in Britain, notably the secretive spying facilities at Menwith Hill and RAF Fylingdales, in Yorkshire.

Environmental movements

Nuclear weapons were not the only perceived threat to the survival of the planet. Concern about environmental damage caused by various pollutants grew during the 1960s. Rachel Carson's book *The Silent Spring* (1962), which drew attention to the use of chemicals in agriculture, is normally cited as the starting-point of serious modern thinking on the environment. A UK branch of Friends of the Earth (FOE) was set up a year after the organisation had been founded in 1969. This helped to publicise the growing feeling among researchers that the developed world's obsession with economic expansion would quickly become unsustainable.

In 1972 a group of scientists and industrialists who called themselves the 'Club of Rome' met to consider the problem; their report, published as *The Limits to Growth* (Meadows et al. 1974), attracted public attention, and in this year the Paris European Council responded to concerns by laying the foundations for future EC action on the environment. In the UK a Department of the Environment (DOE) had been set up in 1970, but originally this owed more to Edward Heath's desire for institutional efficiency than a determination to check environmental damage. The main tasks of the DOE concerned housing and local government, rather than the control of pollution. However, environmental concerns were forced on the British public by the fourfold increase in oil prices during 1973. The sudden focus on the need to save energy helped to stimulate greater interest in the world's resources.

The environmental groups which had arisen in response to the new concerns had three options. They could form their own parties, to win publicity and (hopefully) representation at either national or local level; they could remain as pressure groups, informing and advising the government and organising demonstrations if they were ignored; or they could combine these approaches, fielding candidates in elections while keeping up the pressure through propaganda and other forms of protest. Ostensibly, this last course was taken by the movement as a whole, although the non-hierarchical structure preferred by activists indicates that there are still mixed feelings about wholehearted commitment to the political process. A party called 'People' contested both of the 1974 general elections (without notable success), and in 1975 this group changed its name to the Ecology Party (Rootes, 1995, 66). This was the first western party of its kind, but similar groups were soon founded in other European countries. The German 'Green' party was particularly successful, winning seats in the Bundestag by 1983; in the mid-1980s the UK party also adopted the Green label.

Taking the name of the German Greens was one thing, but it was much more difficult to repeat their success. The proportional electoral system in Germany, and its thriving local democracy, meant that it was far easier to achieve meaningful representation there than in the UK. The most spectacular achievement of the UK Greens came in the 1989 elections to the European Parliament, when their candidates received nearly 15 per cent of the vote. Admittedly turn-out at the election was low, but the fact that the Greens won no seats for their efforts made the UK system appear unjust. The Greens were able to pick up some council seats, but with the powers of local government being eroded these victories could serve only as temporary boosts to morale.

In fact, there was a danger that the frustrations of the Green Party might detract from the growing popularity of the cause itself. The late 1980s saw a surge in membership for environmental groups; between 1988 and 1989 FOE attracted almost 100,000 new supporters (Rootes, 1995, 71).

At the same time pressure group activity seemed to be paying off at last. A MORI opinion poll conducted in April 1987 showed that 81 per cent of respondents wanted the government to do more to protect the environment (Porritt and Winner, 1988, 62). This message was apparently heeded in Whitehall; in September and October 1988 Margaret Thatcher delivered speeches which seemed to indicate at least a partial conversion to environmental awareness. This new departure was followed up in February 1989 by her active participation in a London conference on the ozone layer (McCormick, 1991, 2). At the time Nicholas Ridley, whose credentials as custodian of the environment were dubious, was Secretary of State at the DOE; in July 1989 he was replaced by Christopher Patten. As an economic liberal Ridley was bound to be antipathetic to the collectivist remedies demanded by the environment lobby, but as a One Nation conservative Patten had no such reservations. This appointment was a step forward, but the Prime Minister was primarily concerned to have a good communicator in charge of the department which handled the Poll Tax (Thatcher, 1993, 602). Whatever Thatcher's motives, the advocates of pressure-group activity could now claim that the government would be more receptive in future to environmental arguments; it could also point to the environmental agenda of the EC, which was producing strong directives on issues such as the pollution of beaches (Judge, 1993). By contrast, the Green Party was earning itself bad publicity through the antics of David Icke, the former sports commentator and party spokesman, who revealed in 1990 that he was 'the son of God'.

The tactical split within the movement between party-oriented leaders such as Jonathon Porritt and those who regarded such narrow political activity as a waste of resources mirrored a theoretical disagreement which had been signalled as early as 1972 by the Norwegian philosopher Arne Naess (Dobson, 1990, 47). Naess distinguished two broad categories of environmental commitment, namely 'shallow' and 'deep' ecology. Shallow ecologists are worried about the environment but not to the extent of

agreeing to give up their life-styles. They might urge that
future economic growth must be sustainable, but growth
remains a priority for them. Deep ecologists have escaped
this kind of thinking, which still insists that the needs of the
human race ought to be considered before the rest of the
eco-system. Instead of providing possible solutions to the
crisis which faces the planet, shallow ecologists are seen by
more radical thinkers as forming part of the problem;
despite their good intentions, they reflect the type of arro-
gance which has put the earth's future in jeopardy. By contrast, deep ecologists place human interests on a par with
those of animals, and even plants and rocks; some have
gone further, and laid themselves open to the charge of hat-
ing human beings by advocating sweeping measures of
population control. The potentially damaging implications
of this theoretical split are illustrated by experiences in
France. In 1990 Brice Lalonde, the former presidential candidate of the green party `Les Verts', formed a new group
called Generation Ecologie. Lalonde accused Les Verts of
ecological fundamentalism; since he later refused to con-
demn the Gulf War, even 'shallow' ecology must have
seemed extreme to him (Cole and Doherty, 1995). Like the
divisions between radical feminism and its other variants,
this quarrel seems to originate in the fact that deep ecologists have a distinctive world-view, while it is possible for
members of all other ideological families to show a 'shallow' commitment to the health of the planet. In short, this
reading would suggest that deep ecology is a separate ideology, while the shallow world-view can be held by conservative ecologists, liberal ecologists, and so on.

Deep ecologists have sound arguments to back their
claim that all life on earth has equal value, but nutritional
difficulties might arise from the logic of the proposition that
lentils and human beings deserve equal consideration. The
most prominent leader of the UK Greens, Jonathon Porritt,
once described such views as 'really a bit dotty'. Porritt
pointed out that it is impossible for human beings to sub-
merge their identities in nature; even if one seriously tries to
'think like a mountain', one cannot avoid thinking like a

human (Porritt and Winner, 1988, 238). The UK Green Party has followed a consistent deep ecology line, but Porritt's own views were pragmatic. In 1988, for instance, he expressed a preference for policies 'which will not entail everyone donning hair-shirts or sacrificing the "good things" in life' (Irvine and Ponton, 1988, x). Unfortunately, even his highly pragmatic approach to environmental questions can appear 'a bit dotty' in a consumerist world. The success of moderate 'light-Green' ideas can be measured from the new concern of manufacturers to appear 'environmentally friendly', and the success of businesses such as The Body Shop; by the mid-1980s polls were showing that a majority of the population was more interested in preserving the environment than in economic growth (Wybrow, 1989, 140). By 1990 80 per cent of the population were either using environmentally-friendly aerosols or intending to do so (Young, 1991, 122). Yet politicians and industrialists retained their obsession with votes and profits, and the knowledge that a serious clamp-down on pollution would cost money for taxpayers and consumers added weight to the argument that only cosmetic improvements ought to be introduced. After all, environmental damage is a global phenomenon, and vandalism could always be excused on the grounds that the guilt of other countries was even worse.

The danger that the environment might be used mostly for party gain was highlighted when Patten unveiled a government White Paper (*This Common Inheritance*) in September 1990; despite the glossy presentation, this document was most notable for its omissions. For instance, it was rumoured that a DOE proposal for a tax on fossil fuels had been vetoed by the Energy Secretary (McCormick, 1991, 171). While the priorities of individual departments conflicted with Patten's plans, the ethos of the government as a whole opposed the sort of regulation of industry which an effective environmental programme required. In this climate, Patten was certain to lose ministerial battles. Where the government could point to genuine successes, these often turned out to be measures enforced by the EU, which ministers usually tried to portray as an intrusive and alien organisation. Like the EU, the United Nations' Conference on the Environment and Development held at Rio de Janeiro in June 1992 served as both justification and excuse for the government. When Norman Lamont introduced VAT for domestic fuel in his March 1993 Budget, he claimed that this was intended to discourage consumption in line with the Rio goal of stabilising carbon dioxide emissions by the year 2000. He bluntly told the Commons that 'it is crucial to avoid taking measures that will have a disproportionate impact on the competitiveness of British industry' (Lamont, 1993). Since the UK had been obstructive during negotiations on this subject, Lamont's appeal to green principles in order to deflate criticism was breathtaking (Skjaerseth, 1994, 32). In the face of such cynicism, even Porritt's limited demands seemed unrealistic.

By July 1993 membership of the UK Green Party had fallen to 4,500 (from a peak of around 20,000 only three years previously) (Rootes, 1995, 86). In the general election of 1992 the party received only 0.5 per cent of the popular vote; in the European Parliamentary election of 1994 it fought every seat, but still attracted only 3.2 per cent of the electorate. But in the late 1990s its fortunes began to improve again, as scientific research demonstrated the extent to which the environment had already been damaged. There were also new environmental threats, like genetically-modified crops; and the BSE epidemic in cattle also showed the unexpected hazards which could emerge when human beings tampered with nature. The revival of interest coincided with the introduction of proportional representation in European Parliamentary elections and elsewhere. In 1999 the UK Greens won two seats in the parliament, where many of their continental colleagues were already sitting. In the Scottish Parliamentary elections of 2003, they increased their representation from 1 to 7 MSPs. They also held numerous council seats. Although the Greens had never been a single-issue party, in 2004 they underlined the point by strengthening their policies on social justice. In some countries, this approach had led to the establishment of 'Red-Green' alliances. In Britain, of course, this was ruled out because Labour was anything but 'red', and its vote-grabbing strategy ensured that its environmental policy would be half-hearted until its next spell in opposition.

In the 2005 general election the Greens won a record vote of 258,000. In one seat, the Green candidate received more than 20 per cent of the vote, though he still only came third. With the other parties now offering almost identical policies and sharing the same world-view, the Greens are more distinctive than ever. But representation in the UK parliament is still unlikely unless the voting system is changed. In the meantime, the best chance of influencing UK government policy lies with 'the oldest, strongest, best-organised and most widely supported environmental lobby in the world' — a movement which is backed by around 4.5 million people (McCormick, 1991, 34). However, on key issues this lobby could easily be outgunned; in September 2000, for example, Labour was forced to scrap scheduled fuel-tax increases in the face of organised protests. London's mayor Ken Livingstone was able to introduce a congestion charge, which reduced traffic volumes in the capital. But other cities were slow to follow his example. Margaret Thatcher had once hailed 'the great car economy' in the UK; and although people were now more willing to recycle their refuse there was little sign of a general desire to cut consumption or to travel on foot even for the shortest journeys. After four decades of argument, the level of commitment to environmentalism in the UK was still extremely shallow.

Animal rights

Apart from lobbying in Whitehall, environmentalists can exert pressure through direct action. Greenpeace's attempts to disrupt nuclear testing have been widely publicised, and in 1986 they rattled the French government sufficiently to provoke the sinking of the movement's ship, the *Rainbow Warrior*. In 1995 Greenpeace's protests against the sinking of Shell's Brent Spar oil platform led to a Europe-wide boycott of the company, which eventually gave in to this pressure even though it had the support of the UK government. More recently, Shell has been targeted by protestors because of its activities in countries like Nigeria.

While Greenpeace has revenues which allow it to mount spectacular international campaigns, the importance of local movements should not be overlooked. In the UK during the 1990s protesters against new roads (for example, the one planned at Twyford Down) won widespread publicity, and contributed to the rethinking of the government's transport strategy despite the power of the motoring and road-building lobbies. At the same time demonstrators began to target the trade in live veal calves. These diverse campaigns, which spawned a large number of local groups, were particularly notable for the range of supporters they attracted, and the violent scenes that were often associated with them. Some traced the origins of this kind of protest to the violent clashes between police and 'New Age Travellers' at Stonehenge in June 1985 (Grant, 1995). The Travellers, whose whole lives were a determined protest against the spiritual void in modern society, were certainly able to provide the organisational skills needed for sustained action. However, by themselves they cannot explain the new mood.

Britain is traditionally an animal-loving nation, although this reputation is not easy to square with its long history of bear-baiting, cock-fighting and other cruel sports. Many animal protection organisations date back to the early nineteenth century; the Royal Society for the Prevention of Cruelty to Animals (RSPCA), for example, was founded in 1824. Anticipating much modern thinking, humanitarians such as William Wilberforce supported this body in a logical extension of the campaign on behalf of slaves. Other long-established movements, such as the British Union for the Abolition of Vivisection (1898), have concentrated their efforts against sadistic and unnecessary animal experiments. In the 1970s these groups received an important boost from the writings of the Australian philosopher Peter Singer; his book *Animal Liberation* not only provided vivid illustrations of animal sufferings in the laboratory, but also elaborated a sophisticated moral theory to explain why most of these experiments were wrong (Singer, 1975). Singer based his argument on the fact that animals resemble humans in their capacity to feel pain. This means that only experiments which lead to significant benefits can possibly be justified; as Singer showed, this criterion was unsatisfied in the vast majority of cases. Tom Regan's *The Case for Animal Rights* asserted that animals have inalienable rights, and thus should not be used to satisfy human purposes under any circumstances (Regan, 1983). These powerful claims applied to other activities, such as hunting and the use of animals to provide food and fur. Whatever the intentions of these authors, their work implied that something had to be done to stop the torture and killing.

The protests against the export of live veal calves were based on non-violent civil disobedience, although one activist was killed in a tragic accident at Coventry airport. Even so, the ferry ports of Shoreham and Brightlingsea, which exported the calves, were regularly invaded by up to 1,000 police officers, often confronting members of the public who had not previously been involved in demonstrations of any kind. Animal rights activism was regarded with particular disfavour by the authorities. This arose from the activities of the Animal Liberation Front (ALF), which was founded in 1975. Apart from releasing laboratory animals, the ALF was blamed for the arrival of letter-bombs at the addresses of all four main party leaders in 1982, and the planting of incendiary devices in stores which sold animal fur. Later in the decade, it was accused of planting car-bombs and blowing up the Senate House of Bristol University. These tactics certainly won attention for the animal rights movement, but there was a danger that this publicity would prove counter-productive. In reply, activists could point out that more traditional forms of protest had been ineffective (Garner, 1993, 218–19, 224).

More recently, media attention has focused on a long-running campaign to close down Huntingdon Life Sciences (HLS), branded by its critics as 'Europe's leading vivisectionist'. The campaign, which began after a Channel 4 documentary in 1997, made national headlines and inspired the creation of a new police group, the National Extremist Tactical Co-ordination Unit. Workers at HLS have suffered intimidation, and the campaign also affected HLS's financial backers and customers in the pharmaceutical industry. Special measures were taken to protect the anonymity of investors, and the government stepped in with promises of financial support. It was claimed that less than fifty agitators were endangering the whole of Britain's pharmaceutical industry, worth billions of pounds.

In October 2004 protestors against animal testing dug up the grave of a woman whose relatives bred animals for research. Despite the resulting media outcry, and new legislation designed specifically to curtail its activities, SHAC (Stop Huntingdon Animal Cruelty) remained committed to the closure of HLS, and the government clearly regarded the case as a trial of strength from which it could not flinch. Sections of the media gave outspoken support to HLS, and it can be argued that far from advancing the cause of animal welfare SHAC's shock tactics have prevented it from winning a fair hearing.

The public response to the SHAC campaign was very different from the general attitude towards the protestors against veal calves. This was partly because the veal trade was particularly emotive; in addition to the brutal treatment they received in transit, the calves were separated from their mothers after only a few hours. By contrast, the public was prepared to accept at face value the claim that animals at HLS were treated well. The real difference in the two cases was that people could easily survive without eating veal, while the experiments at HLS were generally supposed to be beneficial to human beings. Despite the well-reasoned case presented by Singer and others, even the remote possibility that their own lives would be improved by animal experiments was enough to satisfy most people in the UK.

Conclusion: the politics of alienation?

In recent years, there has been a significant increase in pressure group activity, at the expense of other forms of political participation. This phenomenon is understandable, at least in one respect. While contemporary political parties focus on specific events like conferences and elections, members of pressure groups can derive a sense of continuous involvement through activities such as fund-raising and petitioning.

In theory, advocates of a liberal democracy can argue that the growth of pressure groups is a healthy sign of *pluralism*. On the liberal view of human nature, people are capable of making rational decisions. But even liberals accept that individuals can see the world from a variety of perspectives, and the principle of free speech allows them to publicise their views. On the most optimistic reading, democracy can only benefit from an increase in pressure group activity, since this will ensure a diversity of views and a better-informed public.

However, pluralist arguments have to be put in context. If pressure groups are becoming more popular while parties decline, this can only mean that the more orthodox forms of political participation are inadequate; otherwise people would be joining parties as well as pressure groups, which they are free to do. By the time of the 2001 general election, Tony Benn was widely regarded as a maverick, but no-one could deny that he had an insider's knowledge of Westminster and the workings of government. As such, he deserved to be taken seriously when he argued that it was better for an independent-minded person to work *outside* parliament.

It is also noteworthy that a good deal of pressure group activity has been provoked by contentious government decisions. The Countryside Alliance, (which supports the right to hunt with hounds) and Fathers 4 Justice (which was set up to fight against a perceived bias in favour of mothers when parents separate) are the best-publicised examples of groups with specific grievances. Such groups are essentially *defensive*. Unlike organisations such as Oxfam, which hope to improve living conditions in deprived areas, they are not hoping to make the world a better place. Rather, they want to prevent it from getting worse, from their point of view. To the extent that Islamic groups have organised to protest against British foreign policy in the Middle East, they fall into the same category. Even people who have committed terrorist acts in the name of Islam often cite the alleged decadence of western culture in justification of their deeds.

The growth of defensive pressure groups casts an ironic light on the party-political scene, which is currently dominated by people who spend much of their time trying to find out what the public really wants. The growth of pressure groups implies that politicians have been asking the wrong questions. For various reasons, it suits their interests to accept the dominance of one ideology — classical liberalism. Yet circumstances change; and while policy makers currently agree with Margaret Thatcher in thinking that 'There is no alternative', a time will come when they have to think again.

List of works cited

Byrne, Paul (1988), *The Campaign for Nuclear Disarmament*, Croom Helm.

Campbell, Duncan (1986), *The Unsinkable Aircraft Carrier: American Military Power in Britain*, Paladin, updated edition.

Carson, Rachel (1962) *Silent Spring*, Houghton Mifflin.

Cole, Alistair, and Doherty, Brian (1995), 'France: Pas comme les autres — the French Greens at the Crossroads', in Dick Richardson and Chris Rootes (eds) *The Green Challenge: The Development of Green Parties in Europe*, Routledge.

Coote, Anna, and Gill, Tess (1974), *Women's Rights: A Practical Guide*, Penguin.

Crewe, Ivor (1992), 'A Nation of Liars? Opinion Polls in the 1992 Election', *Parliamentary Affairs*, volume 45, number 4.

Dobson, Andrew (1990), *Green Political Thought: An Introduction*, Unwin Hayman.

Drucker, Henry (ed.) (1979), Multi-Party Britain, Macmillan.

Garner, Robert (1993), Animals, Politics and Morality, Manchester University Press.

Garner, Robert (1996), Environmental Politics, Harvester Wheatsheaf.

Gilmour, Ian (1992), Dancing with Dogma: Britain under Thatcherism, Simon and Schuster.

Garnett, Mark (1996), *Principles and Politics in Contemporary Britain*, 1st edition, Longman.

Grant, Linda (1995), 'Just Say No', *Guardian*, 3 June.

Greer, Germaine (1970) *The Female Eunuch*, Granada.

Heath, Anthony, Evans, Geoff, Field, Julia, and Witherspoon, Sharon (1991), *Understanding Political Change: The British Voter, 1964-1987*, Pergamon.

Irvine, Sandy, and Ponton, Alec (1988), *A Green Manifesto: Policies for a Green Future*, Optima.

Jones, Mervyn (1994), *Michael Foot*, Victor Gollancz.

Judge, David (ed.) (1993), *A Green Dimension for the European Community: Political Issues and Processes*, Frank Cass.

Lamont, Norman (1993), 'Green Measures', Budget Statement, *Parliamentary Debates*, volume 221, 182-3.

Lovenduski, Joni, and Randall, Vicky (1993), *Contemporary Feminist Politics: Women and Power in Britain*, Oxford University Press.

Lovenduski, Joni, Norris, Pippa, and Burness, Catriona (1994), 'The Party and Women', in Anthony Seldon and Stuart Ball (eds) *Conservative Century: The Conservative Party since 1900*, Oxford University Press.

McCormick, John (1991), *British Politics and the Environment*, Earthscan.

Meadows, Donella, Meadows, Dennis, Randers, Jorgen, and Behrens, William (1974) *The Limits to Growth: A Report for the Club of Rome's Project on the Predicament of Mankind*, Pan.

Porritt, Jonathon, and Winner, David (1988), *The Coming of the Greens*, Fontana.

Regan, Tom (1983) *The Case for Animal Rights*, Routledge and Kegan Paul.

Rootes, Chris (1995), 'Britain: Greens in a Cold Climate', in Dick Richardson and Chris Rootes (eds) *The Green Challenge: The Development of Green Parties in Europe*, Routledge.

Sanders, David (1992), 'Why the Conservative Party Won — Again', in Anthony King (ed.), *Britain at the Polls*, Chatham House.

Sebestyen, Amanda (1985), 'The Politics of Survival — While the Work Goes On', in Robin Morgan (ed.), *Sisterhood is Global: The International Women's Movement Anthology*, Penguin.

Shaw, Eric (1994), *The Labour Party since 1979: Crisis and Transformation*, Routledge.

Short, Clare (1986), Speech Introducing Indecent Displays (Newspapers)Bill, 12 March, *Parliamentary Debates*, volume 93, cols. 937-40.

Singer, Peter (1975) *Animal Liberation*, Thorsons, 2nd edition.

Skjaerseth, Jon (1994), 'The Climate Policy of the EC: Too Hot to Handle?', *Journal of Common Market Studies*, Vol. 32, no. 1.

Sutherland, Keith (2004), *The Party's Over: Blueprint for a very English Revolution*, Imprint Academic, 2004.

Taylor, Robert (1970), 'The Campaign for Nuclear Disarmament', in Vernon Bogdanor and Robert Skidelsky (eds) *The Age of Affluence 1951-1964*, Macmillan.

Thatcher, Margaret (1993), *The Downing Street Years*, HarperCollins.

Topf, Richard (1989), 'Political Change and Political Culture in Britain, 1959-87', in *Contemporary Political Culture*, Sage.

Vincent, Andrew (1995), *Modern Political Ideologies*, Blackwell, 2nd ed.

Wainwright, Hilary (1984), 'Women and the Division of Labour', in Philip Abrams and Richard Brown (eds) *UK Society: Work, Urbanism and Inequality*, Weidenfeld and Nicolson.

Witherspoon, Sharon (1985), 'Sex Roles and Gender Issues', in Roger Jowell and Sharon Witherspoon (eds) *British Social Attitudes: The 1985 Report*, Gower.

Wybrow, Robert (1989), *Britain Speaks Out: A Social History as Seen through the Gallup Data*, Macmillan.

Young, Ken (1991), 'Shades of Green', in Roger Jowell, Lindsay Brook and Bridget Taylor (eds) *British Social Attitudes: The 8th Report*, Dartmouth.

CONCLUSION

Principles and Politics since 1970

The history of UK politics since 1970 shows the consistent importance of principles, yet it also proves the dangers of neat generalisation. The main political parties and the wider public remained divided in their views before and after the supposed 'breakdown of consensus'. Harold Wilson and Edward Heath were both criticised even from within their respective parties before 1975; Mrs Thatcher's victory in the Conservative leadership election of that year did not cause the mass conversion of her party. Thatcherism was never accepted by a majority of the population, but people outside Westminster were far from unanimous in their support for any alternative principles. Reactions to Tony Blair's domestic and foreign policy were equally diverse. Commentators often talk of a 'climate of opinion' as if such a uniform phenomenon could be discovered, but anything more than a cursory examination of the evidence reveals that a wide range of views were held throughout the period. However, some views are more influential than others; and within 'elite' opinion some broad themes may now be recapitulated.

The Conservative Party

Between 1970 and the advent of Mrs Thatcher, Conservative party policies were broadly compatible with conservative ideology. That is, people with a sceptical view of human nature could feel reasonably happy with Edward Heath's approach to policy. Although he did want to inject new dynamism in the economy, and used rhetoric which sounded misleadingly radical, he was keenly aware of the need for social stability. Hence, when unemployment rose to what he considered to be an unacceptable level Heath took action to reduce it; and although the Industrial Relations Act infuriated many trade unionists, the Prime Minister was prepared to hold constructive talks with the unions in the hope of reaching agreement on the best way to address Britain's economic problems in an era of soaring inflation.

However, while conservatives could be reasonably happy with Heath, the early 1970s were highly uncongenial for them. Even those who accepted that Britain's power had greatly diminished since 1945 could only regret the limited alternatives which were available to policy-makers in an increasingly inter-dependent world. On paper, the humane management of relative decline sounded more appealing than a shift towards a free-market approach which would endanger social stability. But the oil crisis of 1973 suggested that radical policy changes would be necessary if living standards were to be held steady, let alone improved. For Heath, membership of the EEC would provide the necessary stimulus for the sluggish UK economy. However, it was difficult for traditional conservatives to share his enthusiasm for an institution which attempted to embrace several contrasting (if not antagonistic) cultures. It bore all the hallmarks of a 'rationalistic' enterprise which conservatives had consistently warned against — sound enough on paper, but likely to disappoint in practice.

Heath's enthusiasm for the EEC was not the only reason for doubting his affinity with the conservative tradition. In 1965 Heath had been chosen as party leader because he was regarded as the candidate who was most in tune with the electoral demands of the 1960s. In itself, this is enough to cast doubt on his conservative credentials; for conservatives, that decade was an unpleasant mistake. In the early 1960s Heath had caused unrest within the Conservative Party by pushing through the abolition of Resale Price Maintenance (RPM), a measure which had defended small shopkeepers against competition from the big retailers. Again, Heath's position was easy to justify in the abstract, and it could be argued that RPM was no longer sustainable in any case. However, Heath felt so strongly on the issue that he was prepared to countenance a serious split among his parliamentary colleagues in order to get his way.

On the basis of this and other evidence, Heath's outlook is best understood in relation to the New liberal tradition. But this is not to say that his opponents within the party were custodians of the true conservatism. Indeed, while Heath's policies were capable of being defended from a conservative perspective, Margaret Thatcher and Keith Joseph were self-conscious radicals whose thinking arose from a model of human nature which contradicted conservatism in several key respects. In particular, when 'Thatcherites' argued that people were motivated by the 'rational' pursuit of self-interest, they flew in the face of conservative scepticism. Although some commentators have made valiant attempts to square Thatcherism with the conservative tradition, this exercise has been singularly unprofitable. Instead of trying to say that Margaret Thatcher's brand of conservatism had much in common with classical liberalism, it would have been much simpler (and more accurate) to accept that she *was* a classical liberal.

Until 1979 Thatcher was on her probation as party leader, but once she had been elected Prime Minister a new approach was quickly established in the key area of economic policy. Identifying closely with only a vigorous minority within the population, Thatcher prioritised inflation rather than unemployment; warnings about the likely impact on society went unheeded. Ministers had anticipated resistance from the unions, but symptoms of discontent like the 1981 inner-city riots took them by surprise. However, the Falklands War turned a disastrous period for British government into a triumphal procession towards re-election for Mrs Thatcher. Afterwards, the party faithful developed a myth from which the 1979–83 period could be seen as a vindication of their leader's principled defiance. Nothing could be further from the truth; equally, though, nothing could be more characteristic of rigid ideological thinking.

Classical liberalism remains the ruling dogma of the Conservative Party. Internal opposition — whether arising from distinctive conservative views, or Heath's brand of New liberalism — disappeared long ago. Even the disastrous split over Europe was a disagreement among classical liberals who reached different conclusions about the EU. John Major lacked Mrs Thatcher's crusading zeal, but that did not mean that he was less assured about the truth of classical liberalism; it was partly a matter of temperament, but also reflected the absence of serious ideological opposition at home or abroad. William Hague, Iain Duncan Smith and Michael Howard were all classical liberals. David Cameron's critics claim that he is trying to abandon Thatcherism, but there is good reason to suspect that the change is more about presentation than substance.

Labour

In 1970 the most influential thinking within the Labour Party came from its social democratic wing. Unlike socialists, social democrats had an unequivocal commitment to peaceful change. They agreed with New liberals in thinking that the state had a key role to play in the struggle to ensure something like equality of opportunity; but by comparison they had a much more positive attitude towards the state, and were more willing to accept a high level of income distribution through the tax system. However, social democrats had cooperated with New liberals in devising the broad outlines of the 1945 settlement. For social democrats, nationalisation of certain key utilities was an essential part of this programme, but they also saw the need for a vibrant private sector which would provide the engine for economic growth and rising living standards.

Unfortunately for Labour, world conditions, and the deplorable record of domestic UK investment, meant that growth was not forthcoming during their years in office after 1964. Harold Wilson was unable to pursue any consistent policy line, and his successor James Callaghan explicitly rejected social democratic priorities after the IMF moved in to prop up the pound. Socialists attempted to fill this ideological vacuum within the party, achieving most success in 1970–74 and 1979–83. Significantly, these were years immediately following Labour's loss of office, when party members had the chance to reflect on ministerial performance. Harold Wilson's victories of 1974 scuppered the first of these efforts, while Michael Foot and Neil Kinnock ensured the defeat of the second. Between 1983 and 1992 Labour returned to a broadly social democratic position. But although opinion polls suggested that the electorate preferred this position to Thatcherism, Labour continued to languish in opposition.

A cool appraisal of the opposition years suggests that Labour did not lose in 1987 and 1992 because of its policy programme; even the party's support for unilateral nuclear disarmament, which was dropped soon after the 1987 election, would have been taken more seriously if it had been given anything like a fair hearing. Opinions differ about the precise influence of the press on voting behaviour, but there is no doubt that the *Sun* newspaper was successful in its attempts to make Neil Kinnock look unelectable. If John Smith had lived longer, the party's response to negative press coverage might have been contained. As it was, his early death handed the initiative to 'modernisers' who were anxious to meet the *Sun* on its own terms.

Before the 1997 general election, Tony Blair disbelieved the opinion polls which suggested that Labour would win a landslide majority. He had some reason to be cautious, because the 1992 experience showed that voters were willing to lie about their intentions. But as soon as the scale of victory was known Blair acted to dampen down any expectation that his government would mark a radical departure from Thatcherism. This was the decisive moment in the Blair premiership. If he had been a social democrat, the result would have assured him that the majority of voters had spent the previous decade searching for a viable alternative to Thatcherism, and that his personality had inspired a level of confidence which Kinnock had never matched. Instead, he decided to interpret the result as an endorsement of 'modernisation'. In short, when he became leader he had taken the view that the electorate wanted 'Thatcherism with a human face'; and no amount of evidence was going to shift him from a conclusion which he had found personally congenial.

During Blair's second term, backbench Labour MPs became more rebellious. Although some commentators have interpreted this development as a sign that parliament is not merely a passive instrument of the executive, the real wonder is that effective dissent was delayed for so long. Mrs Thatcher had known that many Conservative MPs disagreed with her views, and usually she had persevered regardless; but she had never adopted policies with the deliberate intention of irritating her internal critics. By contrast, there have been occasions when Blair had clearly taken up an idea in order to test the extent of opposition on the Labour backbenches. Election promises have been broken by a leadership which continued to claim a 'mandate' on the basis of its manifesto commitments; and the party which kept British troops out of Vietnam eagerly signed up to George Bush's 'war on terror'.

New Labour's record since 1997 does include limited action against child poverty, and the 'welfare to work' programme can be reconciled with the social democratic tradition because it reflects a genuine desire for people to fulfil their talents (as well as the Thatcherite drive to massage the unemployment statistics). However, the most telling fact about New Labour is its approach to the higher rate of income tax which it inherited from the Conservative Party. Before the 1988 budget, even convinced Thatcherites assumed that the top rate would never dip below 50 per cent. When Nigel Lawson announced that it would fall to 40 per cent, Britain's wealthiest citizens openly rejoiced. Despite Labour's protests at the time, the party has made no move to increase the rate of tax on the rich. Indeed, Blair attacked the Liberal Democrats for advocating a 50 per cent tax on the highest earners, using the same (questionable) arguments about incentives which the Conservatives had deployed in their tax-cutting days.

Liberal Democrats

Throughout our period, the Liberal Party and its successors have retained their allegiance to New liberalism, having discarded most adherents of the classical variety by 1945. The party's loyalty to the welfare state and the mixed economy should have ensured easy collaboration with the social democrats who left the Labour Party in 1981; and given the state of opinion in Britain during the 1980s the Alliance should have been an electoral success. But in its early days the Alliance was scuppered by the Falklands War on one side, and tribal loyalty to the Labour Party on the other. Following these setbacks, the SDP encountered difficulties because of the personality of Dr David Owen, who moved away from a distinctive social democratic position under the influence of 'Thatcherism'.

Under Paddy Ashdown the merged Liberal Democrat party reasserted its New liberal position; and, as Tony Blair followed Owen in a Thatcherite direction, after the 1997 general election the Lib-Dems were left in control of ideological territory which was shared by the majority of the UK electorate. However, at this moment of opportunity Ashdown decided to step down. The party continued to make electoral progress under his successor, Charles Kennedy, and in 2005 its opposition to the war in Iraq should have ensured significant gains. It did secure a record number of MPs, but it was natural for senior members of the party to feel disappointed by the outcome. Concern about Kennedy's performance came to a head at a time when the ideological initiative had passed to members of the party who sympathised with Thatcherism. As a result, at the time of writing it appears that Liberal Democrat distinctiveness will be short-lived, and that the party will join Labour and the Conservatives in appealing for the votes of 'rational', self-interested individuals.

A crisis of party politics

The above account shows that the range of political views espoused by the main parties is more restricted even than it was during the days of the 'post-war consensus'. Supporters of classical liberalism can point to developments within the globalised economy which have ensured the lasting triumph of their views. However, in the UK classical liberalism has been assisted by unforeseen accidents. Among many such incidents, the unexpected death of John Smith was particularly significant; but even then, political life would surely have been different if Gordon Brown had not accepted the infamous deal with Tony Blair. As we have seen, although Brown has backed many of Blair's controversial policies, if he had become leader in 1994 it is likely that Labour's policies would have remained within the social democratic tradition.

Thus the effect of all the political upheavals since 1970s has produced a new 'consensus' which is even more narrow than its predecessor, forcing any aspiring politician to adopt classical liberal views. Since public opinion is more diverse than ever before, it is hardly surprising that people have looked elsewhere for the chance of meaningful participation. Pressure groups provide the most obvious outlet for idealism. Ironically, though, a great deal of pressure group activity is now directed against unpopular government decisions. For example, recent general elections have registered victories for campaigners against sleaze, hospital closures, all-women shortlists, and the Iraq war. Although these results demonstrate that the British public can still be roused against perceived injustice, there is little sign as yet of a concerted drive against an elite political culture which has helped to produce a disgraceful spiral of decline in electoral participation. Whatever one thinks of classical liberalism, it is reasonable to expect that people will continue to see the world in different ways; and if the democratic process in the UK is to continue in a reasonable state of health, before too long it will have to generate a political movement which offers voters a genuine alternative.

Index

Adam Smith Institute (ASI) 131, 208
Adams, Ian 19, 195, 197
Adey, Robert 267
Alliance (SDP-Liberal) 95,97, 99-100, 106-7, 110, 123, 152, 157, 160, 272, 293
Alliance Party (N. Ireland) 181
Alternative Economic Strategy (AES) 35, 39. 150, 152, 154, 156
Animal Liberation Front (ALF) 281
Animal Rights 263, 279-83
Ashdown, Paddy 98, 103-5, 108, 110, 164, 293
Asquith, Herbert 29, 53, 80, 171
Attlee, Clement 23-4, 27, 31, 53-4, 82

'Back to Basics' 211, 214
Baker, Kenneth 125-6, 129, 140, 202
Barber, Anthony 60, 62
Barnes, Rosie 98
Barnett, Joel 132
Beckett, Margaret 158, 233, 235-6
Benn, Tony 26, 33, 36, 39-41, 44-6, 71, 90, 121, 139, 146-50, 152-55, 157-8, 160-1, 191, 219, 233, 244, 263, 283
Bevan, Anuerin 25, 28-9, 154
Bevan, Andy 41
Beveridge, William 29, 53, 67, 80-1, 83-4, 99, 132
Biffen, John 64, 112, 123-4
Blair, Tony 5, 9, 102-4, 159, 171, 183, 193-4, 210-11, 223, 229, 234-53, 255-7, 262, 287, 291-4
Blunkett, David 242
Bottomley, Virginia 204
Boyson, Rhodes 135
British National Party (BNP) 188-90, 195

Brittan, Leon 120-2, 202
Brown, George 26
Brown, Gordon 103, 193, 226, 234-6, 243-6, 251, 256-7, 294
Budd, Alan 55
Burke, Edmund 6, 73, 75, 136, 184

Callaghan, James 26, 29, 37-41, 43-5, 69, 71, 87-8, 91, 111, 113, 147, 291
Cameron, David 4, 228-30, 257, 290
Campaign for Democratic Socialism (CDS) 28
Campaign for Labour Party Democracy (CLPD) 41, 146, 148-9
Campaign for Labour Victory (CLV) 146
Campaign for Nuclear Disarmament (CND) 150, 172, 270-3
Campaign Group 157-8
Campbell, Alastair 243-4
Campbell, Menzies 107-9
Carrington, Lord 111
Carson, Rachel 293
Cartwright, John 98
Castle, Barbara 26
Central Policy Review Staff (CPRS) 65, 124
Centre for Policy Studies (CPS) 64-5, 124, 131, 209
'Charter 88' 204
Charter Movement 208
Churchill, Winston 52-3, 73
Citizen's Charter 204
Clarke, Kenneth 126, 192, 202, 204, 213-14, 216-20, 225, 228
Clause IV 22-4, 28, 210, 236-7
Coates, David 41
Coates, Ken 40

Cockfield, Lord 122
Community Charge 123, 129, 157, 161-2
Confederation of British Industry (CBI) 59
Conservatism 2, 11-12, 17-18, 48-53, 65-67, 69-70, 72-3
Conservative Party 4, 9, 11-12, 40, 48-50, 52-6, 63, 66-8, 71-2, 74-5, 79, 81, 86, 94, 100-1, 112, 116-17, 121, 123-4, 135, 137, 162, 174, 186-7, 202-3, 211-13, 217, 220-2, 230, 287-8, 292
Conservative Philosophy Group 69, 135
Cook, Robin 248
Crewe, Ivor 70, 95, 133
Crosland, Anthony 14, 27-30, 33, 39, 41-3, 82, 91, 94, 100, 158-9

Dalyell, Tam 172
Davies, John 59
Delors, Jacques 122, 130
Democratic Unionist Party (DUP) 181-3
Devolution 40, 102, 162, 173-9, 181, 217, 233
Disraeli, Benjamin 53, 137, 185
Drucker, Henry 24, 261

Ecclestone, Bernie 242
Equality 13-15, 22, 27-8, 33, 63, 65, 84, 94, 99, 158, 226, 233, 237, 264-6, 290
European Community (EC) 95, 120-1, 138, 147, 150, 154, 157, 192, 206, 268, 273, 275
European Economic Community (EEC) 30, 32, 57, 59, 62-3, 81, 83, 87, 90, 92, 154, 191, 221, 233, 288
European Monetary System (EMS) 120
European Union (EU) 102, 105, 173, 189-90, 192-4, 216-21, 224, 277-8, 290
Evans, Gwynfor 176-7

Fabian Society 22, 146
Falkland Islands 95, 116-17
Falklands War 119, 184, 271, 289, 293
Feminism 11, 263-9, 276
Field, Frank 149

Foot, Michael 39, 71-2, 92, 147-55, 161, 270-1, 291
Forsythe, Michael 174
Fowler, Norman 124, 129, 202
Friedman, Milton 115
Friends of the Earth (FOE) 273-4

Gaitskell, Hugh 23-5, 28, 83, 236
Gamble, Andrew 63, 124, 133, 134
George, Stephen 191
Gilmour, Ian 68, 70, 112, 119
Gonzalez, Felipe 138
Gorbachev, Mikhail 156-7, 164-5, 271
Gould, Bryan 233
Gould, Philip 256
Gray, John 209
Greater London Council (GLC) 119
Green Party 98, 160, 175, 270, 274-9
Green, Thomas Hill 17, 29, 81
Greenham Common 268-9
Greenpeace 279-80
Greer, Germaine 264
Griffin, Nick 189-90
Griffiths, Brian 212
Grimond, Jo 81-3, 88, 100
Gummer, John 202

Hague, William 218-19, 222-8, 257, 290
Hain, Peter 83-4
Hall, Stuart 134
Hattersley, Roy 30, 42, 153, 158-9, 166, 240, 244
Hayek, Friedrich 53-4, 56, 74, 131, 133
Healey, Denis 35, 37, 39, 41, 72, 87-8, 92, 147, 149-50, 153, 156
Heath, Edward 9, 30, 32, 34-5, 56-9, 61-5, 67-8, 70-3, 75, 86, 90, 111, 115, 117, 119-21, 149, 153-4, 187-9, 202, 208, 215, 220, 227, 273, 287-90
Heffer, Eric 36, 246, 158
Heseltine, Michael 112, 116, 120-1, 129-30, 200-2, 205, 208, 214, 217-18, 270
Hobhouse, Leonard 81
Hobsbawm, Eric 149
Hogg, Quintin (Lord Hailsham) 50-1, 54-5, 70, 73
Holland, Stuart 35
Hoskyns, John 114

Howard, Michael 4, 189, 202, 218, 226-8, 257, 290
Howe, Geoffrey 56, 68, 112-15, 118, 124, 127-8, 130, 159, 200-1
Howell, David 112
Hurd, Douglas 128, 189, 201

Icke, David 275
Ideology 1-12, 16, 43-5, 48-9, 53, 64-5, 69-70, 73, 80, 108, 121, 131, 140, 195-6, 221, 229, 262, 266, 272, 284, 287
Immigration 56, 185-8, 190-1, 224
In Place of Strife 26, 34, 59, 69
Income Tax 5, 35, 60, 88, 98, 103-6, 114, 123, 127, 162, 190, 210, 240, 292
Industrial Relations Act (1970) 34, 36, 59
Inflation 35, 37-8, 59-61, 70, 113-14, 118, 120, 126-7, 132, 160, 203, 206, 253, 288
Ingham, Bernard 128
Institute of Economic Affairs (IEA) 65, 74, 117, 131
International Monetary Fund (IMF) 37, 39, 41-4, 88, 90, 145, 262, 291
Iraq 105-6, 175, 197, 205, 226, 246-9, 255-6, 263, 273, 293-4
Irish Republican Army (IRA) 124, 130, 181, 183

Jay, Peter 38-9, 91
Jenkins, Roy 26, 29-30, 32-4, 41-3, 87, 89-96, 100-1, 104, 116, 121, 148
Jones, Jack 32, 37
Jones, Tudor 154
Joseph, Keith 64-5, 68-9, 96, 112, 115, 289

Keynes, John Maynard 29, 38-9, 53, 67, 69, 75, 80-1, 84, 99
King, Anthony 95
Kinnock, Neil 2, 5, 123, 145, 149-50, 153-66, 232-3, 239, 246, 271, 291-2

Labour Co-ordinating Committee (LCC) 146
Labour Party 9, 11, 14, 21-2, 24-5, 27-9, 32, 34, 37-42, 49, 53-4, 67, 69, 71-2, 79-80, 82-7, 91, 94,

100-1, 107, 123, 132, 139, 144-6, 150-2, 154, 160, 164, 186, 207, 235, 239-40, 242, 244, 257, 263, 270, 290, 293
Lamont, Norman 202, 206, 213, 278
Lang, Ian 174
Lawson, Nigel 112, 118, 120, 124, 127-8, 130, 133, 161, 200-1, 292
Letwin, Oliver 229
Letwin, Shirley 135
Liberal Party (Liberal Democrats from 1990) 21-2, 39, 49-50, 53, 67, 75, 79-84, 87-90, 92, 97-108, 163, 175, 179, 216, 241, 255, 267-8, 292-3
Liberalism 9-12, 15-18, 49, 57, 64-5, 67, 74-5, 80-1, 88, 101, 105, 108, 112, 121, 134-5, 137-8, 140, 195, 210, 215, 221, 227, 230, 240, 249-50, 256-7, 284, 289-90, 293-4
Lilley, Peter 218
Livingstone, Ken 119, 252, 279
Lloyd George, David 79-80, 101

Maastricht Treaty 173, 191-2, 207, 212
MacDonald, Ramsay 23, 29
Macleod, Iain 186
Macmillan, Harold 55, 58
Major, John 101-2, 124, 128, 159, 162, 164, 183, 189, 192-3, 200-20, 225, 227, 232, 241, 252 290
Mandelson, Peter 155, 164, 235, 242
Marquand, David 30, 41, 43, 100
Marx, Karl (and Marxism) 2, 6-7, 13, 25, 28, 41, 69, 74, 139, 182, 185
Maude, Angus 68, 134
Mayhew, Christopher 86
McKenzie, Robert 80
Meacher, Michael 153, 155, 159
Mellor, David 211
Meyer, Anthony 129
Militant Tendency 5, 146-7, 150-1, 154-5, 161, 165
Milligan, Stephen 211
Mitterrand, Francois 122, 138
Monday Club 186, 188
Monetarism 59
Morrison, Herbert 24, 49
Mosley, Oswald 195
Mount, Ferdinand 135
Mullin, Chris 146
Murdoch, Rupert 238

Naess, Arne 275
Nairn, Tom 194
National Economic Development
    Council (NEDC) 55
National Front (NF) 188, 195
National Health Service (NHS)
    124-6, 162-3, 186, 220
Nationalisation 23-4, 27-8, 36, 52,
    82-3, 90, 102, 156, 162, 236-7, 290
'New' Labour 5, 106, 232, 236,
    240-1, 244-6, 251-2, 255-7, 261,
    292
'Next Steps' Initiative 204
Northern Ireland Civil Rights
    Association (NICRA) 180
Nott, John 112
Nuclear Weapons/Disarmament
    92, 96-7, 150, 153, 156-7, 159, 165,
    172, 177, 247-8, 263, 266, 269-73,
    279, 291

Oakeshott, Michael 72-3, 209
Orwell, George 184
Owen, David 30, 42, 75, 91-8, 100-2,
    122, 148, 158, 239, 293

Paisley, Ian 181, 183
Pardoe, John 87-8
Parkinson, Cecil 112
Pimlott, Ben 254
Plaid Cymru 175-9
Poll Tax (see Community Charge)
Porritt, Jonathan 275-8
Portillo, Michael 214, 217-18, 223-6
Powell, Enoch 55-6, 62, 64-5, 72,
    121, 183, 186-7, 219
Prentice, Reg 25-6, 40
Prescott, John 235-6, 242
Prior, James 111, 113
Private Finance Initiative (PFI) 245
Privatisation 117, 122-4, 138, 204,
    208
Public Spending 38, 57, 60, 114,
    119, 210, 228
Pym, Francis 112, 118-19

Quangos 119, 125, 204

Race Relations 83, 186-7, 191
Rawls, John 158
Rayner, Derek 114
Reagan, Ronald 119, 126, 138, 156,
    210, 246, 271-2

Redwood, John 123, 214-15, 218-20
Regan, Tom 281
Revisionism (see Social
    Democracy)
Riddell, Peter 188
Ridley, Nicholas 58, 64, 112, 120,
    129, 275
Rifkind, Malcolm 174
Rodgers, William 30, 91-2, 94, 96,
    100, 148

Sawyer, Tom 155
Scanlon, Hugh 32, 37
Scargill, Arthur 119-20, 155
Schmidt, Helmut 41
Scott, Walter 171
Scottish National Party (SNP)
    172-9
Scruton, Roger 135
Sex Discrimination 30, 264, 266-7
Sherman, Alfred 65
Short, Clare 158, 248, 266-7
Silkin, John 149
Sillars, Jim 174
Singer, Peter 280-2
Sinn Fein 181-3
Skinner, Dennis 158, 161
Smedley, Oliver 81
Smith, Adam 15-16, 131, 171
Smith, Cyril 89
Smith, Iain Duncan 225-6, 228, 257,
    290
Smith, Ian 26
Smith, John 102, 162-3, 166, 172,
    233-8, 291, 294
Social Contract 36-7, 63
Social Democracy 11, 14, 18, 29, 33,
    40-1, 43, 55, 69, 92, 100-1, 144,
    166, 239-40
Social Democratic and Labour
    Party (SDLP) 182-3
Social Democratic Party (SDP) 50,
    90, 92-102, 104, 116, 123, 150,
    152, 158, 166, 233, 272, 293
Socialism 2, 9, 11, 13-14, 17-18, 24,
    27-30, 32, 38, 40-3, 49, 51, 54,
    67-9, 86, 89, 94, 122, 144, 146,
    148, 154, 158, 164, 237, 239, 253
Socialist Workers' Party (SWP) 151
Spencer, Herbert 49, 52-3, 56, 81,
    133
Steel, David 87-90, 93-4, 96-7

Tatchell, Peter 151, 161
Taverne, Dick 42, 86, 233
Taxation (see Income Tax)
Tebbit, Norman 112-13, 116, 123-4,
    136, 229
Thatcher, Margaret 2, 4-5, 9, 12, 30,
    39-40, 42, 44, 49-50, 55, 57-8, 64,
    68-75, 89, 94, 97, 100-1, 104,
    111-40, 145, 149, 152, 155-7,
    160-3, 165, 167, 178, 182, 187-9,
    191-2, 195, 200-2, 204-6, 208, 210,
    212-13, 215, 219, 221, 227, 229,
    232, 236, 238-40, 250, 253-4, 256,
    265, 269, 272, 275, 279, 284, 287,
    289-90, 292
Thatcherism/Thatcherite 56,
    65 – 9, 71, 73-6, 94-6, 99-101, 108,
    111-40, 152, 156, 158-60, 166, 174,
    194, 203-6, 208-11, 215, 220,
    227-30, 234-5, 241, 149-50, 255-7,
    262, 264-5, 287, 289-93
Thorneycroft, Peter 55, 68
Thornton, Sara 267
Thorpe, Jeremy 83, 86-8
Trade Unions 34, 119, 154
Tribune Group 25, 36, 39, 154

Ulster 180-2
Ulster Unionist Party (UUP) 121,
    181, 183, 187
Underhill, Reg 151
Unemployment 16-17, 23, 35, 38-9,
    52, 60, 89, 113, 115, 126, 132, 136,
    149, 151, 155, 162, 203, 206,
    288-9, 292

Value Added Tax (VAT) 35-6, 60,
    114, 213, 278
Victory for Socialism (VFS) 28
Vincent, Andrew 195
Waldegrave, William 129, 203
Walker, Peter 68, 111, 120, 129, 178
Wallace, William 83
Walters, Alan 127-8
Weapons of Mass Destruction 247,
    271
Webb, Keith 196
Westland Affair 121-2
Whitehouse, Mary 135
Whitelaw, William 68, 72, 74, 112,
    128, 182, 236
Willetts, David 135, 208-9

Williams, Shirley 75, 91-2, 94, 96
    158
Wilson, Harold 21-2, 24-6, 29-33,
    35-6, 38, 40-1, 44-5, 54, 56-7, 63,
    71, 75, 83, 86-7, 90, 153, 191, 243,
    290-1
'Winter of Discontent' 37, 112, 145
Women's Liberation Movement
    (WLM) 264
Wyatt, Woodrow 131-2